FIGHTING DESTROYER

FIGHTING DESTROYER

The Story of HMS *Petard*

G.G.Connell

CRÉCY BOOKS

This revised and updated edition published by
CRÉCY BOOKS LIMITED, 1994
First published by WILLIAM KIMBER & Co., 1976

© The Estate of G.G. Connell, 1976, 1994
ISBN 0 947554 40 8

Printed and bound in Great Britain by
Hartnolls Limited, Bodmin, Cornwall

This book is dedicated to
Commander Mark Thornton DSO DSC RN
Commander Rupert Egan DSO DSC RN
and the men who died and served
during the 1st Commission of HMS *Petard*.

Contents

List of Illustrations

MAPS

Acknowledgements

I owe a debt of gratitude to a number of individuals and organisations who helped and encouraged me to write this book, with the British Broadcasting Corporation heading the list. Charlie Chester in two of his regular Saturday morning broadcasts asked for members of the *Petard*'s ship company to get in touch. Because of this radio programme I received a number of letters and visits that helped to put the story together. I am indebted to Jack Hall for his unfailing interest and support during the two years of research and writing, also to the late Alfred Haustead DSM, ex-Chief Petty Officer and Buffer, who served for the entire first commission. Alfred for the last sixteen years of his life endured bravely partial immobility, following a stroke; he supplied a wealth of recollections and guidance, sadly he died on the 31st March 1975, without seeing the completion of the book.

I am grateful to Rear Admiral P. Buckley, CB DSO and his staff led by Mr Parsons at the Naval Historical Section of the Ministry of Defence, for their assistance and placing records at my disposal; the Keeper and staff of the reference library of the Imperial War Museum for their help. I wish also to thank the Keeper of the Public Records Office and in particular the staff of the Rolls and Search rooms for their unfailing courtesy and patience during my many visits to seek and study documents.

To Maureen Lovell who deciphered my early scrawlings, later my inexpert and much amended typed drafts, then converted them into immaculate typescript, I owe a special debt, similar to the one owed to my long suffering family who endured two years of my endeavours that dominated most evenings, overlapping into caravaning holiday breaks.

Finally I wish to acknowledge and thank for his special interest and critical help, Rear Admiral G.C. Leslie, CB OBE MA, Domestic Bursar and Fellow of St Edmund's Hall, friend and advisor to *Petard*'s first commanding officer, and who wrote the postscript placing Part I in its correct perspective.

Introduction

During the summer of 1973, a few days after the start of a holiday tour, with some of the family, taking our caravan through the Yorkshire Dales, the Border counties and on to the West Highlands of Scotland, we paused for a break at the Scottish town, Jedburgh.

Parking the car and caravan outfit by the side of Jed Water, Joan and our two sons, Michael and David, with the dog, explored the river and its banks, while I wandered off into Jedburgh looking for somewhere to cash a cheque and perhaps find a drink. Under my arm I was carrying a rather battered set of Zeiss binoculars, once the property of an officer who served in a U-boat, sunk 31 years before. The binoculars have been in my care since they were taken from the side of a body of a German officer, as it lay in the upper part of the conning tower of his submarine, seconds before it sank, leaving a very young shipmate of mine struggling in a rough Mediterranean sea. The U-boat sank taking not only the corpse of the officer and other crew members, but also the First Lieutenant and an Able Seaman from the destroyer in which I was serving. They were both trapped inside, having boarded the stricken submarine after it had surfaced damaged after a long hunt and attack by our ship.

I was then the Sub-Lieutenant, RNVR in charge of the ship's sea boat that had followed the boarding party who had dived from the forecastle of our destroyer, and had swum through a wind roughened night sea, in the light of the searchlight that illuminated the conning tower of the surfaced and wallowing U-boat. They swam through groups of Germans struggling from their abandoned ship, to board and salvage codebooks and documents; a success that was bought with their lives. At the same time my life was saved because of the earlier action taken by Tony the First Lieutenant.

On the fine sunny late morning of Wednesday, 25th August 1973, with none of these recollections in my head, and only the thoughts and anticipation of a leisurely holiday, the almost forgotten incident came back with sudden and vivid clarity when I discovered by chance, that we had stopped for a break in Tony's home town.

Walking past the ruins of Jedburgh Abbey and the modest war memorial to the dead of two world wars, I had to pause before crossing the road busy with holiday traffic. As I waited for a gap in the traffic flow, I climbed the few steps that lead up and round the memorial to get a better view of the abbey ruins, at the same time glancing casually at the names recorded on the granite face of the small obelisk. I find it difficult to describe my emotions when I realised that the Lieutenant Antony Blair Fasson, George Cross, Royal Navy, whose name appeared with many others, was the same Tony who had saved my life over thirty years before. I stood a little dazed by my feelings and the return of half forgotten memories, in that busy border town, carrying in my hand the trophy I have kept since the night Tony and his companion Colin Grazier died. Colin was also awarded, posthumously, the George Cross for his part in the action.

This extraordinary and accidental spotting of Tony Fasson's name on the border towns war memorial has made it a personal necessity to try and tell the story, a remarkable story, of the fleet destroyer, HMS *Petard* and her ship's company who served in the ship during the first commission that lasted for two and a half years, 1942 to 1944.

Additional authors note to new edition

When this book was originally published I was not aware that the equipment recovered by Tony Fasson and Colin Grazier and later landed at Haifa, under intense security, was in fact an Enigma machine with a complete set of current operating instructions and the TRITON code.

In retrospect it seems that Fasson who had been briefed prior to the commencement of the hunt for *559*, knew what was at stake when he ordered me off the f'x'le to take charge of the whaler while he and Colin dived into the sea to board the stricken U-boat.

This capture of the Enigma equipment contributed dramatically and conclusively towards the defeat of the U-boat campaign of 1943 in the north Atlantic — this face remained a closely guarded secret for 30 years after the end of World War Two.

G.G.C.

PART ONE

27th March 1941 to 9th January 1943

THE FIRST COMMANDING OFFICER

CHAPTER 1

Commissioning and Work-up

On 27th March 1941, a cold grey sombre rain-lashed day, charged with the urgencies and tension that can grip a nation at war, in Walkers' Navy Yard, Newcastle, the long narrow red-leaded hull of yet another fleet destroyer, slid into the industrial polluted waters of the Tyne. No ceremonial distinguished the launching of this addition to the war emergency building programme. Only the builder's officials, tradesmen and yard workers, clad in rain glistened black oilskins, with ordered and practised calm saw the hull safely down the slipway into the river, delivered it to the waiting yard tugs, who nudged and manoeuvred the lifeless slender hull alongside the fitting out berth. From this berth the ship would finally sail for her first commission fourteen months later.

The launching hardly altered the pace and tempo of the work in the adjoining slipways, fitting out berths or workships and foundries. The roar and rattle of riveting, the cascading red gold of molten metal barely faltered and only imperceptibly, as the heart-stopping sight that normally stirs all shipbuilders and seamen, the spectacular entry of a new ship's hull into the water element took place. Such was the crisis urgency of the ship construction programme in the second year of the war.

A small, hardly noticed group of men at the launch, stood apart and clear of the civilian experts overseeing the operation, and watched *Petard* move down the slipway into the river with a proprietary interest. The eight men in naval uniform, had at their head Lieutenant Commander (E) B.R. Faunthorpe, Royal Navy, appointed as the engineer officer of the ship. He had reported to Vickers Armstrong at Walkers' Navy Yard a month earlier to oversee on behalf of the Admiralty the final stages of the hull construction, the launching, and fitting out.

Faunthorpe had with him a specialist warrant officer, the future ship's torpedo gunner. Mr J.A. MacAllen, Gunner (T), was responsible for the electrical equipment and the ship's armament. The remainder of the group who made up Lieutenant Commander

Faunthorpe's staff, working from offices that had been supplied by the Builders, consisted of other specialists who would eventually sail in the ship. These were engine-room artificers, with Chief Engine-room Artificer Peters, the engineer officer's right hand man, and the senior of five engineer artificers. The remaining two members were the petty officers in charge of the ship's naval stores and the ship's office.

The ship that took shape over the next fourteen months following the launch of the hull on the wet cold day in March 1941, came from the Admiralty Constructors' war emergency design of fleet destroyers, and was one of eight destroyers of the 'P' or Pakenham class fleet destroyers, and like her sister ships, 1540 tons, length 388 ft and beam 35 ft. Steam turbine engines developed 40,000SHP, and twin screws gave a top speed of 32 knots. She proved to be extremely stable and manoeuverable in bad seas and at high speeds. Of traditional hull design, with a handsome trawler bow and single funnel, *Petard* was not initially disfigured by a lattice mast; this was fitted later in her life and only after the completion of the first commission. The foremast: a tripod base carried a topmast with two single yardarms and a crow's nest, giving a satisfying finish to a hull design; last to be seen in the destroyers of the 12th Flotilla. A small 286 radar aerial topped the mast head truck.

The main armament was at first sight a shock and a disappointment. Four QF 4 inch Mark V guns of First World War vintage on high single HA/LA mountings that allowed elevation up to almost 90 degrees, were fitted in all the 'P' class ships. These gun mountings had rather odd shaped gun-shields, fitted on the A, B and X mountings, more for their psychological effect on the gun crews, rather than the protection the lightweight thin steel plates could give against blast, shell or bomb splinters. Some shelter was given from wind and spray to the gunlayer and trainer, also the communication and fuze setting members of the gun crews. It was apparently not considered necessary in *Petard* to fit a gun-shield to Y gun on the quarter deck. The protection given by the after superstructure and the blast shield extended from X gun deck above was supposed to be sufficient for this gun and its crew. These rather ancient guns gave *Petard* only limited range and hitting power against surface and ship targets, but with well trained and experienced gun crews she partially overcame this deficiency by delivering a high rate of fire. The guns proved to be very effective against air targets when firing a fixed fuze barrage against diving aircraft. The rate of 22 rounds per minute from each gun saved the ship many times during her service in the Eastern and Central Mediterranean. The fixed ammunition weighing 44lbs per round had to be fuzed and loaded by a team of two fuze setters and four loaders; there were no mechanical aids to assist the gun crews of HMS *Petard*, only highly drilled muscle power and a concentration that could not be diverted from serving the gun in action. One four barrelled pom-pom for close range anti-aircraft protection was mounted abaft the funnel and four oerlikon guns on single mountings were fitted one each side of the bridge and searchlight platform. The searchlight was a powerful 36 inch lamp; the platform also carried the short mainmast with one small yardarm for the W/T aerials.

Eight torpedo tubes, divided into two quadruple mountings on the centre line of the iron deck or waist of the ship, one ahead and the other abaft the searchlight platform were in the best traditions of the fleet destroyer.

To fulfil her anti-submarine role, *Petard* carried 100 depth charges that could be delivered over the side in patterns of eight or twelve from two stern traps and two sets of throwers fitted on each side of the quarterdeck.

The 'P's with the 'O's were to be the last classes of destroyers to be built with the officers' accommodation provided in the after part of the ship.

Accommodation was arranged following a long established tradition with the ratings living in the forward part of the ship and the officers separate and aft, and not suited to modern warfare. The crews of the stern armament lived remote from their action stations, and this applied similarly to most of the officers whose action stations were mainly on or near the bridge. At night and in bad weather closing up for normal sea watches or action stations could be a hazardous evolution, with gun crews rushing aft and into officers moving forward to their stations. Only the Captain had a sea cabin forward, immediately below the bridge. The afterguards' accommodation was both spacious and comfortable, and although the ship was built during the war, the furniture in the cabins and wardroom was constructed rather surprisingly of wood. All nine officers had large single cabins that also served as their offices. In contrast the messdecks were crowded and had few comforts. 211 ratings, senior and junior, had to sling and sleep in hammocks; the open between deck spaces forward were divided into many small messes of about eight to ten ratings whose off duty life centred round one small scrubbed wooden table fixed to steel bars suspended from the deck above at the inboard end, and to the ship's side at the other. Two padded benches (mess stools) completed the furniture apart from the limited and rather primitive crockery and mess cooking utensils, (Tingear).

The leading seaman of the mess or senior longest serving member of the mess normally had the coveted hammock billets above this domestic altar. The messing arrangements were called the canteen system. Each mess had an issue daily or on as regular a basis as operational conditions permitted, bread, meat, flour, tea, sugar, tinned milk and other basic items from the ship's victualling stores. Each man was also allowed a cash victualling allowance; this was spent by the appointed caterer for each mess at the ship's NAAFI canteen on cheese, fresh fruit and vegetables when available and other foods as decided by the mess. Any credit was shared out between the mess members, and overspending had to be settled by the mess sharing the debt. If a mess was dedicated to cash savings and to living only on the victualling office (Pusser's) rations, they could have a rather bleak and hungry time, before making up for their self-imposed austerity by spending the accumulated saved ration allowances on a heroic run ashore. Each mess had a responsibility for preparing their individual meals which were cooked in the ship's company galley located on the upper deck and between the legs of the tripod base of the foremast.

The wardroom had a separate galley in the after superstructure, and a wardroom cook, who organised and prepared the wardroom meals under the direction of the petty officer steward.

In the after superstructure the officers also had their heads and bathroom with hot and cold water; in their cabins wash basins were supplied with hot water from old fashioned copper containers that had been on issue to the fleet for a century or more. Some two-thirds of the after structure was taken up by three electric winches and the hoists to the two four inch main armament ammunition and the depth charge magazines, and space for the ammunition supply parties to manhandle supplies to 'X' and 'Y' guns and the depth charge crews.

The ship's company forward, in contrast to the officers, had primitive heads and bathrooms, a design that had changed only in minor detail since the 1914-1918 war. The bathrooms for the senior ratings as well as the juniors consisted of a space below decks of about 10 or 12 square feet with a few tip-up galvanised basins supplemented by buckets for washing, bathing and dhobying.

The insulation of the ship against heat or cold was primitive and almost non-existent. There were no wooden decks, so in the tropics, conditions between decks, with the sun beating down on iron decks and ship's sides, made life below in a closed down state – portholes and deadlights shut – intolerable except for limited periods, and that only where special provision was made to force in air from the upper deck. In winter or cold conditions, the derisory insulation could not prevent massive discomfort from condensation.

The hull and superstructure were painted dark wartime Home Fleet grey, the ship's pennant numbers, G56 picked out in large white capitals on either side of the bow, and the flotilla colour or markings on the funnel painted in broad red and white bands.

Bertram Aloysius Faunthorpe, Lieutenant Commander (E) RN, responsible for seeing that the Admiralty specification for the *Petard* was carried out by the contracting ships' builders, Vickers Armstrong, came from the West Country, Westward Hoe, the area that had traditionally provided so many other of England's servants in her fighting and colonial services. From public school Bertie had entered the Royal Naval Engineering College at Keyham, Devonport where he had acquired his skills as both a naval and marine engineer. His relaxed, slightly donnish appearance and attitudes tended to emphasise his intellectual ability, so that it came as some surprise to find that he was also an extremely practical engineer, capable of improvisation and manual skills in situations of emergency or damage from enemy action or maritime hazards.

He had a tremendous, also wicked, often Rabelaisian sense of humour, an enjoyment of the ridiculous, liked his liquor; his company was savoured and enjoyed by women. The music which was the civilising feature of the wardroom was entirely due to his influence, and came via the small portable gramophone, (Bertie's) a permanent fixture screwed to the mess side-board, and Bertie's stock of records. Of necessity this stock was a small one and could not be replaced as they became worn and casualties of bad weather and enemy action. The record that survived all others, and very much his favourite and remembered by his mess-mates, never to be forgotten, the Spinners' Chorus from *The Flying Dutchman*.

Bertie, like most of the wardroom, was a bachelor, and at thirty-five the oldest officer in the ship. Because of his age he had to put up with irreverent and affectionate ribbing by his juniors, enquiring and asking him to describe what it felt like to be '35 years of age'! He was a master of bar games and particularly those based on dice. Single and double cameroons game of dice awaited the watchkeeping officers relaxing after sea watches or action stations, who were kept up-to-date with their progress in complicated variations of these dice games, with charts and tables, kept with care and detail by Bertie and his conspirator and other non-watchkeeper, the ship's doctor, the Irishman Prendergast.

Bertie was a little older and senior in rank as a lieutenant commander than the captain who eventually arrived to take over the command of the *Petard*. Lieutenant Commander Mark Thornton, DSC RN, appointed to the command of the destroyer from 28th April 1942 had seniority as a lieutenant commander dated 16th November 1938. Bertie's seniority dated from 1st July of the same year. Bertie's age and seniority, with his personality strengths, were a steadying influence in periods of tension and near crisis during the early days of *Petard*'s working-up programme following the departure from the Tyne.

Lieutenant Commander Mark Thornton, DSC RN, *Petard*'s first of two commanding officers during the first commission was a long serving professional naval officer, a product of a training which had commenced in early teenage. He came to the ship after a brief rest, from another fleet destroyer HMS *Harvester*, where he had won a DSC for sinking a German submarine *U32*, and like so many other captains of destroyers and escorts, he had been driven to the limits of mental and physical exhaustion because of demands made during the first desperate two years of war at sea.

In appearance he had a body frame of medium height, square and powerful. He seemed to have immense strength, a thick muscular neck supported a head square and flat at the back and top, covered by thick grey closely cropped hair. His face, rugged and battered like a boxer's, completed the total impression of the granite man. He terrified many, and in particular those who formed the junior section of the wardroom. He was a great if unorthodox and daring seaman, he taught new embryo officers much about seamanship, lessons that made men react instinctively in action conditions.

It was clear in the early days when Mark Thornton pressurised the builders to complete the ship for sea trials, at the same time driving hard to turn a new and in the main raw ship's company into the semblance of a reliable and effective crew, that he traded heavily on mental resources that had been under prolonged stress, and only briefly rested.

His gentle wife, living in rented accommodation so as to be near and to make the most of his short breaks from sea service, was because of her anxiety about him, a confirmation of first impressions gained by some of his officers. A few days before the ship sailed for Scapa Flow, Mrs Thornton having tea with the officers, shyly asked her hosts to take care and to look after Mark. To young men, new and very junior officers, it seemed inconceivable that such a request fitted any forseeable eventuality, when the Captain seemed to be a ruthless powerhouse of a man. It was not until seven months later that the reason for the hesitant plea seemed to fit the situation and the man.

For the immediate present, the actions of Mark to further his determination to achieve seagoing and fighting efficiency in the shortest possible time, dominated everyone's lives. The Captain was served by two mature senior officers, First Lieutenant and the Engineer Officer, strong and experienced personalities, professionals like himself, who saved him from his own excesses and the disaster that could have been the end product of some of his more extravagant exercises imposed on a tired and at times near desperate ship's company.

Early on the Tuesday morning of the second week in May, an air of expectancy, tinged with anxious curiosity, gripped the now enlarged advance contingent who were preparing *Petard* for her acceptance trials and the reception of her ship's company. All the officers and senior chief and petty officers, specialists and heads of departments, had arrived during the last few days to join the ship. The advance party with one or two exceptions were now living onboard, with the main living spaces and domestic services being hastened towards completion by the builders.

Although the messdeck continued to be littered with the builders' equipment, tools, airlines for compressed air drills and chisels, ship's fittings waiting to be bolted or welded into position, the hammock rails festooned with electric leads for temporary lighting, it was now possible for the ship's company to occupy the crowded spaces.

The First Lieutenant, with the coxswain, Chief Petty Officer

Traves, the chief bosun's mate, Petty Officer Alfred Haustead, and his other senior rating head of department, Chief Gunner's Mate and instructor, Chief Petty Officer A.L. Hobbs, after long hours of work on the nominal roll received from the manning depot, HMS *Victory* at Portsmouth, prepared the ship's watch bill, and for each member of the arriving ship's company, his individual station card. These cards gave every seaman, stoker or communication rating his mess, part of ship, watch, action and defence station, damage, collision and abandon ship station. The work of fitting qualifications, experience and service from the information supplied with the nominal roll by the drafting authority was complicated and subject to the problem shared by all fighting units in the second year of war, of not having more than a handful of trained war experienced men to fill the many vital action stations on a watch and station bill.

The task of slotting in names and qualifications from long impersonal lists off the ship's nominal roll was on this Tuesday morning personalised as the party of men who had travelled up on the long overnight train journey from Portsmouth to Newcastle would soon be marching onto the fitting out jetty. Hostility-only conscripts, volunteer or pensioner reservists, regular engagement seamen, stokers and communications ratings would identify themselves as the Chief Gunner's Mate called out their names from the nominal roll, and become recognised as individuals.

The arrival of two large canvas covered, 3 ton Royal Navy transport lorries with civilian drivers, signalled the impending approach of the marching body of about 200 ratings with their petty officers.

From the lorries, about half a dozen seamen and stokers descended, baggage party in charge of the piles of kit bags, hammocks and suitcases. As this small party lowered tailboards to prepare for unloading, it did not pass unnoticed that they were to a man badgemen 'old hands' who had not missed the trick of avoiding marching to their ship.

The First Lieutenant, second in command and senior executive watch-keeping officer, Lieutenant Antony Blair Fasson, RN, moved down onto the jetty, dressed in his No 1 uniform to receive the ship's company. He was joined by the Chief Gunner's Mate tall, straight and immaculate, a product of the gunnery school at Whale Island; the Coxswain in his role as the regulating Chief Petty Officer, sat at a small table placed on the jetty, with all his station cards ready for distribution. The Chief Bosun's mate made up the fourth of the reception party and, as befitting his special responsibilities of being in charge of all the upper deck, standing and running gear and rigging, boats anchors and cables, wires and hawsers, his short stocky figure was clad in well scrubbed overalls, with his 'pusser's' knife, the Chief Buffer's badge of office, slung round his waist by a plaited codline lanyard.

Suddenly the ship's company were in sight, marching in fours with the characteristic relaxed gait that all sailors acquire, with oilskins folded over their left arms. No one, who saw them marching through the crowded busy shipyard, over the train and crane rails, failed to feel a sudden lift and a catch in the throat. Even the yard workers who had seen it all many times before, reacted to the sight of the *Petard*'s men marching into the yard to man their ship. Ragged cheers and shouts, laced with rough Geordie humour, came from the yardees on the slipways, ships longside the fitting out berths, yard roadways and workshops, greeted and encouraged the marching men. The column wound its way through the yard roadways on to the jetty where the ship that they had come to man, lay ready to receive its ship's company.

The column halted, ordered by the petty officer in charge of the draft to form two deep and right turn in two ranks facing their ship.

After the formalities of saluting and reporting his draft to the First Lieutenant, the petty officer was ordered to fall the men out to collect their hammocks and baggage from the transport and to fall in again. While this was going on, the advance party now gathered on the upper deck of the *Petard* looked down with interest and a variety of emotions at their newly arrived shipmates. Some looked for 'old ships', others for the number of service badges, rank as well as qualifications, trying to assess the amount of experience and training in the draft.

The men on the jetty in their turn, as they collected their large yellow canvas kit bags and hammocks and stood at ease in the re-formed two ranks, looked at their ship for the first time. To about fifty, this was their first ship, to others regulars and hostility only, *Petard* was the first destroyer in their sea-going experience, but there were in the ranks a sprinkling of smallship, destroyer men. From these in the main, came the ribald and shouted enquiries to the few ratings of the advance party standing on the irondeck and forecastle. The *Petard* looked now nearly the complete ship, superstructure, masts and funnel in place, boats at their davits, guns and torpedo tubes shipped, with civilian as well as base naval armament experts carrying out final adjustments and tests. The draft could see and hear the continuing dockyard builders' activity, long lengths of air hoses and power cables in untidy bunches linking the shore to the ship and snaking the length of the decks and into bulkhead doors, down hatchways, serving workmen fitting ammunition lockers, cutting holes for last minute equipment, and much else that still required to be done before the ship sailed for her first engine and sea trials. Packing cases stood singly or in piles on deck and the quay, the first arrivals of a small mountain of engineering, naval and armament stores, that would have to be struck down below in orderly sequence, into store-rooms and between deck stowage.

The brief moment of relaxation was terminated by the Chief GI calling the draft to attention and to report to the First Lieutenant that the draft was ready for the rollcall and embarkation. Before this was done Tony Fasson introduced himself and welcomed the draft to the *Petard*.

In a few short sentences he outlined the immediate tasks for the new and final arrivals. The senior ratings, followed by the junior seamen, stokers and miscellaneous ratings, were to collect their station cards from the coxswain as their names were called out by the Chief GI, with their kit and hammocks file onboard where guides would lead the way to the separate messes for the various ranks and rates. Breakfast was ready and available from the ship's company galley. They all had an hour to eat, stow away kit and hammocks, shift into working rig, overalls, and standby to obey the pipe to fall in for receiving details of the next few days' routine, meet their divisional officers, the petty officer captains of the tops, allocated jobs and the routine for the day.

As the last man filed over the brow and stepped down onto the iron deck carrying his hammock and bulky kitbag, *Petard*, now with her ship's company, seemed to come alive.

The next morning the white ensign was hoisted and the ship formally commissioned. At 1100 hours, before 'up spirits' for the issue of rum was piped, the call to 'clear the lower deck' was heard through the ship for the first time. All officers, senior and junior ratings were ordered to muster on the forecastle, facing aft. It did not take long for the coxswain to move swiftly through the between spaces of the ship, to check that no one had failed to hear or obey the shrill pipe of the quartermaster's and bosun's calls and to report to the First Lieutenant that the lower deck was cleared, that all officers and ratings were mustered on the forecastle. The mainly overall clad mass of seamen and stokers with their chief and petty officers stood in a packed crowd on the narrow forecastle, on and between the anchor cables, the twin capstans and round the four inch 'A' gun. The officers stood in a small blue clad knot within the mustered ship's company and with Bertie in his white grease stained engine-room overall, made a contrasting enclave.

Tony Fasson called the assembled company to attention, then disappeared rapidly aft over the decks covered with dockyard litter, to report to the captain, returning within a few minutes as simultaneously Lieutenant Commander Mark Thornton appeared on the anti-blast flare of 'B' gun deck, above the heads of his ship's company.

Tony shouted from the forecastle, the formalities of reporting that everyone was present, and at the Captain's invitation stood the *Petard*'s crew at 'Stand easy'. Mark Thornton looked down at the men he was to lead and command, his square powerful physique dominated the men gathered on the deck below, making a strong, and for some a fearful, impression on the majority who were seeing their commanding officer for the first time.

Using short uncomplicated sentences, the Captain introduced himself – proclaimed with a complete and an unsophisticated conviction that he knew that every member of his ship's company shared his impatient pleasure in receiving a seagoing appointment, and above all to be in a new fleet destroyer. He was now hellbent to get to sea, finish the working up and training period so that he could get back to the war, and seek action with the enemy as quickly as possible. To achieve this objective the Captain left no one in any doubt of his intention to work himself and his ship's company tirelessly with only the briefest opportunity for 'make and mends' or leave. As a final footnote to his short address to his officers and ratings, Mark, probably to reassure the new hands and bolster the courage of the apprehensive, proclaimed that his war experience to date had proved that the enemy could not kill him, and he would survive the war. This immunity he knew would be shared by his new ship and her ship's company.

The somewhat dazed company had little time to ponder on the short, sharp statement of his objectives, by the man who now assumed the responsibility for their future and lives, before Fasson called the new ship's company to attention for the second time, ordered off caps; the Captain then read the Articles of War, followed by the commissioning warrant. Stores, naval, victualling and armament began to arrive in a continuous flow by rail, road and by barge. All had to be checked, embarked and most manhandled through narrow bulk-head doors or down hatches to stowage positions. Very few of even the largest and heaviest items could be eased aboard and into position by the dock-side cranes. Time had to be found for men to be exercised at their action and armament stations. Guns, main and secondary, torpedo tubes, control stations with firing and communication circuits had to be tested and double checked.

The First Lieutenant organised and controlled all this feverish activity, and into the tight schedule on each day of the remaining time at Walker's Yard he made it possible for one watch, half the ship's company, to get all night leave. Most men gratefully found their way to the Newcastle pubs and dance halls for brief respite from the hard physical demands made on them within the crowded confines of the *Petard*, and were able to enjoy the entertainment to be found in the war blacked-out Newcastle, but some found the after effects of the northern beer an additional trial when reporting for work at both watches of the hands at 0730 hours the following morning.

Fuel tanks were filled and boilers flashed up; with steam raised and passed into the turbines, longside engine and steering machinery tests and trials commenced. These, with minor problems only to be rectified, led on to the first of a short series of steaming acceptance trials in the North Sea. There was a headlong atmosphere of urgency and to many the awareness of the inevitable remorseless return to the grim realities of long days and nights of war at sea.

Sea and acceptance trials completed, *Petard* in June 1942, reported herself ready to sail for her working up exercises prior to joining the fleet. The day the ship sailed from the Tyne, she lay ready to slip, with steam and main engines at immediate notice, at low tide alongside the fitting out jetty of Walkers' Navy Yard. The jetty towered over the ship's waist and iron deck crowded with the ship's company who had been 'cleared from the lower deck' to hear their Captain bid farewell to the builders.

Most of the ship's company looking up, could see Mark Thornton as he stood on the brow linking the forecastle to the shore, already slung to be hoisted clear by the waiting crane so that *Petard* could slip and proceed to sea. He stood impressive in his sea gear, the naval cap crowning his massive head at a characteristic angle. Mark roared at the assembled builders' executives and workmen, thanked them for their workmanship and achievement in handing over a fine ship to fight the King's enemies. In return he promised that he and his ship would hound the enemy and bring him to action; the ship's builders could expect a steady stream of trophies that would follow *Petard*'s successes. Good stirring stuff that finished with a call of three cheers from both sides, but many of the new ship's company were left with feelings of apprehension and the Geordies were looking sympathetic.

There was a certain uniqueness about the ceremony; the spokesman for the builders, who replied to Mark's short speech, was not an executive, but one of the workmen chosen by ballot. *Petard*'s captain with a special flair for the occasion, presented the workman standing in his soiled overalls, with an engraved pint tankard, an action that was appreciated and gave enormous pleasure to a surprised workforce.

Petard moved away stern first, then turning without the aid of tugs in the narrow river, the screws churning the brown water violently as Mark forced the ship round in its own length to point down stream to the sea. She slipped swiftly down the Tyne for the last time, into the grey North Sea, turning to port and steamed north at speed towards the Orkneys and Scapa Flow.

From the Flow the ship sailed each day to exercise engine-room, upperdeck, gunnery, torpedo and signal departments. To become a fighting ship the *Petard* and her company had to learn to live with the sea in all its conditions. Although it was June, the weather ranged from poor to appalling, with only rare fine days that seemed miraculous because of the contrast and their beauty. More often the ship's company's lot was a long day at sea in bad conditions with gun crews struggling to keep their feet to engage surface and air targets, driven on by their remorseless captain. The day would finish by a return to Scapa and a struggle for an hour or more to pick up and secure to a mooring buoy in the teeth of a westerly gale, sleet and snow flurries at times adding to the torment, as luckless buoy jumpers with bruised hands and bodies strove to secure the mooring cable to the buoy ring.

The weather plus inexperience in the engine-room and wheel-house as well as on the forecastle, at times submerged the buoy and its seaman before the ship was secured. For the gunnery control officer, who was also the forecastle officer, these failures and the pressures from the Captain and the First Lieutenant made anxious responsibilities for a new and raw reserve sub-lieutenant.

Mark brought back to the base, day after day, an exhausted ship's company; he stayed at sea as long as there was light to see; all night when there was an opportunity to exercise night encounters, and anti-submarine offensive training. The weather conditions could and would not deter him. In harbour even after a late return he would continue with damage control exercises, physical training and any other activity that could not be fitted into the day's programme at sea.

On the rare occasions when secured early enough for the wardroom members to sit down for a meal together, the mess was more than once startled by the spectacle of Mark leaping to his feet and beating the after bulkhead with his fists until the metal boomed like a drum, and at the same time roaring 'I must have action with the Enemy now'. It seemed impossible for him to contain his tremendous physical and overtaut strained nervous energy.

Two or three days and nights were spent at sea in generally foul weather: the ship steamed north and south under whatever lee that the islands of the Orkneys and Shetlands provided, so that gunnery practice against air and sea practice targets, officer of the watch with fleet manoeuvering exercises, could continue. The pace never slackened and Mark was tireless in his pursuit for maximum efficiency in all departments. A raw ship's company was gradually being transformed into a fighting unit, building on the professional skills of the few regular officers and senior ratings with a sprinkling of action experienced reservists. Gun crews with their control teams began to achieve a degree of competence and ability to fight the ship by day or night in all conditions of sea and weather.

Day and night action stations, damage control, the very many exercises of towing, being towed, boarding parties, collision and ramming stations, depth charge and torpedo drill, as well as the whole range of a fighting ship's general drill, followed in endless and repetitive cycles. The ability to live, cook, feed, keep body and clothing clean and mind alert in a small highly manoeuverable close packed ship came to all the recent landsmen with varying degrees of ease, depending on the individual, but all had to learn fast how to survive. This applied to both officers and ratings.

The entire ship's company was involved; none escaped the

exhausting pressures put on them. The engine room learned to react to sudden calls for full speed, emergency stops and full astern without blowing the ship apart. Even the bleak weather failed to make the upper deck parties envy the stokers in their inferno below. The communications department in their turn, because of their close proximity to the Captain had cause to envy the seaman when V/S and W/T fell below requirements.

There were however setbacks that must have strained both Tony's and Bertie's qualities of leadership and loyalty to the full. The ship had returned and secured to her buoy with improved speed and squared off for the night. It was too late and dark for shore leave to the canteen at Flotta. The ship's company with the exception of the duty men and watch were quickly piped-down, all were looking forward to a short but comparatively warm night in little used hammocks, free from alarms within the relative shelter that Scapa Flow could offer. Aft in the wardroom and cabins, officers were catching up with writing reports and other documentation, without which no training or even a war seemed possible. Most were anticipating a few hours in their bunks with a degree of pleasure. Only the officer-of-the-day, his standby and watchkeepers viewed the remainder of the night with less enthusiasm.

The sudden gut rendering rattle of the action alarm destroyed all this. Officers clawed their way up ladders pulling on protective clothing as they ran out onto the iron deck and the pitch dark to their action stations. From forward, the wind blew a whiff of acrid smells from some sort of explosion and the sound of angry murmurs from men's voices, a disturbing situation, as men usually moved to action stations silently and fast. This time men were struggling out from the forward messdecks through the heavy canvas darkened ship screens in some confusion, not all dazed with sleep and alarm from an unidentified danger, but also anger. As the action stations closed up, reports started to come through that there had been an explosion in the stokers' messdeck, followed by an inrush of water – no casualties, and that the Captain was at the scene.

Before the standard operational signal could be passed to the base Flag Officer warning the base and all ships present of an emergency, an order reached the bridge from Tony, also at the scene of the incident, fortunately in time to stop an alarm signal being passed by W/T and signal light. By this time the bridge and gunnery control officers were receiving information that the action station alarm was an exercise initiated by the Captain, and that the stokers' messdeck was in a shambles.

After a delay of about twenty minutes the First Lieutenant arrived on the bridge ordering action stations to fall-out and with the exception of the duty watch, everyone was to pipe-down and turn in immediately. The duty watch was to report to the stokers' messdeck.

In the wardroom, officers who had returned from their action stations, except for No.1, learnt from a terse and angry Bertie briefly what had happened. Mark had apparently decided to stage an emergency exercise by simulating a limpet mine explosion without consulting either his Engineer Officer or First Lieutenant. His intention to catch his ship's company at rest after the ship had returned to harbour could not be faulted, and the fact that the ship survived its first two and a half years' commission was due to his relentless training; only the timing of this particular party was perhaps questionable.

The ship and its company was having its first short breather; the opportunity of a little undisturbed sleep during the work-up period, and following a spell of continuous day and night exercises, dominated by a captain who would allow no let-up, or concessions to the weather conditions. Very few were yet able to appreciate that the rough tough rather frightening character who seemed tireless and perhaps just a little mad, was a splendid seaman with many surprising sides to his character. The qualities that he did lack and perhaps for understandable reasons at that time in his career, were perception and patience. He did not pause to consider if that particular night was the right one for testing his command's reaction to yet another surprise emergency exercise, when he ordered a reluctant duty petty officer to follow him through the darkened hammock packed seamen's messdeck to hurl a thunderflash down a hatch into the sleep filled stokers' messdeck below.

As the startled sleepers leapt or fell out of their hammocks, the welter of alarmed and shouting stokers were drenched by a massive jet of freezing sea water from a fire hose held by Mark Thornton and the duty petty officer standing at the top of the hatch. Not even the seamen in the messdeck above, wakened by the explosion and the uproar, could appreciate the validity of the exercise when they found as they turned out of their hammocks, the Captain directing a hose down into the mess below. To describe the reaction of the

J. A. MacAllen, Gunner (T) (Malaya)   Lieutenant Commander Mark Thornton, DSC, RN

Petard off Ras el Tin, Alexandria

Able Seamen Mizon and Emmott, pom-pom crew

Leading Seaman Russell,
Captain of 'B' gun

Lieutenant Commander (E) B. R. Faunthorpe (Bertie), Chief E.R.A. Peters and colleague

ship's company as being that of bewilderment would be to underrate the situation for the next few days. It discredited for a time the ability of a fighting destroyer captain.

A few days later the ship left Scapa Flow for the last time and was heading her way south down inside the outer Hebrides, bound for Loch Long and torpedo running trials.

Leaving Scapa Flow at the conclusion of the first part of the working up period, the event was marked by one of those extraordinary calm warm exquisite days that make the Highlands and Isles places of special magic, and that so often follow periods of bad and hellish water. The ship first sailed west along the top of Scotland, rounded Cape Wrath and south down inside the outer Hebrides heading for the Little Minch and the sea of the Hebrides, on passage to Loch Long and a programme of torpedo running trials. The ship's company closed up at defence stations and everyone working on cleaning ship and armament overhaul. It was an interlude before the horror of war caught up with the new vessel of destruction. New as well as experienced seamen of *Petard*'s crew responded to the sunshine and beauty of the sea and islands, the air seemed like some wonderful gift from the Celtic gods. The ship's company was relaxed and the recent tensions and pressures were receding into the background.

The ship steamed swiftly south, dipping gently into the slight swell, and through waters of teaming brit and the attendant mackerel. Groups of magnificent and savage gannets plummeted out of the sky into the shoals; surfacing to gorge their catch, taking off with mighty wings thrashing the sea, to repeat the spectacular vertical plunge with outstretched neck and half closed wings. At times groups of ten and more, close by and distant, crashed down into the sea to harvest the waters. A number were operating ahead of the ship; men crowded to the rails to see the splendid and dramatic dives by these beautiful sea birds.

For the next few days the ship was engaged on torpedo running trials on the test ranges in Loch Long. Torpedoes were run and calibrated with an associated spin-off, officers of the watch could practise ship handling to pick up the tin fish. Sea-boat crews and upperdeck parties improved and learnt new seamanship skills through recovering and hoisting back in board heavy and awkward torpedoes.

The ship anchored off Greenock for several nights, and for the first time since leaving the Tyne, all night leave was piped for a watch at a time. Almost all made their way to Glasgow. The city a rough tough place in the blackout, its pubs never the places where drink could be used as the catalyst for social occasions, were in a wartime setting of general drabness, dreadful tiled establishments dedicated to grim and drunken consumption of endless scotch and chasers. There were of course the exceptions, where relaxation could be enjoyed in hostelries that compared with the best south of the border. The city was full of servicemen of all branches and nationalities, seamen of fighting and merchant navies who crowded the bars, dance halls and places of entertainment. Arguments and alcoholic spurred rivalries were an accepted hazard, and the women hard pressed by many transient partners. The runs ashore with the chance of a drink, a meal and some entertainment made a change that was needed, and steadied many of *Petard*'s ship's company for whatever lay ahead.

There were a great many ships in the Clyde and Firth, a constant movement upstream to discharge from incoming ocean and coastal convoys or fast independent ships that sailed unescorted outside the convoy system. Besides the discharge of the raw materials of war and supplies for the civilian life of the United Kingdom, great vessels were embarking troops with supporting stores and arms, then moving down into the Firth to anchor inside the boom defences. Others arrived already loaded with troops and stores from other UK ports. These ships were naturally the targets of rumour and great speculation, as it was obvious that a troop convoy was in the process of being formed. Speculation reached fever pitch when it was known that *Petard* had finished her brief work-up period and was to take her place in the fleet as a member of the 12th Destroyer Flotilla. The ship was topped up with stores, victualling, naval and armament, to full capacity. Ammunition barges moved in to both sides of the ship as she lay at an allocated buoy.

Petard's full outfit of 4 inch fixed ammunition, semi-armour piercing, direct impact, anti-aircraft and starshell was embarked and passed down into the magazines. Upper-deck ready use lockers were filled, and under the control of the Gunner (T) Mr MacAllan, the Chief Gunner's Mate, A.L. Hobbs, and his party, with the gun crews, worked through the night to fuze anti-aircraft shells. Pom-pom and oerlikon ammunition was also embarked, torpedo warheads were shipped.

CHAPTER 2

Bound to the East Mediterranean Station

To confirm any doubts that remained whether the ship would join the escort of the convoy anchored in the Clyde, and at the same time to focus the rumours on probable destinations, the ship's company were issued with white tropical kit. The cruiser HMS *Hawkins* of 1914-1918 vintage and the armed merchant cruiser HMS *Ranpura* arrived, anchored in the Clyde and prepared for early departure. Their ships' companies seemed to share buzzes similar to those that prevailed in the *Petard*.

All speculation came to an end with the convoy conference held in the headquarters of the Flag Officer Clyde. The conference attended by the convoy commodore, commanding officers of the escort ships, and the masters of the twelve ships forming the convoy, learnt that the departure date was to be 30th July 1942, with a final destination Port Suez via the Cape of Good Hope.

At 07.45 hours of 30th July, HMS *Hawkins*, (Captain G.A. French RN) and HMS *Ranpura*, Captain H.T.W. Pawsey RN, preceded by two destroyers, *Petard* and *Catterick*, Lieutenant C.H. Highton RN, sailed and passed through the Clyde boom, deployed south of Arran, to await the emergence of the ships of Convoy WS 21 from their anchorage. At precisely 08.30 hours SS *Narkunda*, with Commodore E.C. Denison MVO RNR and his staff embarked, passed the boom-gate vessel at the head of an extended column of twelve great ships. Some of the ex-passenger liners loaded with military stores and troops, bore names remembered from the days of peace.

One of *Petard*'s company regarded the familiar lines of the SS *Almanzora* in the long line of ships, with affection and nostalgia. Born in Portugal and brought up there with many others of British stock, he had travelled in her and the sister ships of the Royal Mail Line many times to and from school in the UK, on the scheduled services to Spain, Portugal and South America. These journeys with the ship full of unescorted school children of both sexes, a special trial for the ship's masters and their crews, were a high spot for the youngsters.

The *Almanzora* with her company colours now covered by the drab war grey like the other ships in the convoy, began to increase speed as ships took up their pre-planned positions in five columns, numbered 01 to 05, deployed abeam.

01	02	03	04	05
SS *James Lykes*	SS *Circassa*	SS *Narkunda*	SS *Malosa*	SS *Almanzora*
SS *Curacoa*	SS *Largs Bay*	SS *Tomaroa*	SS *Rangittini*	SS *Samaria*
	SS *Aorangi*		SS *Volenden*	

With *Hawkins* steaming ahead of the SS *Narkunda* and the Commodore in the centre column 03, the *Ranpura* covering the rear of the formation, and *Petard* and *Catterick* giving anti-submarine cover ahead and to port and starboard of the convoy, the scheduled speed of 13 knots was reached as the ships rounded the Mull of Kintyre and headed for the rendezvous with the main part of the ocean escort.

The additional escorts, seven fleet and Hunt class destroyers, with the senior officer of the anti-submarine screen, Commander J.E. Broome RN in HMS *Keppel*, sailed from Londonderry to rendezvous with the convoy at 0600 hours six miles off Oversay the morning after the departure from the Clyde. The convoy moved west into the Atlantic and into rapidly deteriorating visibility. Fog enveloped the convoy with a varying degree of density for the next two days bringing immediate continuing tragedy, and near disaster to the outward bound Convoy WS 21.

In worsening conditions with ships losing sight of each other from time to time, in the swirling grey wetness of the fog, the merchant ships struggled to keep station and in touch with the next ahead and those in the adjoining columns. Fog buoys were streamed and towed to help the ships astern to keep station by steering up to the plume of spray thrown up by the buoy when the towing ship, the next ahead in the column, became blotted out by the closing down of the fog blanket.

During the 48 hours of navigational nightmare, two escorting Sunderland flying boats of Coastal Command were shot down out of the fog by the gunners in the crowded transports; at the same time a maritime disaster of titanic proportions was miraculously avoided. An incoming convoy, unsighted or reported by the primitive radar, passed so close to WS 21 in the dense murk, that HMS *Ledbury* covering the port column 01, immediately after picking up a few flying boat survivors, collided with the port wing ship of Convoy MG 86 as the two great formations of ships blundered past unseen on reciprocal courses.

After the first doom haunted days, the ships steamed south into improving weather, and gradually those embarked in the transport and the escort ships crews began to shake off the depression that had gripped the great company of ships. For the next few days the Commodore exercised by day and night his convoy in emergency drills and turns, the close escort responding with changes in anti-submarine screening formations executed as necessary at high speed. Defensive and offensive exercises to counter submarine, surface and air attacks, were carried out frequently. In the *Petard*, the Captain was in his element and could be appreciated in his capacity as the professional and tireless fighting seaman. The new and junior watchkeeping officers under his eye quickly became proficient, able to keep station on the zig-zagging convoy and position as part of the appropriate formal anti-submarine screen, ordered by the escort commander. They learnt to observe quickly and without the need of unnecessary signals, changes of bearing and distance carried out by the escort commander's ship and other escort destroyers and to respond quickly and smoothly by adjusting *Petard*'s station without driving the engine room watch frantic with frequent changes of engine revolutions. Bearing and distance could be gained or lost by subtle and almost instinctive orders to the helmsman for course and rudder alterations.

Above all else Mark Thornton, and Tony as the senior watchkeeper, taught officers, bridge signal staff, lookouts and gun crews to use eyes and binoculars constantly; no one dare be caught relaxing or off guard, Mark's fury could be devastating and terrible. The radar fitted in *Petard* was still relatively primitive, the air and surface warning set had limited range and capability to give accurate bearings, and the single gunnery ranging set could only be used when the optical rangefinder in the gunnery control director was trained and elevated on the target. There were no radar monitors either on the bridge, charthouse or plot. The ability to keep a good visual lookout was basic and vital.

The pressure was on the three sub-lieutenants as embryo watch-keepers at sea, but the Captain quickly gave his trust. They learnt that when Mark grunted 'Got the weight, Sub?' and if satisfied by the response, retired to rest or to eat in his sea cabin below the bridge, he neither nagged or flustered the OOW by constant enquiries or orders up the voice pipe. He was always on call and never choked off the nervous or uncertain officer who may have called him onto the bridge unnecessarily, even if roused from a brief sleep and up onto a dark rain lashed bridge.

Although the Captain's actions continued at times to alarm, they were in retrospect somehow complementary to the steady and solid influence of his senior executive officer Tony Fasson. During the long journey round the Cape to Port Suez the ship and her company acquired through the drive of these two, the instinctive skills that must have contributed to the *Petard*'s survival in the months and years ahead.

Progress south continued with few U-boat alarms and only one or two major alterations of course to avoid probable positions of the enemy reported in the intelligence signals received daily from the Admiralty. The ship's company became conditioned to a two watch defence station routine that kept half the armament continuously manned. Full Action Stations were closed up at the dangerous periods of dawn and dusk. The asdic crews settled down to a continuous anti-submarine search that would never be relaxed at sea until the ship returned to England $2\frac{1}{2}$ years later. It was the asdic crews of the escort ships that broke the steady routine from time to time with reports of probable sub-contacts and caused a flurry of one or more destroyers ordered to investigate and attack.

Apart from exercising the depthcharge crews, the Commodore and his convoy carrying out defensive and emergency turns away from suspect submarine contacts, there was little sign of the enemy except for the appearance of the occasional Focke Wulf reconnaissance aircraft. Even this diversion ceased as the convoy moved further down towards the South Atlantic.

The distant covering force appeared from time to time, first as dimly seen shapes and masts on the horizon, then to close the convoy – perhaps to reassure the troops who crowded the transports. The force would then drop back over the horizon in the direction that possible surface raiders could approach.

Continuing far out from the mainland of Portugal the convoy approached the latitude of the Azores; first the *Petard* and then the *Catterick* were detached and sent on ahead to Ponto Delgada to fuel from an oil tanker based there for the purpose of fuelling escorts of ocean convoys. *Petard* arrived at noon on a calm, warm and sunny day, 5th August; secured immediately to the oiler, and commenced to embark bunker fuel up to the full capacity of her tanks.

The guard-ship lying at her anchor was the British designed 'H' class Portuguese destroyer *Vouga*. She looked resplendent and rather incongruous in her peacetime livery, with awnings spread and officers and ratings uniformed in immaculate whites. The officer of the guard from NRP *Vouga* was soon on the visiting warship's quarter-deck, wearing sword and medals, presenting his commanding officer's compliments and an offer of assistance to the Captain of the *Petard* during the ship's brief fuelling stop.

The visitors scored a minor success as the British ship's duty officer was able to respond to the officer of the guardship in colloquial Lisbon Portuguese. This resulted in an immediate and pressing invitation to visit the *Vouga*, to sample its wines. A splendid but perhaps fortunately brief session playing 'Cardinal Puff' was spent by about six members of HMS *Petard*'s afterguard in the Portuguese wardroom sitting round the open hatch, of what in a British ship would be a magazine, but in this fortunate neutral was a shipborne wine store. The blazing hot afternoon was better suited for a swim and a brief siesta than the sampling of wines from Portugal, the Azores and Madeira. Only the completion of the fuelling and the need to return to protect the vital convoy continuing on its way south, broke up a party before it could seriously get under way. The hosts had to see their guests take their ship out of Ponto Delgada at speed to relieve the escort partner, *Catterick*, who in turn later entered port to fuel.

By dawn the 5th August, six destroyers of the screen had withdrawn and proceeded eastward to Gibraltar, leaving the senior officer of the destroyers for one day further before he also complied with the WS 21 Convoy plan and left on the 6th August in HMS *Keppel*.

Only *Petard* and *Catterick* remained as anti-U-boat screen, with the cruisers *Hawkins* and *Ranpura* to fight off any German surface raider that might locate the convoy. The two destroyers, to extend their fragile cover against possible U-boat intrusion, placed themselves about five miles ahead and out at 45 degrees from the two leading wing ships of the formed convoy. As they carried out independent zigzags across the line of advance, the two ships were at times outside visibility distance from each other. Asdic equipment range was limited so the ability to keep a constant all-round visual watch for periscopes or submarines on the surface was vital; with little support from the poor ranging ability of the radar sets available to the escorts, and the danger that if used, they could indicate the position of the convoy to the enemy.

The weather remained perfect, light breezes, a calm sea and the sun blazing down from a cloudless sky. The ships' companies of the warships and the troops embarked in the convoy revelled in the long days of hot sunshine; the sea, a lovely blue reflection of the sky, erupted from time to time as schools of dolphins and porpoises leaped ahead and around the ships. Flying fish rushed and skimmed across the water away from the advancing vessels, and at night occasionally landed on the low decks of the two destroyers to startle into alarmed awakeness seamen sleeping in the cool of the upper deck away from the hot closed down atmosphere of the crowded messdecks.

Noon, 7th August 1942, position 18 degrees 50 minutes north, 22 degrees 10 minutes west, course 175 degrees, speed 12½ knots, weather clear and calm, visibility excellent, Convoy WS 21 proceeding with no reports of enemy sightings. The escorts at two watch defence stations, closing up to full action stations at the vulnerable periods of dawn and dusk. As WS 21 approached the first port of call Freetown, Sierra Leone and the point where ocean shipping routes converged, the probability and threat of enemy submarines being present, increased: Mark Thornton allowed no one, on or off watch, to relax from keeping a constant lookout. He gave an example in his own typical fashion by standing for long hours on the upper yard, back braced against the mast and truck, secured only by a single tack-line, passed round his body and mast. From this elevated position, high above his command, his range of visibility was increased; he ensured the constant alertness of the officer of the watch, bridge staff, lookouts and the occupant of the crows-nest below his feet, by bombarding those he thought needed stimulation with missiles from the stock in the pockets of his shorts. At the risk of frying their brains under the sun, some officers of the watch felt it prudent to wear their steel helmets.

One day out from Freetown, the escort received reinforcements from the destroyer HMS *Velox*, but there was nothing to prevent the safe arrival of the convoy at the end of the first leg of the passage to the Mediterranean. WS 21 anchored in Freetown roads on 10th August, 12 days out from the Clyde. On this same day, General Montgomery relieved General Auchinleck and assumed the command of the 8th Army in the North African Middle East desert.

The next few days in Freetown, while the convoy ships were

being fuelled and topped up with provisions, made it possible for the escorting warships to give shore leave. Most, and this included *Petard*'s company, seemed to find their way for one or more visits to the stupendous beach that flanks this eastern boundary of the South Atlantic, and for a few brief hours, enjoyed the illusion of freedom from the confines of shipboard life, relaxed in the sea, sun, sand and shade of the lovely stretch of coast. There were few other attractions in or around Freetown apart from the free show given by the magnificent naked and muscular washerwomen in the river that passed under the road from the town to the beach. The wenches were regarded with a lusty lechery, tinged with a fearful bravado by the passing enforced celibate seamen, brought to this place with relish by the local taxi-men. The sailors in their turn were subjected to obvious Rabelaisian comment and laughter by the naiads, whose uninhibited body action and gestures doubtless lured some to sample a brief but perilous liaison.

At 1400 hrs, 12th August, HMS *Ranpura* weighed anchor and sailed alone from Freetown. Three days after *Ranpura*'s departure the convoy sailed at 0900 hours, 25th August; WS 21 was now increased in size to 17 ships by 5 additions with destinations, Cape Town, Kilindini and Bombay. The escort consisted only of the now familiar *Hawkins* with the same anti-submarine screen, *Catterick* and *Petard*; the sky was overcast, visibility good, little wind, temperature at noon a modest 76 degrees for this area so close to the Equator.

The next morning *Petard* caused the only alarm in an otherwise anxiety free passage to the Cape. At 0800 she reported to the *Hawkins* and Convoy Commodore that she was in asdic contact with a suspected submarine and was about to attack with depth charges. As the convoy made an emergency 45 degree turn away from the direction of the reported contact, *Petard* went in to deliver the first action depth charge attack of her commission.

With the ship's company at action stations, tensed and expectant for their first enemy encounter; the *Petard* turned back after delivering the charges, moving slowly towards the area where four great circles of disturbed sea marked the spot from which had come the underwater hammer blow explosions. With the asdic equipment searching out ahead, in and around the area of the first contact the asdic teams were not long before declaring the contact as non-sub, so *Petard* at speed returned to her position sweeping ahead of the convoy once more on course for Cape Town, everyone feeling a little self-conscious for the alarm caused to the convoy.

This brief fruitless activity tested the training of the depth-charge crews, part of the Gunner T's area of responsibility. Mr J.A. MacAllen, the *Petard*'s warrant officer, torpedo and electrical specialist, led the ship's torpedo department. His division also maintained the electrical supply and equipment for the gunnery, asdic, torpedo, navigation, radar and domestic requirements, and crewed the torpedoes and depth-charges. He was in charge of all the ammunition and explosives. 'Malaya' MacAllen, Gunner T or 'Guns', had been promoted from Chief Petty Officer Torpedo Instructor to warrant officer on 1st July 1937 to wear the thin gold and highly respected stripe that was the mark of the long serving naval professional and expert. He received his affectionately used nickname because he had come to *Petard* from his last appointment, a shore base in Malaya, an area of the British Empire that had obviously impressed and delighted the Gunner, and about which he never tired of yarning, and reminiscing to his wardroom companions who were deprived, in his estimation, for not having visited that exotic land.

'Malaya' joined the navy as a boy seaman, and as a professional, viewed with understandable reservations the seaman-like qualities of those members of *Petard*'s ship's company who were not Royal Navy regulars. Although this was now 1942, and the war was in its third year, the Gunner (T) was meeting for the first time after his long stay in Malaya, civilians either as volunteers or hostilities only conscripts serving in the King's ships at sea. He fairly quickly came to terms with those who were serving as ratings, but he found it more difficult to accept the two sub-lieutenants he found sharing the wardroom as mess-mates and senior in rank.

The very great number of temporary and often action experienced volunteer reserve officers that now helped man the fleet, were something entirely new to Mr MacAllen, his two wardroom shipmates were his first contacts with this breed of outsiders. He had been brought up and trained in the virtues of exact and meticulous drill and procedures. Accurate book-keeping and compliance with the King's Rules and Admiralty Instructions dictated all his actions. His attention to maintenance routines of electrical, torpedo and depth charge equipment was exacting and dedicated.

The same attention he also paid to the servicing and inspection of magazines and ammunition, with strict accounts of all ammunition fired in practice, with the counting and return of spent cases and cartridges to the magazines for eventual return to armament depots for recycling.

The Gunner T was a short compact man, with a long almost aggressive jawline, and could clearly show by the tilt of the head and thrust of the chin, that his sense of fitness and good order was being offended. He took himself and his duties with great seriousness, carried himself with considerable dignity, but missed being pompous. The meticulous insistence on detail and naval procedure brought him very early in the working up period at Scapa Flow, into conflict with, of all people, one of the new sub-lieutenants RNVR. The sub-lieutenant had come to take up his appointment as the Gunnery Control Officer, via the training centre for temporary commissioned officers RNVR, HMS *King Alfred*, direct from two years service in the old 'C' class cruiser, HMS *Coventry*. The cruiser in her role as an anti-aircraft ship, had been almost continuously in action areas of the war since the first weeks in 1939, through into the campaign in Norway. Within the Narvik fiord, the ship suffered 65 recorded direct air attacks within 14 days. The air bombardments ranged in duration from 15 minutes to a three hour battering by relays of aircraft. The gun crews served their guns with a combination of immaculate and instinctive drill, plus an ability to use their initiative to get the best out of the out-dated guns and the mountings in changing action situations.

The *Petard*'s GCO was hellbent to see that the new ship's gun crews, using the same type of gun and mounting, should benefit from the lessons learnt in the *Coventry*, and join the Mediterranean conflict, capable of defending herself against heavy air attack. So he insisted that gun drill and practice firing had to be subordinated to serving the guns as if in action conditions, and this had to include keeping the decks clear of expended cartridge cases that could jam under the gun mountings and put guns out of action, or cripple the loading members of the gun team trying to keep their feet as the ship rolled and pitched in a seaway or heeled under helm for sudden and violent avoiding action or change of course. To do this required the immediate disposal of the cartridge case as it was ejected from the recoiling gun. If it meant that most of the valuable brass containers found their way over the ship's side, so be it. It is probable that the GCO, preoccupied with his conviction that the training had to be realistic, was less than tactful, and no doubt brash in his dealings with stalwart Gunner, who was desperate to account for and to return all spent cartridge cases to Naval Armament Stores.

Fortunately it was a situation that Number 1, Tony Fasson, was well equipped by training and character to handle; long before the ship left home waters, he had ensured that the best of the GCO's battle experience was being harnessed to the Gunner's attention to detail and the rules, and that the end product resulted in a gunnery team of first class quality. In the process Mr MacAllen and the GCO learnt to appreciate their dependence on each other.

Malaya had none of these problems with the second of the two RNVR sub-lieutenants, first, because his appointment as the Asdic Control officer and the Second Navigator, had less chance of impinging on the Gunner's responsibilities, and second that Kenneth Brooksbank was in temperament less volatile than his fellow RNVR, the GCO. His training as a school-master and as a professional career educationalist helped him to accommodate and reconcile the varying personalities represented in the nine individuals who made up the population of the wardroom. Except for the commanding officer, Ken was the only other married officer, and the one university graduate. Both these things gave him a special undefinable status within the small group of officers. He also had a calm and unflappable attitude to the irritations of naval routine and shipboard life; it was one of his strengths that served the ship well in the months that lay ahead. Brooky, as he soon came to be known to his mess-mates, was at HMS *King Alfred* with the GCO, having arrived there after a period at sea as a CW rating, following his enlistment as a volunteer in early 1941.

It was through Brooky, that the wardroom occupants quickly found in Malaya a personality that was full of character, sustained by a sense of humour, and once he had evaluated his colleagues and trusted their ability, became a firm and loyal friend.

The convoy proceeded through the South Atlantic wastes, untroubled by alarms, real or false. There was little to test the watchful alertness of the ocean escorts; in each ship the closing up for dawn and dusk action stations followed with monotonous regularity. Day and night defence stations, required the ships' companies to be on a continuous four hours on, followed by four hours off watch. The two short, two hour dog watches between 1600 and 2000 hours ensured a change round in the 24 hour cycle.

Petard with *Catterick* again scouted far ahead to port and to starboard of the convoy's line of advance, often out of sight of each other and the convoy, continued their search for submarines and surface raiders beyond the visibility range of WS 21, in superb weather conditions, through seas of matchless blue, returning back from time to time for visual contact with the formed body of 17 great merchant ships steaming in their majestic columns, the attendant *Hawkins* ahead, her long low grey warship silhouette, a contrast to the classic lines of the stores and troop laden liners. It was difficult for many of the new and untried members of *Petard*'s company to appreciate or visualise the devastation and horror of war that would engulf nearly all who were bound for the Mediterranean. Only a few very short weeks of life remained for many sailing in the south-bound armada.

On 18th August, *Petard*, and later the *Hawkins*, as the convoy followed up over the horizon astern, exchanged recognition signals and pennants with the armed merchant cruiser HMS *Alcantara*, carrying out her long and lone patrol of the South Atlantic convoy and fast independent shipping routes. *Alcantara* soon disappeared astern exchanging signals, laced with coarse seaman humour, with her sister ship of the Royal Mail Line, the SS *Almanzora*, sighted in the convoy columns; the signal decks of all ships that were in sight range of the light signal exchange, shared and enjoyed the robust dialogue.

The next day, in position 10 degrees 37 minutes south, and 10 degrees 10 minutes west, HMS *Ranpura* rejoined the escort from Takoradi, bringing with her, an additional ship to join the convoy. Two days later, *Petard* and *Catterick* were detached from the escort to proceed to St Helena for refuelling from the Royal Fleet Auxiliary tanker, *Fortal*. While the fuelling was taking place in the open roadstead, the fortunate members of the watch below were given three hours shore leave.

The two destroyers found and resumed their places as convoy escort, early in the morning of the next day, 22nd August at 0130 hours; a feat of precise navigation and plotting by the escort commander and the ships carrying out the rendezvous, something taken as a normal exercise of professional navigation skills, carried out without the assistance of the relatively primitive radar equipment. The darkened ships continued on through the night on their unmolested way south towards the Cape.

The hot sun drenched days followed each other, allowing the men in the crowded troopships to enjoy tolerable conditions; many were able to live and sleep on the open upper decks, as the ships thrust a way through the southern ocean. As an added bonus, the convoy and escorts were able to observe, in near perfect conditions, on 26th August at 0500 hours, the total eclipse of the moon, something that very few present in the ships would ever have the opportunity of seeing again.

The 26th August having started with a celestial spectacular, was to be a day of activity for the convoy. At 0800, following a signal from the convoy commodore, the Durban bound section of seven ships, under the command of the vice-commodore bore away east then north-east with the *Ranpura* in attendance. Later, shortly after mid-day, *Petard* was ordered to take *Catterick* with her and leave for Simonstown to refuel, and on completion to proceed with the *Catterick* in company to sail direct to Durban, and await orders to rejoin WS 21. In the meanwhile, *Hawkins* altered course for Capetown and shepherded the remaining ships towards Table Bay. All were safely anchored by 1540 hours on 27th August in the main anchorage while *Hawkins* berthed on the coal jetty to store, fuel and to give her ship's company leave during the next three days.

The two destroyers had meanwhile arrived in the early hours of the same day at Simonstown, berthed together on the oiler, and gave each watch six hours' leave in succession, the last to expire at 2100 hours. The *Petard*'s company, like their destroyer mates from the *Catterick* found ashore food, drink and entertainment that surpassed anything that could be found in the humid and primitive bars of Freetown. The attractions proved so seductive that three of *Petard*'s men all gunlayers, were still carousing in a dive, out of reach of the patrol sent to look for them, when their ship followed by the *Catterick*, slipped at 2345 hours, and led out to sea. Proceeding at 23 knots the two ships made a short passage, arriving at Durban at 2 o'clock on the afternoon of 29th August.

On passage the First Lieutenant released the news that the ship would be long enough in harbour for everyone to have 48 hours leave. The news was received with varying degrees of excited anticipation. The reputation that the citizens of Durban had acquired, was by now in late 1942, legendary with British Home forces.

A few of the ship's company had experienced the delights of the open handed generosity of this English-speaking white community, and their description of what could be expected in this lovely city on the Indian Ocean, free from any restrictions, food rationing and other shortages that were the way of life in a blacked-out United Kingdom, further stimulated the excitement of those visiting South Africa, and Durban for the first time.

Durban lived up to all expectations, near incredulous leave takers were collected from the ship in luxury cars, and taken to stay in lovely homes in the suburbs, along the coast or up country. Visits to the nature reserves were laid on, surfing and barbecues on the magnificent beaches, dancing through the night in both public and private open air gatherings.

Officers and men soon became adjusted to the continuous offers of lifts, from almost anyone with a car and seats to spare. Near delirious sailors drooled on for months afterwards recalling gorgeous long-legged suntanned goddesses who collected open-mouthed matelots from the pavements of Durban, for long hours of near fantasy on beaches and house parties. The astounding thing was that it was all true, actually happening to the ships' companies of the two destroyers. The experience was enjoyed by officers and men, and did much to sustain morale, for the long months ahead, of those who paused for a while on the way north to the war and carnage in the Eastern Mediterranean. The South African ports, Cape Town, Simonstown, Port Elizabeth and Durban all gave thousands of servicemen on their way, many of them to their deaths, a brief interlude of forgetfulness from the realities of a situation, over which they had neither control nor a say.

From Cape Town, on the 30th, the main part of what remained of Convoy WS 21, escorted by the faithful *Hawkins*, sailed at 1030 for the next leg of the passage to Port Suez, bound for Aden. As the convoy of 10 ships with the commodore, Captain E.C. Dennison, RNR, now embarked with his staff in the SS *Samaria*, moved into the Indian Ocean and steamed up the coast of Cape Province and Natal, the *Petard* was still giving leave to the fortunate, and carrying out a short engine-room overhaul.

Petard had to sail from Durban so to be able to rendezvous with the Aden bound convoy at 1500 hours on 3rd September in position 30 degrees south and 32 degrees 06 minutes east, some sixty nautical miles due east from Durban. The day and time of sailing came with inevitable and remorseless speed. Watched by many of *Petard*'s friends and hosts standing with the large crowd that always gathered on the jetties and docks of Durban, to see warships and transports depart, the call of 'Sea dutymen to your stations' and 'Hands stand by wires and fenders' was piped and obeyed. A reluctant ship's company prepared to sail their ship from the delights and temptations of Durban, suffering also from envious chagrin as *Catterick*, the partner of the long haul from the Clyde was to remain behind on the station. The ship sailed a little before 1000 hours with some of her crew looking for the last time at civilian and female friends, but at the moment of sailing all were responding to the shouts and cries of goodwill with no concern of what the future held.

The convoy was not long coming into sight, steaming a course away from the African mainland towards the southern tip of Madagascar, and avoiding the Mozambique Channel. *Petard* steaming a course to intercept, shepherded two transports that sailed with her out of Durban, made the rendezvous on time. The merchant ships joined their designated stations within the columns indicated by flag signals from the Commodore's ship at the head of the centre column. *Petard* to carry out the orders passed by light transmission from the *Hawkins*, moved at speed to take up her solitary station 8 to 10 miles ahead of the convoy and for the next six days, with the ships of WS 21 hull down far astern, she steamed wide and erratic zig-zags, carrying out a constant anti-submarine asdic watch, across the course up the eastern seaboard of the island of Madagascar.

The Mediterranean war station now loomed close; Mark Thornton and Tony Fasson felt rightly that the approaching realities of war had to be driven home after the long soft cruise in conditions of perfect weather and smooth seas escorting WS 21, followed by the five days' enjoyment of the fleshpots of Durban. So started a series of rough tough simulated action situations, commencing the 'evening hate' at the second dusk action stations at sea out of Durban, the convoy approaching the Tropic of Cancer latitude.

In a temperature of 90 degrees plus, the decks smeared with soft soap to make foot holds difficult and even impossible and the ship given an artificial list of several degrees, the ship went to action stations in the dog watches with all hell breaking loose. Lighting went off the main switchboard, thunder flashes exploded and hoses poured sea water down into dim emergency lit between deck spaces to torment and exercise the supply parties operating in action and damaged conditions. As the exercise reached a climax the ship's siren jammed itself into an open position, the steam operated shriek of the destroyer's sound signal tortured everyone's ears and alarmed the convoy miles astern. While the engine room party struggled to subdue the siren by turning off seized steam valves, a message via the telephone link aft reached the bridge that the wardroom chef had collapsed at his action station, one of the supply party located in the wardroom flat. The doctor rushed aft over the sloping and slippery decks with the siren still screaming overhead, to see what had happened to the man, Mark passed down orders that the unfortunate chef should be taken below into the Captain's day cabin and placed on his bunk. The doctor found that there was nothing that he could do; the chef had died in the heat and uproar of the evening exercise.

Shortly after the body had been removed from the Captain's cabin and placed in the sickbay, the ship reverted to defence stations, some of the mess cleaned from below decks living spaces, the siren silenced and the fault traced, but the repercussions of that evening's dusk action stations activity continued. During the middle watch, the Captain asleep in his sea cabin had a shake from the coxswain bearing a message from the doctor. Because of the extreme heat and closed down conditions it was imperative that chef's corpse should be buried at sea immediately. Half an hour later on the dark quarter deck a small group stood round the still form of the chef sewn into his hammock by the Buffer and his yeoman, waiting for the Captain to read the committal prayers for burial at sea. As the ship slowed, with starboard screw stopped Mark struggled with the aid of a shaded blue light from a signalman's torch to find the appropriate section in the ship's prayer book. This he failed to find, so Chef was committed to the Indian ocean with an extemporized prayer from his Captain and the Lord's prayer from his messmates.

Later during the forenoon when the Captain and the First Lieutenant had studied the fleet prayer book and order of the funeral service at sea, a second funeral party was ordered. With the ship's company mustered aft and a firing party in No.1 uniform and accoutremented, Mark Thornton gave the wardroom chef the funeral service and burial honours that were his right.

Only one other incident disturbed the passage of the troopships. During the morning of September 5th, for an hour the *Petard* hunted a suspected sub-contact, and dropped two patterns of depth-charges before the Captain was satisfied that it was probably a non sub-contact. HMS *Ranpura* hauled her familiar silhouette over the horizon on the 8th and resumed escort duties, in time to permit the escort commander in *Hawkins*, to detach the *Petard* after first light on the following day, to refuel at Diego Saurez.

The ship completed taking in furnace fuel and fresh water during the first watch and slipped out of Diego Suarez immediately, to steam through the night, catching up with the convoy at 0945 hours on September 11th.

At 1430, the convoy split into three sections, the main portion consisting of six ships, *Aorangi, J. Lykes, Samaria, Bantam, Lookout* and *Silver Walnut* with *Ranpura* and *Petard* continuing as escorts, steamed on for Aden. Three ships turned away bound for Bombay, later to be joined by the cruiser *Enterprise* for the passage across the Indian Ocean. The *Hawkins* with the three remaining ships, altered course for Mombassa where they arrived during the morning of October 13th. As *Hawkins* turned away at the break-off position this was to be the last that *Petard* would see of her until they would rendezvous again in February 1944 in circumstances very different to the peaceful almost casual manoeuvring of the large troopships as they diverted to final destinations.

The 16th September saw the arrival of WS 21 with *Petard* and *Ranpura* at Aden. The searing heat of the port made life in the ships, particularly in the smaller ones, a test of endurance, and although the stay for the *Petard* was to be for less than 24 hours, awning stanchions had to be erected and the forecastle, irondeck and quarterdeck awnings spread. These and the constant running of sea water from the hydrants over the steel decks and ship's sides only just made life between decks tolerable.

The town of Aden, set against a backdrop of harsh, bare, sun-blistered, dead volcanic peaks, tempted few ashore when leave was piped. Some who did go found their way to the beach where swimming was possible inside a sharkproof wire enclosure – others sought the few bars, shops and bazaars that served the garrison. A few found time to visit the area along the foreshore where the beautiful hulls of the Red and Arabian sea dhows were built.

In the early hours of the morning 18th September, *Petard* left the convoy as she slipped out of Aden; at 20 knots steered towards Perim Island and the Red Sea, hurrying over the last leg of her journey to join the 12th Destroyer flotilla. Convoy WS 21 sailed later with only the *Ranpura* remaining as escort to Port Suez. The three day run up to the Suez Canal gave Mark Thornton the opportunity to exercise independently, so gun crews toiled in the blazing Red Sea sun, firing live ammunition at simulated air targets made from smoke shell, rockets and star shell. Gun crews worked up their rate of fire in anticipation of having to defend their gun sector and ship against mass air attack. Surface gun-fire was exercised by engaging remote uninhabited islets and rocks.

The First Lieutenant and the Chief Bosun's Mate, Petty Officer Haustead, organised the cleaning of the superstructure, paintwork of the gunshields, bridge and other upper-deck painted surfaces; washed down by sweating seamen. Seaboats and the motor cutter were repainted, guardrails' wire scrubbed and oiled, all running gear, slips and bottle screws checked and greased, in fact all and everything that would come under the critical eye of the 12th Flotilla leader and the other flotilla ships when the new ship joined them at Port Said. Nothing could be done to the ocean stained ship sides, but the Buffer made his preparations for a complete ship sides repaint as soon as the opportunity of a free day in harbour would allow Tony Fasson to give the go ahead. Stagings for seamen to wash and paint from, were constructed and rope lanyards spliced and fitted, paint fannies and brushes with the drums of paint were located and earmarked in the ship's naval and paint store.

Petard entered the canal at Port Suez looking travelworn but workmanlike. With the canal pilot embarked, the special seadutymen and coxswain, Chief Petty Officer Travers, on the wheel, settled down for a long stint at their stations. The canal had been recently cleared of the latest crop of mines dropped by the Luftwaffe and a check sweep preceded the *Petard*'s passage north through the desert canal. The war time conditions had reduced the traffic up and down the canal to a small and interrupted trickle, so the small Egyptian army posts of two or three men sheltering under their palm roofed shelters on the canal side at five kilometre intervals, in almost all cases greeted the passage of the destroyer with interest and shouted greetings, a break in their otherwise routine and very dull duties. The replies from the *Petard*'s men probably matched the Sudanese soldiers' Arabic and pornographic greetings.

The new fleet was in its infancy, a handful of cruisers, two scratch flotillas of destroyers, a number of sloops, minesweepers and other craft replaced the proud fleet of battle ships, aircraft carriers and cruisers, with attendant fleet destroyer flotillas, that previously had denied the larger Italian fleet the freedom of the Mediterranean. The new Commander-in-Chief, Admiral Sir Henry Harwood, who three months earlier had relieved Admiral A.B. Cunningham, remained at the naval headquarters at Ras-el-Tin, Alexandria to organise the rebuilding the fleet shattered by massed German stuka squadrons during the retreat out of Greece and Crete.

The Buffer's and Bosun's mates' pipes summoned the ship's company to fall in on the upper deck as Port Said drew closer; the rig of the day, white singlets and shorts for officers and men, contrasted with faces and limbs, sun and weatherbeaten from the $7\frac{1}{2}$ week voyage out from the Clyde. Under the direction of the captains of the tops, the port seaboat was turned out ready and manned for lowering to secure the port anchor cable to the head buoy; similarly on the starboard side, the motor cutter manned and davits turned out for lowering, also ready to secure the wires from aft to the stern buoy; the ship's Mediterranean ladder rigged and waiting to be slipped over the side, on the pipe. Forward on the fo'c'sle, the port cable had been unshackled from the anchor, replaced by a munro shackle and the cable lead forward; lowered through the bull-ring, waiting to be taken to the head buoy, following the picking up wire already rove for securing to the buoy by the seaboat's crew. Before the ship entered the canal, the starboard anchor had been eased out of the hawsepipe and held by the blake-slip, for immediate release in the event of an emergency.

The ship's company fell in, two ranks facing outboard to port and starboard, in their parts of the ship, fo'c'sle, irondeck and quarterdeck, as the ship moved at reduced speed into Port Said, to run the gauntlet of cruisers, destroyers and smaller ships at their moorings. The First Lieutenant, with the Buffer and his piping party of bosuns' mates, stood out on the bridge wings to direct the mooring of the ship as the Captain brought the *Petard* up to her buoys. By chance or design of the King's Harbour Master, the new arrival to the station, piping as she went the senior ships or acknowledging the pipes of those with commanding officers junior in rank or seniority to Lieutenant Commander Mark Thornton, had to pass down the critical and curious line of ships in harbour to reach her berth at the seaward end of the canal just inside the anti-submarine nets of the boom and ahead of the *Pakenham*, 12th Destroyer Flotilla Leader, Captain E.B.K. Stevens, DSO, DSC, RN.

Petard managed a tolerably efficient and seamanlike evolution as she acted out her ordeal of securing to head and stern buoys under the interested and critical gaze of the flotilla staff officers and the ship's company of the *Pakenham*. The sea and motor boats were lowered together on the pipe from the bridge, and went ahead and astern to their respective buoys, taking with them the picking up wires from the fo'c'sle and quarter-deck. Within a short space of time *Petard* was secured almost abreast of the statue of the builder of the canal, de Lesseps.

The motor cutter lay longside the Mediterranean ladder that had been lowered into position, again in response to a pipe and in time with the hauling out of the lower boom. Within a quarter of an hour of the ship being secured, Mark Thornton was piped ceremoniously over the side into the motor cutter, coxed by Leading Seaman Tipping, and underway to cover the short distance to the *Pakenham* to report in formal and traditional terms to Captain D12, the arrival of his ship to join the 12th Destroyer Flotilla. The day was 22nd September 1942.

CHAPTER 3

The 12th Destroyer Flotilla
The German Submarine

At the end of the third year of war, the number of destroyer flotillas had multiplied, but because of sinkings, casualties, refit requirements, and above all else, operational demands in the far-flung theatres of war, no flotilla was a complete unit of one type or class of destroyer. The proud and powerful Tribal class now only functioned with reinforcements from older, as well as newer and very different, types of ships: surviving flotilla leaders of destroyer classes, with Captains (D) and staff embarked, were administering and leading flotillas of eight destroyers from many different class origins; as well as ships manned and flying the flags of allies, Dutch, Norwegian, Polish, Greek and the Free French.

The 12th Flotilla was no exception; *Petard* joined her parent flotilla for the last few months of the 12th Destroyer Flotilla's short existence; a miscellaneous group of destroyers, of different types and nationalities. Although all eight ships of the 'P' class fleet destroyer were now built and in commission; *Pakenham, Penn, Partridge, Panther, Porcupine, Pathfinder, Paladin* and *Petard*, not more than four at any time found their way into the Eastern Mediterranean to serve together. In September 1942, there were only three 'P's' in the 12th, *Pakenham, Paladin* and the *Petard*, some 'E', 'H' and 'I' class and the Greek ship HHMS *Queen Olga*, a British built 'H' class, armed with four mighty German 5 inch guns. These guns gallantly and skilfully manned by their Greek crews, were a constant problem and worry to her commander; to Captain D12 and his gunnery staff officer; spare parts were unobtainable, they had to be manufactured in the ship or the destroyer's base ship, HMS *Woolwich*. Ammunition could only be found in captured enemy dumps; foraging parties followed the Eighth Army into the desert, seeking replenishments for the magazines of the *Queen Olga*.

The availability of ammunition or spares were of little concern to the *Petard*: the next few days, in between forays into the sea area off Port Said and Alexandria, the ship was preoccupied with a series of checks and inspections by the flotilla staff and specialist officers;

due to culminate with a formal inspection by the Captain D12 in person, Captain E.B.K. Stevens, DSO DSC RN. Somehow the ship had to be painted; this was exercising the mind of Tony Fasson, he knew that the Buffer was getting anxious and restive while days slipped by, and the day of the inspection, 3rd October, approached.

Two days after the arrival at Port Said, 24th September, a division of the 15th Cruiser Squadron, *Arethusa* and *Orion*, escorted by six destroyers, *Pakenham* (Captain D12) *Paladin* and *Petard*, *Jervis* (Captain D14) *Javelin* and *Kelvin* sailed out of Port Said in a hurry to investigate a high speed surface contact, reported by the radar stations established on the coast between Port Said and Alexandria.

Driving his ship at high speed; part of a cruiser and destroyer squadron, seeking action at sea; Mark Thornton was at last back where he had so impatiently wanted himself and his new ship to be; the ship and her company standing to, at action stations; gun and torpedo crews clad in overalls, anti-flash gauntlets, head and face covering, with steel helmets rammed firmly in place. Bridge party, navigator, officer of the watch, torpedo control officer, yeoman, signalmen and lookouts, supporting the steel helmeted captain, standing clear and a little above, at his bridge conning position. Above the bridge in the gun control director, looking down over the whole length of the narrow speeding hull sat the director's crew, the GCO, director trainer Petty Officer Alfred Haustead, director layer Petty Officer Charles Williams and the optical rangetaker Petty Officer Clarke, ready to train to elevate, and range the director on to the enemy as soon as it was sighted.

Everyone in *Petard* was aware of being the new ship in a force of ships that had seen action many times; this added to the build up of tension as the routine gun and torpedo control instrument and communication checks were carried out; ammunition supply routes were opened up for immediate action; water-tight doors and openings closed down, with engine room and magazine crews enclosed at their action stations.

The squadron steamed up to the area off Paphos where the suspected enemy surface contact had been reported, everyone keyed up and expectant, even the most reluctant of the ship's company feeling a sense of exhilaration as the two sections of destroyers responded under full power to the flag hoists from the Rear Admiral 15th Cruiser Squadron to take up extended search formation, screening ahead of the cruisers. The search across back and over the area drew a blank; but as the realisation that a surface action was now unlikely, the partial sense of an anti-climax and relief before it could establish itself, was thwarted by the appearance of three inquisitive Ju 88 aircraft flying low across the horizon, showing a definite and menacing intent to deliver a torpedo attack on the force from the direction of the setting sun. Directed by the C-in-C who had received the RA 15th cruiser squadron's negative report, *Arethusa* and *Orion* reversed course and sped towards the east, back to Port Said, as the destroyers laid a heavy smoke screen barrier across the line of retirement between the cruisers and the Ju 88s. The smoke screen seemed to have the desired effect, for when *Pakenham*, leading *Petard* and *Paladin* in line ahead, doubled back into the smoke to engage the torpedo bombers, the marauders were flying parallel some four miles from the edge of the smoke wall. *Pakenham* flying the signal for the ships to turn 90 degrees to starboard in succession opened fire on the aircraft as Captain D12 executed the signal; moments later following round in D12's wake *Petard* was in gun action for the first time. Before turning back together 90° to starboard into line abreast, in response to DF12s 'Blue Nine' flag signal, the ship had fired three controlled 4 inch gun salvos at a range of about eight thousand yards.

The result of *Petard*'s first but brief gun encounter could not be assessed for effectiveness, except that her shell bursts seemed to be with the others from her consorts, near and around the Ju 88s; the short action was an easy introduction to the many engagements that lay ahead in the immediate future.

The three ships dived again into the smoke, working up to full speed of a little over thirty knots to rejoin the squadron; in *Petard* the short but inconclusive gun action had improved confidence, the GCO and the Chief GI finding little fault in the drill or performance of crews and guns and even the Gunner T feeling pleased, as only one of his cartridge cases had been ditched. Perhaps only the Captain felt frustrated by the lack of real action, but Mark Thornton was to get his fill before the end of 1942.

In the gathering dusk a flight of Beaufighters passed over the ships heading towards the west setting sun to try and remedy what the shipborne gunfire had failed to do; down the German Torpedo aircraft. By 2300 hrs the squadron had passed the boomgate vessel guarding the way into the Suez canal and were secured again to the buoys vacated 16 hours earlier.

The next three or four days were scheduled for a short self-refit, so with notice for steam extended to 12 hours, authorised by Captain D12, the First Lieutenant had his opportunity to paint ship. The Buffer was given his head, charged to complete the job in 24 hours; Petty Officer Alfred Haustead was ready with an evolution planned so that no department could escape their quota of men.

From both watches of the hands at 0730, few escaped the painting marathon, the minimum special sweepers were fallen out; the GI had to fight hard to get a few hands to service his guns, and only on condition that they also painted the gun-shields and mountings. The Buffer with his paint lockerman was everywhere; checking paint supplies and progress, his eyes seeking out painters' holidays.

Whenever the motor cutter was spare from routine runs, he would be away out circling the ship, sometimes with the First Lieutenant, to check the effect, progress and watching out for any slackers sitting out the warm Mediterranean sun; a bellow from the short stocky figure standing in the sternsheets of the cutter roused those hoping for a post-mid-day tot and meal break slumber, who thought that a staging under the fo'c'sle flare or a spot on top of a gun shield or inside the bridge wings would shelter them from the Buffer's energetic seeking eye.

Painting ship in Port Said, in the late September sunshine was not a bad job; Tony Fasson had put a target, ship's sides, funnel and masts to be completed before leave would be piped; the remainder to be finished off on the following day; by 1530 the pipe, return paint and secure; liberty-men to clean, came after a day of progress that satisfied the First Lieutenant and even his henchman, the Buffer.

October 3rd, saw the day devoted to the formal inspection by the Captain 12th Destroyer Flotilla. He was received by the Commanding Officer, Lieutenant Commander Mark Thornton with his ship's company fallen in by divisions and in their parts of ship, dressed immaculate in white singlets and shorts, under the hot sun.

As Captain D12 walked round the ship and reviewed the officers and men paraded for his inspection, his staff officers examined the ship's books, records and equipment making an assessment to form the basis of his comments to the ship's officers gathered in the wardroom at the conclusion of the inspection. The report on the inspection was satisfactory, but not enthusiastic, there seemed to be

rather less warmth in the relationship between the leader of the
flotilla and the newcomer, than existed towards the remainder of the
12th Destroyer Flotilla. This may have been due to past differences
or clash of personalities, known only and understood by the
professional naval establishment, but incomprehensible to the
temporary and volunteer officers.

Because of this indefinable antithesis, when the flotilla
reorganisation was published in orders, it came as no surprise to
find that the fourth sub-division of the 12th Flotilla was to comprise
the single Greek ship *Queen Olga* and the *Petard*. Paradoxically the
outcome of the order was the rapid growth of a close and warm
relationship between the two ship's companies; only terminated
when the *Queen Olga* was sunk on the first major operation when the
two ships were not together, in close support of each other.

The inspection by the Captain D12 seemed more appropriate to
a peacetime routine, than to a war situation of a single squadron of
light cruisers and attendant destroyers, a few other smaller craft;
driven out of the main fleet base, Alexandria, because of the
proximity of the foreward enemy airfields behind the
German/Italian lines before El Alamein. These ships were the
successors to the proud fleet of battleships, cruisers, aircraft
carriers and destroyers that had dominated the Mediterranean
from east to west; a fleet that had supported General Wavell's
defeat of the Italian desert army, and cowed the larger Italian fleet,
later to be nearly decimated but not defeated by the German
Luftwaffe when the reversals came in the land fighting.

The reduced British force still continued the domination of the
larger Italian fleet and prevented the Italian ships putting to sea
except for short and furtive dashes that seemed designed to avoid
action at all costs. The flanks of the sea route to Malta from the east
were bounded on the south by the great bulge of Cyrenaica, now
again entirely in enemy hands and lined by desert airfields; to the
north the airfields in Crete combined to make operations at sea to
supply the beleaguered island a costly and hazardous enterprise;
forcing convoys through an air dominated sea gap of a little more
than two hundred miles wide. The reduced Mediterranean fleet
continued to fight ships to Malta with often desperate losses of men
and ships.

A continuing cause for concern was the squadron of Vichy
French ships under the command of the honourable but obstinate
Frenchman, Vice-Admiral R.E. Godfroy. The squadron had been

at its berths within Alexandria harbour since the fall of France in June 1940. Although the ships had only sufficient fuel to allow the reduced crews to continue living on board, and vital parts as well as spares for the main armament had been landed, the ships continued to be an embarrassment to the British operational fleet, particularly at this stage of the war, with the increase in French political and military confusion that accompanied the period preceding Operation Torch, the Allied invasion of the French held territory in North Africa.

Most of Port Said was out of bounds to service personnel, making the task of protecting unarmed libertymen, officers and ratings, a practical proposition and necessary in the cosmopolitan and explosive urban area where Axis agents and sympathisers proliferated. The out of bounds area also reduced a little the risk of venereal disease; treating men that contracted VD, within the confined spaces of crowded troopships and men-of-war, in an era when treatment was still comparatively primitive, was a special problem that had to be minimised. Because treatment could be painful and prolonged and also the stigma of the CDA mess, men tended to hide the fact that they had caught a dose, aggravating a difficult situation. Brothels that existed within the inbounds area were few in number, but regularly supervised by the Army Medical Corps, but because they were few, and to the afficionado, lacking in variety; it was inevitable that many strayed under the cover of darkness, persuaded by gharrymen with promises of greater erotica in surroundings of Arabian splendour. Few of the premises, from which the fortunate were later extracted by the large and armed Naval, Royal Marine and Army patrols, made any pretence of offering anything better than those within the 'in bounds' enclave; most were seedier, and all very much more dangerous.

The relatively stiff punishments for being caught in and out of bounds area, laid down in the C-in-C Mediterranean's station orders, added to the not infrequent muggings and deaths of luckless voyeurs, did little to deter libertymen from nightly excursions into the hinterland of Port Said. The *Petard*'s libertymen were no exception; few nights passed without the duty officer receiving from the town patrol, one or more collected from an off limits area.

Members of the wardroom, on one occasion were part of the collection returned by the Royal Marines Patrol, for one Bertie Faunthorpe the consequences were disastrous. The escapade terminated whatever slim chance remained that his name would appear in the next list of promotions to Commander, the last chance as he approached the end of his promotion zone. A party of four, Bertie, the doctor Prendergast, an RNVR Sub Lieutenant on passage and the GCO, from dinner in the mess, via a *felucca*, visited the one large entertainment centre open to officers and other ranks, the Eastern Exchange on the canal side promenade. Here, the management with a reluctant tolerance allowed men and officers of the fleet to add their own ideas to the entertainment fare on nightly offer.

On the particular night that Bertie and his companions arrived, an impromptu circus or rodeo was just coming to an end under the joint persuasion of the management and the reinforced town patrol; gharry horses that had been unhitched and removed from protesting gharrymen by their fares, and persuaded through the foyer onto the dance floor, were being herded back to their frantic owners, assisted by some of the more responsible revellers. Working their way down into the crowded hall, the party from the *Petard* found their usual table and seats close to the stage, by the side of the fountain and fish-pool that fronted the low stage; settled down for a late evening break from shipboard life.

The cabaret, a diversion from the general uproar and extensive drinking, had started; an unchanged bill of Gulli Gulli men, a few tired dancers, singers and Gabby. The star of the show sang and danced a little, but her main asset, appreciated and waited for nightly by her fans, was her superb body. Gabby, taller than any of her fellow performers, was probably Lebanese, and in her late twenties; with legs and torso of voluptuous and exquisite proportions she wore only three post stamp size Union Jacks that served to emphasis her magnificent nakedness.

Gabby had her priorities right, no one had any illusions that the Union Jacks would change immediately into Italian and German ensigns to suit the fortunes of the contestants in the Western Desert. She understood all the subleties of ranks, ratings and seniorities; with unerring certainty without wasting time, she knew where to find the table in the audience, make the best killing in terms of commission for drinks ordered by hosts deprived of all power of rational moderation by the proximity and promise of her warm scented physical presence at their table. Her visits were little more than a tease, closely escorted by her ponce, lover or protector, and she left always after achieving the cash target. The Doctor had built up a dangerous and alcoholic ambition to discover and analyse the adhesive with which Gabby secured, so firmly, the minute Union Jacks to her brown moist skin; so far she had adroitly avoided the advance of his questing hands, but on this night Doc was determined to fulfil his hitherto frustrated mission.

His other passion when under the influence of social drinking was to wash his socks and feet in public. These passions of the Irish doctor in a bizarre way helped to spell the end of Bertie's promotion prospects; with the aid of a bar of pusser's soap he was doing his usual dhobying routine in the fish pool with complete dedication and concentration, necessary when the night's drink intake had increased the risk of falling head first among the outraged goldfish. He failed to notice that Gabby had left the table before he could resume his research of her microscopic apparel, until after he had completed the messy foot ablutions. His determination to carry out the mission was overlooked by his three companions, when he disappeared. Only when the shrieks of an outraged female came in ascending intensity from the direction of backstage, that his whereabouts were located.

Bertie lead the rush to Gabby's dressing room, to find the gorgeous creature on the floor with the diminutive, scruffy bearded doctor sprawled over her body, prising the third and last of the tiny flags from her crotch. The situation was chaotic, a screaming Gabby, a swearing Irishman, and a corridor filling up with menacing coloured gentlemen; mainly excited Egyptians, with many curious beer stimulated men of all the three services in support. Bertie quickly had the naked squirming Gabby in his willing fondling arms, as the two sub-lieutenants prised the dedicated doctor away from her reluctant body; for a while the situation looked capable of getting out of hand, and perhaps critically dangerous; but suddenly Gabby inexplicably calmed down, perhaps Bertie had solved the problem with his calming hands; sensibly in the lull, with promptitude, the officers left, even the normally liable to be belligerent, when stimulated with drink, doctor followed.

Outside the blacked out Eastern Exchange, the quartet embarked in a waiting four horse gharry; Bertie fired by his brief contact with Gabby's scented squirming brown body, could not be diverted from directing the equipage towards the Port Said branch of the very much grander and better known establishments, in Cairo and Alexandria, of 'Mrs Mary'. In Port Said the Mrs Mary collection was housed very far out of bounds, and there with a grim certainty the duty Royal Marine Patrol located a senior and distinguished engineer officer of His Majesty's Royal Navy in deshabille, upstairs with a lady of the establishment. Poor Bertie had not got Gabby out of his system before he was persuaded by a huge polite but forceful colour sergeant to rejoin his volunteer reserve mess-mates downstairs where they had been interrupted from a leisurely selection entertainment.

The reserve officers were dealt with by Tony the following day, and with no stake in the career structure of the Royal Navy, the lecture from a mature and respected brother officer had considerable effect; but the restriction of future leave possibilities were easier to ride than the body blow poor Bertie had to suffer by his final elimination from the commander promotion lists. The naval establishment and old boy net had received its final blessing from the reports received from Mark Thornton and Captain D12. A splendid, very professional engineer had not met the stringent requirements of his peers. It had been very obvious to Bertie's volunteer officer mess-mates that he was for reasons that were never explained clearly, *persona non grata* with the Captain D12 during his formal inspection of the ship, or to the flotilla Staff Engineer Officer, a term colleague of Bertie's from the RNE College. The irony of the decision to exclude *Petard*'s engineer officer from the promotion lists, was the endorsement of his professional ability to keep his ship as a seagoing fighting unit after severe damage, something that his senior flotilla officer was unable to match.

Queen Olga with *Petard*, sailed in and out of Port Said for the next few days, either on anti-submarine patrols, or exercising with one of the Allied submarines in the area to improve the two ships underwater hunting skills. This kind of routine suited the ship's company, hard work at sea during the day, with nights in, and leave ashore in Port Said. Only the Captain was visibly chaffing with frustration, driving him on after dinner one night in the wardroom to repeat his bulkhead beating performance, last enacted in Scapa Flow, to cause some concern to his ship's doctor.

On the 12th October the ship sailed in company with the *Pakenham* to Haifa for escorting duty with the cruiser *Arethusa* from Haifa to Alexandria. The passage was only remarkable for the sighting shortly after leaving Port Said, a flock of many hundred pink flamingoes; the fantastic and unusual cloud of birds were for some inexplicable reason, apparently flying away from the marshes of the delta area towards the northern limits of the Sinai desert. Perhaps the birds had been driven from their natural habitat by some by-product of the war.

At Haifa, everyone in *Petard* was tempted by the attractive appearances of the white houses that climbed up from the harbour in irregular and interesting disorder, a contrast to the very flat landscape of Port Said and the canal; the town did not fail in its promise of bars and cabarets, only the dreadful stench of great piles of animal skins laying on the open quay under the hot sun, spoiled the enjoyment of the new port of call. For those who could not leave the ship, the wind when it shifted to blow the smell towards the shipping at the berths made it a night of unforgettable nausea. On the 13th, *Arethusa* sailed with the two 'P' class destroyers as escort, bound for Alexandria and exercises on passage with three more cruisers, *Cleopatra* wearing the flag of Vice-Admiral 15th Cruiser Squadron, *Orion* and *Euralyus* with attendant fleet destroyers. The force concentrated on exercises and tactics for the protection of convoys against air and sea attack, through the day and following night, arriving at the end of the swept channel for Alexandria, at dawn.

The *Petard* remained a week in Egypt's principal port, now again the main base for the Mediterranean Fleet. There were obvious signs that some new operation was in the offing in the desert; Alexandria was virtually clear of the army; the movement of tanks and vehicles that clogged the area round the canal and the vicinity of Alexandria and to a lesser extent Port Said, had almost died away. It was rumoured that the army was bracing itself to repel a renewed attack from Rommel and his Afrika Korps, but all suspected and hoped that the army would soon launch an assault against the combined Italian and German armies, driving them back over and from the Egyptian frontier. The new general, Montgomery, now commanded the Eighth Army in the desert; stories of his style and activity to encourage his command had percolated back to the fleet.

For the *Petard*, the seven days in Alexandria were of special pleasure. With the army virtually absent, the great variety of restaurants and places of entertainment were available, anxious to please and attract the liberty-men; the Greek, French, Italian, Lebanese and other communities gave the city of wide boulevards and thronged thoroughfares an attractive flavour and made it a lure, often an exciting one, to the servicemen. The large and well organised fleet club provided meals and entertainment for those who hankered after the more familiar fare from the British Isles.

Because the ship was left out, or remained in harbour as a reserve, and not involved in the current naval activity along the North African coast towards Tobruk, Tony Fasson had the ship's company under full stretch with athletic and recreational activities, his first opportunity since commissioning. The whalers were lowered and the crews away under oars; later sailing, first for instruction then during the dog watches for recreation. Tony arranged with the shipwright to construct waterpolo goals, which were soon rigged out from the ship's side as she lay at the detached mole inside the defended entrance to the harbour. Intertop sides and a competition was organised that included the sub-division sister ship, *Queen Olga*. The largely novice *Petard* side learnt for the first time from their Greek friends the variety and effectiveness of underwater tactics, during frenzied and hilarious matches. Tony had immense energy; he was a good athlete, took part in all the activities he promoted, football, hockey and the rest. He had the special knack of being able, without patronising or any loss of authority, to mix and relax with the junior ranks. A firm disciplinarian who could enforce the traditional and accepted code with understanding, a light touch and considerable charm; his decisions regarding punishment, often severe for breaches of discipline or leave breaking, were accepted by the offenders without lasting aggression or umbrage against the First Lieutenant. With the junior officers in the ship he was a genial and attractive companion; it was Tony who made life tolerable for those who may have fallen short of the formidable Captain's standards.

On 23rd October, the ship was bound for Port Said but delayed and turned aside not far from the end of the Alexandria swept approach channel, to investigate a possible submarine reported by a minesweeper.

Not long after entering the area of the suspected enemy, Brooky and his asdic operating team were in contact. The water conditions made the search difficult allowing the submarine to escape for lengthy periods from the probing of the asdic equipment. During the long afternoon the ship made occasional fresh contact and two direct depth charge attacks, but with no effect. After the second attack, firm contact with the elusive submarine was not regained despite a long two hour search round the last position marked on

Able Seaman Craven, pom-pom crew, and (*top*) Able Seaman Fortune, oerlikon gunner

Signalman Lampard

'X' gun fuse setters

Surgeon/Lieutenant H. W. F. Prendergast (Doc)

Lieutenant H. K. Brooksbank (Brooky)

The Gunnery Control Officer

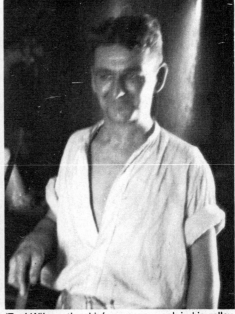

'Tug' Wilson, the ship's company cook in his galley

the semi-automatic plot; an angry and disappointed Captain finally had to report that the submarine had escaped. Darkness had by this time fallen as the hunt had slowly moved westward parallel to the coast, toward El Alamein and the area where the two opposing armies faced each other in the dark across huge desert minefields. Not long after *Petard* had broken off the fruitless search for the undersea adversary; set course for the canal, the night sky away on the starboard quarter exploded into an inferno of artillery fire, that stretched from the sea to back beyond the unseen desert horizon. The sheer immensity of the man-made torrent of fire and explosions lighting the entire south eastern sky cowed and numbed the observers safe and many miles away in their ship. For the next few days news from the desert was scarce and the world held its breath.

At 0550, 30th October a Sunderland flying boat on patrol north of the delta area reported that it was in visual contact with a submarine steering westwards. An urgent signal followed on the heels of the sighting report, to the destroyer *Hero* on passage from Haifa to Port Said; diverting her to the position of the submarine 60-70 nautical miles north-north-east of Port Said. The Sunderland, surprisingly unsighted by the submarine, continued to report the position and homed *Hero* towards the enemy. From Port Said, *Pakenham* leading *Petard*, *Dulverton* and *Hurworth*, raced at high speed to back up the *Hero* seeking the now dived submarine. By 1000 the ships were on the scene to take over from *Hero* who had been intermittently in contact, but had not delivered an attack with depth charges. Captain D12 set up a square search with his four ships round the zone where *Hero* had her last firm contact.

The asdic conditions were bad, the water disturbed by varying density and temperature bands, aggravated by the huge freshwater discharge from the Nile delta, favoured the hunted U-boat.

Soon after the start of a meticulous quartering of the sea area, contact was regained to start a twelve hour search for a kill; with the U-boat to be lost and found with agonising frequency. The four ships on the hunt, now that *Hero* had been released to continue to Port Said, were able to build up a composite plot of the submarine's actual position when the ships were in contact, establishing a datum for projecting possible moves and position when she had wriggled out of the reach of the probing asdic beams. Watched over by the circling Sunderland, a series of intermittent attacks were made by depth charges, the attacking ship being conned onto a cross-bearing of asdic contacts by two ships passing ranges and bearings to the third ship moving in to drop her charges; the fourth ship moving round the perimeter to ensure if possible, that the submarine did not escape under the additional water disturbance caused by the depth charge explosions. All the ships delivered attacks during the afternoon and evening, on to both firm and doubtful sub-echoes, but with results that were not apparent. The wind was beginning to rise, breaking up the smooth sea surface, so that any debris or oil slicks that might give a clue to a damaged submarine became harder to spot in the broken water.

Mark Thornton seemed to develop a sixth sense; several times when all contact and positive indications seemed to have been lost, he conned his ship and asdic team back on target. Utterly tireless he never left the bridge or plot, nor allowed any break in concentration; he was well served by Brooky with his asdic ratings who were determined to get the elusive German. The ship had delivered four depth charge attacks during the long day; tension remained high as course and speed was under constant change trying to pin down the unseen enemy. At slow speed every eye scanned the sea for a periscope that could catch the ship with a torpedo as she probed and listened; when revolutions rapidly increased and the thrust of the screws could be felt, muscles contracted and men braced themselves against the coming shock of the underwater thudding charges. Darkness fell; *Pakenham* with *Hurworth* moved to the south of the area, following D12's interpretation of the intelligence from the combined plot information, but Mark remained up wind with *Dulverton* in support.

The *Petard*'s Captain's instinct had its reward; at about 2200 the ship was again in firm contact, and Brooky was able to confidently identify a sub-echo moving at 3 knots. Mark Thornton turned his ship to deliver a deliberate eight charge attack with settings to sandwich the submarine between explosions above and below. *Dulverton* was informed by the small blue directional 'Heather' signal light of the intention to deliver a depth charge attack down wind; she responded that she was also in contact and confirmed with bearings and ranges that matched those appearing on the *Petard*'s plot; the entire ship's company felt that the long hunt was nearly up. The ship moved in at her attacking speed, 18 knots, courses adjusted to allow for the submarine's course, speed, and the falling rate of the depth charges through the water after discharge from the traps and throwers. The interval between the firing of the charges and the moment of explosion seemed to be an eternity; when they came the darkness of the night made the crashes devastating and a threat to the ship as well as the underwater quarry; the silence that followed, unbroken except for the rising wind and sea noises, seemed menacing.

As the ship nosed forward into the wind and the dark; suddenly and simultaneously 'B' guns crew, the bridge and gun director teams detected the unmistakeable smell of diesel fuel; cries from the asdic hut came almost immediately; they could hear for the first time a submarine blowing its tanks. All eyes were straining to pierce the darkness out to the port bow bearing given by the asdic team; suddenly a flurry of white breaking sea could be sensed rather than seen; the Captain calling for the searchlight to be exposed, but before the 36 inch beam could be trained onto the area, the port large signal lantern operated by the Yeoman of Signals Chapman, opened its white beam onto a conning tower showing in the breaking sea. Seconds later the searchlight added its blinding brilliant light; the wallowing *U-559* with a white horse painted on the fore part of the conning tower was revealed with a pitiless clarity: a few white scurrying figures appeared out of the tower to fall, slide and crawl along the casing into the sea.

In answer to Mark Thornton's commands for the armament to open fire, only the pom-pom and one of the port oerlikons could bear or depress low enough to open up; the U-boat was too close for the 4 inch 'B' and 'X' guns. Pom-pom shells hit the submarine casing and tower but it was clear that the U-boat was stopped and its crew abandoning their ship; any further gunfire would cause unnecessary damage if the submarine was to be captured; the cease fire bells rung by the First Lieutenant standing close by the Captain on the bridge, stopped the deluge of fire from the secondary armament. More orders followed from Mark Thornton in rapid sequence; for the U-boat to be boarded before it sank from damage or scuttling charges; the GCO to get out of the director, down onto the fo'c'sle to prepare to lead a party to the submarine casing; the sea boat to be lowered and manned at full speed.

The ship was by this time stopped and hove-to, lying with the wind broad on the starboard bow, forming a partial lee for the *U-559* that lay very low in the roughening sea about 60 yards off the port bow. It was a black moonless night, with stars masked by dense cloud, not unusual for the Mediterranean in late autumn. Only the conning tower and the sea between, was illuminated by the searchlight and the two large bridge signal lanterns; outside the small zone of harsh brilliant light and unseen, the *Dulverton* moved round the *Petard* and her prey, to ward off any other U-boat attempt to revenge the stricken *U-559*. The time was 2245.

The GCO/Sub-Lieutenant with jellied legs and numbed brain clambered out and down onto the heaving slippery iron deck of the fo'c'sle, calling for the 'B' gun crew above him to pass down a rope ladder and nets for climbing down onto the submarine. It quickly became obvious that it would be an unnecessary and hazardous risk to place the pitching and rolling destroyer closer to the nearly submerged U-boat, the gap was too large to jump; the large starboard wing signal lamp illuminating the fore part of the fo'c'sle as well as the conning tower; lit up the GCO in his dilemma, as the voice of the Captain roared out of the darkness behind the blinding lights; ordering him to dive over the side from the high fo'c'sle flare and to swim to the U-boat through water where the faces and arms of crewmen struggling for their lives showed up whitely in the brilliant beam of the searchlight.

The GCO started to strip off his outer protective clothing as men moved up onto the fo'c'sle and into the light to join him; one, a young able-seaman Colin Grazier, calling out over the wind that he would swim across with the Sub-Lieutenant, and stripped off his overall. At that moment Tony Fasson scrambled out of the darkness from the starboard side aft, where he had been organising the clearing away of the starboard sea-boat for lowering, he also was tearing off his uniform, already capless and kicking off his half-wellingtons, he ordered the GCO aft off the fo'c'sle to complete the lowering of the whaler and to get it round to the submarine at top speed. As the GCO slithered and raced off the fo'c'sle the First Lieutenant and able-seaman dived naked into the night sea and swam towards *U-559*.

It was a difficult operation to lower the starboard sea-boat as the wind, sea and rolling of the ship smashed the boat against the ships side; after a struggle and some delay the boat was lowered without serious damage, cleared from the ship's side and manoeuvred round the bow of the ship through groups of shouting German seamen, in the dark and considerable seaway. The sea-boat reached the U-boat; the heavy sea and the fact that the casing was awash and lying very low in the water made it extremely difficult to get longside without crashing down on the submerged pressure hull. The boat was hampered by this time by a number of German

seamen hanging onto the gunwhales. The boat's crew were
astonished to see in the searchlight beam a third member of their
ship's company hanging onto the guardrail attached to the after
end of the conning tower; this was the small naked figure of
Tommy, the boy NAAFI canteen assistant. He had dived in from
the waist of the ship and followed Tony and Colin before anyone
including the frantic canteen manager, could stop him. Young
Tom, holding on by one hand as the sea broke over his small frame;
with his other arm and hand he held against his body a few charts
and documents that had been passed up to him from inside by
Tony and Colin Grazier. These items he managed to pass into the
bow of the sea-boat as it surged forward, back and crashed onto the
pressure hull.

The gun platform and the guard rails were now almost
submerged; Tommy clambered back onto the conning tower that
had been holed in several places by the earlier gunfire; he yelled to
the boat's crew that there were two bodies lying by the hatch down
into the control; one of the bodies appeared to be that of an officer;
he could see down into the vessel as the lights were still on, Colin
Grazier was on the ladder leading down to the control-room, and
the First Lieutenant was at the bottom trying to pass up what was
vital enigma equipment — he was going down to give them a hand.
The GCO ordered him not to do so, the U-boat seemed to be fast
getting lower in the water, he was to tell Tony and Colin to get out
immediately, and that he was coming inboard to give them a hand.
The seas broke continuously over the portion of the hull that
remained visible, the conning tower, and poured out through the
pom-pom shell holes. It was a bizarre crazy scene, brilliantly lit by
the slowly circling destroyer that continued to try to give a lee to the
now obviously sinking submarine. From the sea came cries of
drowning U-boat men, a number still clung to the side of the whaler
as the crew struggled to keep it alongside the conning tower and at
the same time keep it afloat.

As the GCO jumped into the sea to clamber on and up the tower,
the U-boat disappeared, leaving nothing to be seen amongst the
breaking waves; he was pulled back into the boat as the crew called
the names of their shipmates. Only Tommy responded, his head
bobbing up almost alongside the sea-boat to be hauled in
immediately, to join the few German seamen who were pulled in
with him. The boat's crew continued to call Tony's and Colin's
names and to search for them; although one or two more Germans

were found, there was no sign of the British sailors. After a short interval *Petard* moved alongside the sea-boat, her sides draped with scrambling nets up which more of the enemy had clambered to safety and captivity; but it was clear now that the inrush of water down the conning tower hatch had trapped Tony and Colin; by some miracle Tommy had avoided being carried down also as he yelled for them to get out of the submarine.

The lower-deck cleared, all hands manned the starboard whaler falls, the sea-boat was hoisted at the run; the ship with *Dulverton*, searchlights extinguished, moved at speed away from the area and the danger of other U-boats that may have been converging to give assistance to their flotilla mate. Elation and excitement surging through the ship at the triumphant end of a long hunt for the undersea adversary, the night struggle on the surface and the capture of prisoners, was short lived; turning to a sickening feeling of loss and a helpless inarticulate sadness, when it was known that the Tony and Colin Grazier had failed to get out of the U-boat. The loss was more poignant when after a count was made between the two ships; the Germans that had survived the 16 hour hunt, an hour in the darkness of the sea, numbered five officers, including the commanding officer, and 35 other ranks. The German engineer officer confirmed that he had opened the submarine seacocks before obeying the order to abandon ship; ensuring that the vessel would sink suddenly and without warning to those who were strangers to the feel and stability of submersibles.

The ship had lost a competent professional naval officer, a mature and a popular personality; the young regular service able-seaman, a fine intelligent physical specimen, a good athlete and an asset to the shipboard life, had married shortly before the ship sailed from Scotland a lovely girl, the attractive pair were regarded by the ship with an envious affection.

Pakenham signalled the C-in-C that the U-boat finally sank at 2343 in position 32 degrees 01 north, 32 degrees 01 north, 32 degrees 52 minutes east, one hour after it had been depth charged to the surface. *Petard* with *Dulverton* in company, was ordered to Haifa; prisoners were to be landed, and the documents, charts and code books, the enigma machine that Tony and Colin had salvaged in return for their lives, to be handed over to naval intelligence officers flying into Palestine especially to collect the secret documents and machine that surprisingly had not been destroyed or ditched by the U-boat captain. The fact that these had fallen into Allied hands was a closely guarded secret for the remainder of the war; for this reason the citations for the George Crosses awarded posthumously in recognition of the incredible disregard for personal safety shown by Antony Fasson and Colin Grazier, gave no hint of the setting of the action or details of their exploit. This information was also omitted from the citation that accompanied the George Medal awarded to Tommy Brown, who was then at sixteen the youngest recipient of that gallantry medal. His part in the boarding of the *U-559*, and the capture of secret and vital items, also remained unknown to the wartime public media.

It was only after the investigation held by the Captain into the reasons why and how, the canteen assistant had appeared on board the sinking U-boat, that Tommy's correct age became known; up to that time he had been regarded as the youngest in the ship and subject to some good-humoured teasing, but everyone believed he was at least 17 years of age. How he managed to disguise his correct age when he received a draft issued by the NAAFI service to join *Petard* is a mystery; he could only have been 15 years old when the ship was commissioned. Once his true age became known, to his great distress, he received his discharge from the ship at Alexandria a few days after the sinking, and was shipped home. The gallant and reckless boy was killed two years later; he died trying to rescue an infant sister who perished with him in the flames that engulfed his family's tenement home in North Shields.

A rather subdued ship gave leave over the next four days at Haifa; some of the ship's company were able to go to Jerusalem for 48 hours, staying as the guests of the Palestine Police at their compound. On the 3rd came the news that the Eighth Army had broken through the enemy lines at El Alamein after days of bitter fighting; Rommel's Afrika Korps was retiring westward and out of Egypt. The ships of the fleet were ready and expecting to start support action along the sea flank of the British Army – in fact units at sea were already escorting supply vessels to enter the desert ports as they were recaptured. *Petard* left Haifa to join *Hero*, *Kelvin* and *Javelin* under the command of Captain D12 in *Pakenham* on a hunt for a submarine reported seen in position 33 degrees 00 minutes north, 32 degrees 30 minutes east, about 60 miles north of the position where *U-559* had been sunk. The ships hunted the submarine for the entire day, 5th November, in very bad asdic conditions; only after all five ships had lost contact and failed to regain touch after the last firm location of the elusive U-boat, did D12 call off the hunt and return to Port Said with his frustrated hunters; entering harbour in the early hours of the morning of 6th November.

For the week following Antony Fasson's death, his place was filled temporarily by the navigator, Lieutenant-Royal Navy, A.H.L.S. Black, the ship's 'Number 2', a quiet man who did a competent job as the pilot. The pilot, however, suffered a disadvantage; something that in the early weeks of the commission was not at first apparent to the temporary volunteer reserve 'wavy navy' officers, unversed in the subtleties of the social order within the ranks of the regular commissioned officers. Black was one of the four regular service executive officers in the ship distinguished from the reserves by their straight gold braid stripes, but he was the odd man out; the only one who had not entered the professional service as a Dartmouth cadet.

Poor Black was not even in the running for the vacant appointment as second-in-command and First Lieutenant. He left the ship a few hours after arrival in Port Said, swopping appointments with the Second-Lieutenant of the *Kelvin*, Lieutenant David Dunbar Nasmith. David was a Dartmouth entry, senior term officer, senior cadet captain, winner of the Sword-of-Honour, and son of a famous World War One Admiral, and holder of the Victoria Cross. He was an outstanding dedicated young officer; marked down for accelerated promotion, earned by his single minded concentration and his professionalism.

The ship was doubtless fortunate to get David as a brilliant replacement for Antony Fasson, but it was not easy for him to follow Tony. His dedicated and pusser approach to his job was in contrast to Antony's lighter and warmer touch.

In the consequential changes of duties following Black's departure and Dunbar Nasmith's arrival; Brooky became the navigator, while still retaining the job of asdic control officer. Peter Wood, the sub-lieutenant SANVR, moved into the second navigator's billet and deputy signals' officer. Robert de Pass, the ship's sub-lieutenant because of his RN regular service status, retained the torpedo control, signals' officer, and ship's office jobs.

Mark Thornton with a special pride was able to honour the promise made to the workers of Walkers' Navy Yard, the builders, to send trophies from the ship's action successes. A German U-boat seaman's life jacket was on its way to Newcastle.

CHAPTER 4

Convoys

Trouble was brewing over Admiral Godfroy's Force X in Alexandria harbour: the French fleet partially demilitarised with reduced complements and restricted bunker fuel, still constituted a threat to the free use of the port by the British Mediterranean fleet; the ships were capable of being moved by their skeleton crews and sunk in blockading positions.

Operation Torch was under way; the Allied invasion of the French territory at the western end of North Africa, designed to pinch the Axis desert forces between the advancing Eighth Army moving west from the breakout at El Alamain, and the combined British First Army with the US 11th Corps moving east from Algeria. The confused loyalties of the French were complicated by the antagonisms between the Free and Vichy French leaders, both in Metropolitan France and the French North African colonies. The French Navy especially was in a peculiar psychological state since the surrender of France in 1940. Most senior officers, these included Admiral Godfroy, regarded Admiral Darlan as their titular head, and were loyal to Marshal Petain as the head of the French Government. They disliked the British for the attacks on the French fleet at Oran and Dakar, and also for the defeat of their land and sea forces in Syria.

From the start of the Torch landings on 8th November, Admiral Darlan in Algiers found himself under strong pressure from the Allied command to order all French forces in North Africa to cease fighting the Allies; intense political, military and personal intrigues at Algiers continued throughout the 8th, 9th and into the 10th; the rivalries of the French military and naval commanders, their agonising soul searching over their loyalty to Marshal Petain in occupied France, was complicated further when the Marshal disowned the Admiral on the 9th.

Finally on the 10th the American force commander General Mark Clark, persuaded the Admiral to accept the role of Governor General of French North Africa, and to issue an immediate order for French forces to cease hostilities against the Allies: Darlan was to be the political head in North Africa and General Giraud the military commander of all French forces.

Admiral Godfroy had been given an ultimatum on the 8th; his ships were to come under Allied command. Unless he submitted, the ships would be taken by force or sunk at their berths. The situation was critical and in many ways a repeat of the confrontation in 1940, when under the guns of the British battleships, the French ships were forced to land the obdurating pads from the guns of the main armament, reduce their ships' companies by two-thirds, and disembark furnace fuel.

After months of negotiation the French Admiral had received permission for the old battleship *Lorraine* to be moved into drydock for a quick but vital underwater refit; the ship actually moved into dock on the day that the ultimatum was delivered; placing the battleship in a position where if blown up by her crew, it would put a dock, vital to the Mediterranean fleet out of commission for many months. The large cruisers of the French force could be moved the short distance from their moorings, and sunk in positions inside the entrance to Alexandria Harbour that would effectively block the fleet and supply base for the 8th Army at a crucial period when the army had just broken out to the west, from El Alamein.

To prevent this happening and to back up the ultimatum, light units including motor torpedo boats, were deployed inside the harbour, to torpedo the French ships at the first sign of any attempt to slip moorings. From Port Said, the 15th Cruiser squadron sailed in the early hours of the 8th, for Alexandria to confront the French ships. The cruisers, *Cleopatra*, *Orion*, *Arethusa* and *Euraylus* with *Pakenham* leading a flotilla comprising *Petard*, *Paladin*, *Hero*, *Kelvin* and *Javelin*, stood off Alexandria, cleared for action, dreading the need to massacre the proud but largely emasculated French ships and their crews. During a long 48 hours, the squadron prowled outside while the wranglings of the political and military leaders continued far away in Algiers. Early on the 9th, *Petard* and *Paladin*, were ordered into the harbour to moor with stern on to the detached mole, so as to be able to train torpedo tubes on the large French cruisers. It was an unreal situation; little activity could be seen in the French ships, but steam rising from the supply systems to the fo'c'sle and quarter deck capstans and smoke from funnels, indicated that some preparations had been made to shift berths. *Petard* with *Paladin* stood to at action stations into the second day, ready to back up the Royal Marine boarding parties that were held ready ashore for rushing Admiral Godfroy's ships, or as a final act, to sink the ships.

With considerable relief a signal was received, late in the afternoon of the 10th, as the last few hours of the extended ultimatum ran out, announcing to the squadron Admiral Godfroy's agreement to accept Admiral Darlan's order to place his ships under Allied command.

That same evening *Petard* slipped out of harbour and joined *Queen Olga* as she escorted from Port Said westward, a small convoy of one store ship and one petrol carrier, bound for Mersa Matruh, in anticipation of the recapture of that small coastal town. The supply force, preceded by three minesweepers sailed cautiously into a heavily minded area, steering parallel to the coast line that was fast disappearing into the darkness, as night fell. Behind the minesweepers, *Petard* led the petrol carrier, followed by the store ship, with *Queen Olga* bringing up the rear; each ship steering on and up to the shaded blue stern light of the next ahead in the column. *Petard* at the head of the column steered on the central ship of the minesweepers, who were in arrow formation; streaming wire double oropesa sweeps to port and starboard. The two wing sweepers stationed themselves inside the floats marking the position of the otter boards at the extremes of their senior officer's port and starboard sweep wires, steamed in swept water; leaving only the senior ship to lead, totally unprotected, into unswept mined water.

There were few in *Petard* or the ships following, that did not in their imagination fill the sea with bobbing horned mines, cut by the sweepers steaming resolutely into the night and the unswept enemy minefields; all prayed that the Italians, who had laid most of the fields, had honoured the international agreement to manufacture only moored mines that were automatically rendered safe once the mooring was severed. It was a nerve-racking experience proceeding through seas populated with unseen mines floating on the surface; there was no room for doubt that mines were being cut loose by the sweep wires; explosive cutters fitted at intervals between the ordinary static steel cutters on the wires, could be heard from time to time exploding under water, activated as mine moorings were swept down the wires into the waiting jaws of the cutters.

Men closed up at 'Action Stations' on the upper-deck and bridge, pulled their duffle coats closer against the night cold coming off the desert, fidgeted blew and checked the air in the inflatable lifebelts worn underneath outer clothing, where should the worst happen they would not impede the shedding of heavy protective clothes. Those far below decks with actions stations in the engine and boiler rooms, magazines, ammunition supply parties as well as the W/T office envied their shipmates up and out on the upper deck; went about their duties in strained anxiety against a sudden and total convulsion of their compartment into oblivion, or at the best into a hideous scene of agony, fire, steam, darkness and flying white hot metal. They consoled some of their fears with the thought that a mine explosion would spare some, allow a few to escape from between decks; that their station below was out of the cold, they were all better off than the merchant seamen who manned the petrol carrier following astern, and who had the certainty of instant oblivion that would engulf all, should a mine ignite the high octane spirit carried in the tanks.

Throughout the entire night, sounds of distant desert warfare could be heard; far off flares and flashes of explosions lit the sky intermittently indicating that by-passed pockets of enemy forces were being engaged by mopping up task groups of the Eighth Army. From time to time aircraft could be heard overhead but not identified, and twice flares were dropped in proximity of the small convoy; attacks did not develop, perhaps because the inquisitive airman failed to spot the ships he suspected below or that he had identified the ships as friendly. The ships held their fire to avoid giving away their position even though the flares falling in a long line to port and at 45 degrees to the line of advance, seemed to expose them defenceless to unseen attack from the air or a patrolling submarine.

About an hour before dawn the smell of baking bread tantalised the nostrils of the tired, tensed and cold gun and torpedo crews, aft and down wind from the ship's company galley under the foremast tripod, where the ship's cook, Petty Officer Inkpen, and his assistant cook Tug Wilson were starting the daily early morning ritual of bread baking, a routine that continued without a failure or delay during the entire commission; a remarkable achievement that no operation or action succeeded in stopping.

Dawn appeared in the eastern sky, astern of the supply convoy; the minesweepers were still in immaculate sweeping formation ahead, and the shapes of the ships beginning to emerge clearly in the morning light as the ship's company, standing to at dawn action station alert, forgot all thoughts of breakfast, as the cry from the bridge starboard look, 'Aircraft in sight, bearing green 40, angle of sight 30' drove men back to reality of the situation. All guns obeyed the order to 'Follow director' onto the unmistakeable outline of a Ju 88 identified by the lookouts and confirmed by the director's crew, peering through their powerful optical instruments after being conned onto the target by the GCO following the target indicator.

The German aircraft flew under the cloud ceiling from the north, across and ahead of the minesweepers, perhaps on a reconnaissance mission behind the Eighth Army lines. The aircraft had crossed the line of advance of the convoy, when it banked steeply to port, flying down the line of the ships as if the crew had suddenly and by accident spotted the formation below. The Ju 88 circled the ships twice, keeping out of range of the *Petard*'s guns, before continuing on its earlier course towards the desert coast line. There could be little doubt that the position, course and speed of the convoy would now be reported to be followed sometime later in the morning by an air attack.

The Captain ordered a semi-relaxation of action stations so that his men could have breakfast before the ordeal to come; none of the gun's crews were however permitted to go below decks, not only because of the imminent attack, but also the continuing high risk from the mines that now could be seen floating on the sea surface; some had obviously been cut free by the sweepers, but many more were old mines that had broken from their moorings in bad weather or earlier sweeping operations. Those that were in close range weapon range, were fired at first by the mine sweepers as they passed, followed by the ships of the convoy and escorts; a few were sunk, others that passed close down the ship sides caused considerable alarm in case the enthusiastic gunners exploded one of the lethal black spheres, to spray the low open decks with shrapnel.

The final destination of the convoy was by this time in doubt; signals that had been received during the night and continued to come in as the morning wore on, indicated that enemy elements still remained in and around Mersa Matruh; the jetty and anchorage were under intermittent shell and mortar fire making mine and blockship obstruction clearance a hazardous operation; the prospect of unloading the store ship and the petrol carrier successfully without unacceptable losses, seemed doubtful. Orders were expected for the convoy to delay arrival or to return to Alexandria or Port Said until the situation at the desert town stabilised; the signal was in fact in course of transmission and being received in *Petard*'s W/T office, when the 286 radar office reported a formation of aircraft approaching from the north, and at the moment of contact, were a little more than 16 miles distant.

Petard hoisted flag signals indicating that she was in radar touch with enemy aircraft, as her guns and gun control director trained round to starboard and the expected bearing from where the attack was to come. All ships in the formation braced themselves for a massive bomb assault; the two merchantmen could only rely on short range weapons manned by a few DEMS ratings and the civilian crew. *Queen Olga*'s mighty 5 inch main armament was incapable of elevation to engage high flying aircraft; her close range weapons did not include a pom-pom and hardly exceeded the fire power of the merchantmen.

The three Algerine fleet minesweepers were armed with a single 4 inch Mark V gun on the fo'c'sle and a few close range weapons, so the burden of engaging the approaching formation until the aircraft broke away to deliver individual low level bomb runs fell upon the *Petard* who had the only gun control equipment capable of tackling a formation attack.

The bridge lookouts sighted 10 Ju 88 aircraft flying in from the north, a little ahead of the starboard beam, on a course taking them ahead of the westward bound ships. It seemed obvious that the attack would come from ahead down the line of ships astern of the minesweepers; the formation commander obviously calculating that freedom for the ships to take avoiding action would be inhibited by the width of the path being swept through the mined area; for the same reason the number of guns that could be brought to bear on the aircraft would be reduced by the fact that the *Petard* was unable to turn beam on to present her full battery of four 4 inch guns; only the forward guns were able to fire. The sky continued overcast with a high cloud base giving the ships one advantage of excellent visibility, and no sun or low cloud to blind or hide the bombing approach. The responsibility for breaking up the high level attack rested entirely on the ability of the *Petard*'s gunnery in the initial stages, there was at that moment no signs of fighter protection called for from the desert air command; it had been asked for when the ships had been first sighted by the reconnaissance plane.

The diamond formation of Ju 88s turned to port when about twenty thousand yards ahead of the Algerines, and began the bomb approach, as they turned. In the *Petard* the voice of the First Lieutenant came over the headset on the GCO's head, repeating the Captain's order to open fire when ready; the director crew had for some time been tracking the planes, the layer and trainer holding their aim on the leader's aircraft; optical and radar ranges had been matched and fed continuously into the transmitting station, together with the GCO's estimate of the formation's height and speed, leaving the gunnery transmitting station converted into elevation and training bearings for the gunlayers and trainers to follow on the gun dials, and a continuous prediction of fuze settings for the ammunition.

The enemy formation flying at a height of 9000 feet, speed 280 knots, loomed large in the directors crew optical rangefinder and fixed binoculars. The GCO gave the order 'commence commence commence'; over the wind seconds later, came the voices of the communication numbers of A & B gun crews shouting the repetition of the order, followed by the crash of the breech blocks as loading numbers forced home into the guns the first of the fused ammunition of fixed shell and cartridge case. The fire bells tinkled in the director and at the guns, as the formation arrived at 14000 yards range; the director layer steadied on his sights, pressed the firing pistol and A and B guns crashed out together, followed by the bell like sound of the ejected brass cartridge cases hitting the decks to roll into scuppers or hitting deck obstructions.

The salvos continued at the rate of 12 per minute; it was several seconds before the fall of shot buzzer warned the anxious director crew that the bursts from the first salvo were about to appear and adjustments could be made to correct aim and fuze settings. Two black puffs appeared a little ahead and below the formation as the leading Ju 88 passed over the bursts; a reduction in speed estimate with a slight increase in height was made in time to catch the third salvo as the aircraft flew remorselessly on to their bomb release position. The second salvo burst, again ahead and below the enemy while the ships below sweated it out, willed and cursed the *Petard*'s guns to knock the menacing immaculate formation off course and concentration; the minesweepers had wisely held their fire, without AA gun control equipment they would have wasted ammunition and confused the spotting by the *Petard*'s gun control team.

The ship's gun crews that could not engage, with the other

upperdeck action parties with restless bowels, ground their teeth as the salvos from the two forward guns continued in measured time; shell bursts began to appear in the formation but with apparently little effect on the steadiness of the German aircraft intent on their bomb run. All four of the director control team strived to make adjustments in time for the following third and succeeding salvos to burst and disrupt the formation, but without obvious results; one plane dipped to the right for a second, but before anything could be made of the side step, came the brain freezing sight of 40 to 50 minute black dots released together from the bellies of the Ju 88s.

A strangled shout from the GCO warned the Captain and bridge of the bomb release; these passed out of sight of the director crew who remained glued onto the aircraft; guns were ordered to cease fire, followed by the order for all guns to stand by to defend their individual sectors and come under the control of officer of the quarters or gunlayer for sector barrage fire against diving aircraft. The bombs raced downwards towards the convoy, trapped because ships could not take avoiding action; passing with a sighing roar over the *Petard* to fall in a huge widespread water convulsion that blotted out the petrol carrier, but with the centre of the bomb pattern a little to port of the column of ships. The great eruption of water, sand and smoke hung for a moment like an obscene curtain before subsiding as the sturdy fuel carrier emerged from the starboard fringe, water pouring off her low decks, followed by her sister supply ship similarly drenched but without damage.

There was no time to ponder why the bombs had missed the tethered targets; the formation broke to port, starboard, ahead and astern as planes began to position themselves for individual shallow dive attacks towards the ships, concentrating on *Petard, Queen Olga* and their two charges. In *Petard* the four 4-inch crews stood ready in their sectors ready for the layers and trainers to fight their guns over open sights, with loading numbers bracing themselves, hugging ammunition ready fused to burst in a short barrage at 2000 yards, to load at a rate of 22 rounds per minute or better, now that the guns were released from director control. The Captain of the pom-pom, Leading Seaman gunlayer, Trevor Tipping, the trainer Able Seaman Mizon, and the loaders Able Seamen Hooper, Craven and Emmott with the crews of the oerlikon guns, spat on their hands waiting their turn to fend off the attack that was to come from all points of the compass.

While the planes started to turn in towards the ships to

Doc examining Able Seaman Holmes, the ship's star footballer

Ship's Company at Port Said, October 1942. The ship's name is held by 16 year old Tommy Brown, GM, Naafi Assistant

Petard hunting *U-559*, 30th
October 1942

Depth charging *U-559*

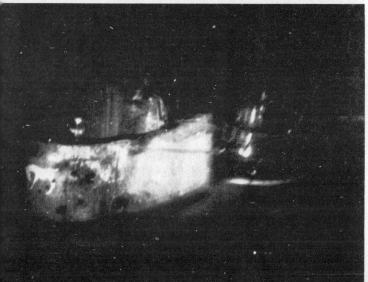

U-559, conning tower surfaced
to surrender, 2249/30th
October 1942

Mark Thornton and Robert de Pass at Tobruk, with the suspect Ju 87 that had bombed the ship in the preceding weeks

Leave in Cairo: the coxswain (third from left) leads a party to the pyramids

Submarine *Uarsciek* after surfacing caught in searchlights from *Queen Olga* and *Petard*

Uarsciek at dawn with prize-crew preparing for the tow

Petard prepares to tow the Italian submarine *Uarsciek*

commence a co-ordinated assault, the Captain signalled by light to the two merchantmen to maintain course and speed of 8 knots, but to disregard his movements. As the signal was being passed he reduced speed to almost stop, turning out to starboard and dropped back longside the petrol carrier, then astern resuming the formation speed in station between the two merchantmen remaining slightly out to starboard by about half a cable.

As the manoeuvre proceeded all hell broke loose; every gun in the four ships was in action against the diving Ju 88s. The uproar from the four-inch guns in *Petard* crushed the ear drums as rapid fire blackened the sky with shell bursts, mixed with tracer from the pom-pom and other close range weapons, and crossed and criss-crossed dangerously over the ships. Bombs exploded everywhere in the sea and the air seemed to be filled with flying shrapnel, much of it hitting and ricochetting off the ship's steelwork. In the midst of the maelstrom of gunfire, smoke, aircraft noise, bomb flight and explosions, the ships continued to proceed inside the narrow swept channel; the sweepers were from some unknown reason omitted from the attack, and from 3 to 4000 yards, the spectators of the savage attack on the convoy and escorts.

Quite suddenly it was all over; four Spitfires were in amongst the preoccupied German aircraft, all ten were in flight, some low skimming the sea heading north, endeavouring to reform as they disappeared towards Crete with the fighters from the desert command in close pursuit. The ships were able to take unexpected early stock of the effects of the air attack, and somewhat surprised to realise that no one had received a direct hit or had suffered severe damage from near misses. The 80 plus bombs hurled at the ships had only caused numerous splinter holes in the sides, superstructure, funnels and boats, but no splinters from bombs or tracer shell from her sister ship or the escorts had ignited the highly inflammable petrol carrier, turning it into a funeral pyre. The luck that combined with the uncharacteristic ineffective bombing by the Ju 88s, seemed a good omen to the *Petard*'s ship's company who were still trying to shake off the gloom that had gripped the ship since the deaths of Antony Fasson and Colin Grazier.

The signal for the force to retire and retrace its way back to Port Said, had been decoded by the W/T office during the action; Mark Thornton, his ship again leading the column, hoisted a signal for the convoy and escort to execute a Blue 18 turn, a turn together 180 degrees to starboard; the minesweepers turning separately in formation with sweeps still streamed, later to overtake the convoy steaming on an opposite course to the original for Mersa Matruh.

The signal for the force to retire was amended, the two merchantmen were to turn aside and enter Alexandria, and only *Queen Olga* with *Petard* were to continue on to Port Said, arriving there eventually late PM on 12th November, everyone feeling lucky to have got away without casualties or serious damage from an abortive operation.

During the next day, 13th, the three sub-lieutenants in *Petard*, one RN and two RNVRs, received full watchkeeping certificates, documents that not only described them as being capable of taking charge of a watch at sea in any major war vessel, but confirmed that they had all somehow measured up to the Captain's exacting standards.

Leave was given to each watch after working hours on the 13th and again on the 14th. During the first day ammunition lighters moved in longside and magazines were topped up, replacing 4 inch and close range ammunition expended holding off the Ju 88 attack. During both days a strong buzz began to build up of a major seaborne operation in the offing. The rumours began to gain substance when on the morning of the 15th a sudden round of activity started the day, the commanding officers of the eight fleet destroyers moored in pairs on the buoys opposite the Eastern Exchange, were ordered to repair on board the cruiser *Euryalus* for a conference.

At noon immediately after the return of the commanding officers, all ships were brought to one hour's notice for steam, and prepared for sea; in *Petard* at 1400, lower deck was cleared so that Mark Thornton could speak to his ship's company and explain the purpose of the forthcoming Operation Stoneage. The operation was to fight convoy MW 13 through the enemy dominated gap between Cyrenaica and Crete to resupply Malta.

The Captain with immense relish made it clear that in his opinion it was inevitable that the operation would be opposed by heavy German and Italian air attacks; there was also the strong probability of surface and submarine opposition to the convoy's passage; the main units of the Italian battle fleet were a force still to be considered. On the credit side there was now the fighter cover that would be available from the forward bases of the desert airforce, and be in position to give cover as the ships approached the island. The Captain reminded his men of the earlier supply efforts and that only part of the stores embarked for the beleaguered island had so far reached Malta, even the convoy fought through by Sir Philip Vian in March, that culminated in the classic and brilliant sea action, the Battle of Sirte, succeeded in disembarking only 5000 tons out of the original 25000 tons that had started out in the holds of the four ships in that convoy.

The Convoy MW 13 was again to consist of four ships carrying about the same tonnage of supplies, critically required to maintain life in the island; Mark Thornton in his most belligerent mood stated his determination that his ship would play a leading part in achieving the objective of Stoneage; he coloured his speech by repeating the conviction expressed in his first address long months past in Newcastle when the ship was commissioned, of his certainty that he would not be killed by the enemy and that his ship would survive with him; in a kind of afterthought and a remarkable effort to encourage his apprehensive ship's company, they were told that in the unlikely event of the ship being badly damaged, there would be no need to abandon ship until the sea could be seen to begin to pour down the funnel.

There was plently of time to mull over the Captain's words and to swop impressions with their Greek comrades; *Queen Olga* lay as usual longside, sharing the same head and stern buoys. Many of her ship's company had listened to the British commanding officer haranguing his men, and it was difficult to determine whether he had alarmed his Greek listeners more than his own people.

The long day wore on without the order to slip and proceed being made; this manufactured a further crop of rumours, the most hopeful of which was that the merchantmen had been held up at the southern end of the canal; the most likely reason was an attempt to confuse the enemy a little, by making it appear that the operation was postponed or even about to be cancelled. Nothing happened that night, and it was not until late in the afternoon of the 16th, that the destroyers were ordered to slip and follow Captain D12 and *Pakenham* out through the boom, leading *Euryalus* who slipped her moorings moments after the last destroyer had got underway. As the evening wore on, the cruiser and the eight fleets formed up and waited for the Commodore of MW 13 to lead his four merchantmen in the falling dusk, past and through Port Said, to join the waiting war ships at the end of the searched approach channel. The formed unit, convoy and escorts, then turned west and sailed to rendezvous the remainder of the 15th cruiser squadron waiting with the close escort of four Hunt class destroyers and another ten Fleets.

At early dawn of the 17th, the convoy, close escort, cruiser squadron and fleet destroyers, set off to the west, towards Malta. The four merchant ships were in two columns, with the four Hunts in close screening positions to give anti-submarine cover, and with their twin 4 inch mountings, effective AA protection against high level and dive bomb attacks. Two cruisers headed the convoy, *Cleopatra* wearing the flag of Vice-Admiral 15th cruiser squadron and the *Euryalus; Orion* and *Arethusa* formed a sub-division astern. The 18 Fleet destroyers in a two flotilla organisation, D12 and D14, were deployed in an extended anti-submarine and torpedo bomber screen round the entire convoy and cruiser formation. With a speed of advance of 12 knots the force zig-zagged westward into a raising sea and worsening weather. The departure of convoy MW 13 was well known to the Axis sympathisers that infested both Port Said and Alexandria, and it was not surprising that reconnaissance aircraft were continuous in their distant patrols from first light of the 17th.

Steady progress was made during the morning with only one incident that involved the *Petard*: an alert bridge wing lookout spotted a rubber dinghy in the broken sea well abaft the beam, only moments before it may have been lost from possible visual contact. The ship turned to starboard out of her screening station to investigate, and shortly afterwards was retrieving from the sea, five RAF crew men who had been shot down the day before, carrying out anti-submarine patrols south of Crete. The airmen were in good shape and only suffering from mild exposure; to the surprise of his rescuers the navigator raced up to the bridge chart house to confirm his estimated position and to win a bet off his fellow survivors; his obvious satisfaction in his navigational ability made his long suffering crewmates threaten to petition for him to be cast adrift in the raft again to continue his slow drift towards the North African coast, to prove his estimate and bet on the landfall.

By mid-afternoon the first air attack developed from 6 Savoia bombers of the Regia Aeronautica; flying very high under the cloud base they delivered a precision bomb attack on the convoy ships and the close escort of Hunts. The formation was subjected to furious anti-aircraft fire from the cruisers and the destroyers with gun mountings capable of high angle elevation, which included the three 'P' class fleets. The bombs fell with uncomfortable accuracy in the midst of the four merchantmen, but apart from splinters and a few injuries, the ships escaped from serious damage. Other attacks came as the afternoon continued, from small groups of Savoias and Ju 88s, but the gunnery and manouverability of the ships taking avoiding action, proved a match for the aircraft that did not press home their attacks with any real determination.

At dusk there did come an attack from torpedo aircraft that caused considerable trouble and alarm. Six Ju 88s circled the dark horizon, low over the sea, then came in from separate points of the compass to surprise the outer escort screen. Firing everything they had, the destroyers first tried to blind the oncoming planes with flash ammunition, fired with a set 2500 yard fuse to burst as a barrier backed up by tracer from pom-pom and oerlikon mountings: the planes broke through, flying at masthead height or less over the outer destroyer lines, they met the second and inner barrage fired from the cruiser's heavier armament, supported by the Hunts' 4 inch twin guns and the massed close range tracer fire from the cruisers, Hunts and the merchantmen. Undoubtedly some of the aircraft were hit and damaged, but none were seen to fall in the deepening gloom; all dropped their torpedoes; the ships with sea room to turn and con the tracks, avoided the deadly tin fish.

The short violent action was over, with no ship crippled, but some damaged – mainly the destroyers hit by shell splinters from the close range barrage put up by the cruisers and Hunts; a constant hazard for the outer screen destroyer, but one that had to be endured. The risk was always present of being hit in the back by the ships under protection and the inner screen of warships, while facing outward towards the direction of the attack.

The night went quiet without further alarm, as the ships of Operation Stoneage continued steaming towards the narrowest part of the gap between Africa and the Island of Crete heading into a strong westerly and a short breaking sea. Soon after first light, the air attacks recommenced from both Italian and German aircraft in small groups but caused little more than anxiety; all were put off accurate bombing by the concentrated gunfire of the escort and the Beaufighters that now patrolled over Convoy MW 13, and by the fact that the cloud ceiling limited the height of the attacks, cloud that was high enough to prevent it being used effectively as cover, and there was no sun to blind the defenders.

The sturdy supply ships ploughed purposefully on in good formation, carrying out exact zig-zags without allowing the sporadic air attacks to divert them from their confident progress. One rather more determined attack was launched by 6 Ju 88s on the outer escorts, the three ships on the tail of the starboard screen, including the *Petard*, the last ship. It was an attack pressed home against the combined fire from the three ships and the two rear cruisers, but even this failed to do more than produce a few near misses as the ships took violent and high speed avoiding action once the bombs were seen to be released.

Late in the evening of the 18th after the escorting fighters had departed, came the first enemy success; against the evening sky 26 Ju 88 torpedo carriers were seen to break into three groups, and keeping well out of gun range began to position themselves for attacks from the outer wings of the ship force and from astern as darkness fell, leaving the fleet straining to pierce the darkness, waiting for the wave hopping advance of the roaring planes. Suddenly out of the clouds over the ships came two long lines of flares in the form of a cross centred on the convoy, dropping slowly drifting downwind, exposing the ships plunging through the rising sea in a merciless brilliant white light. Desperate efforts were made by the ships nearest to the descending parachutes to shoot the flares out, but with little success; unseen from out of the wind and spray flayed darkness came the roar of the torpedo bombers intent on the ships silhouetted against the flare paths.

Every ship on the screen opened up blind into the night, setting up a barrage of bursting shells low over the sea in the hope of catching the planes as they flashed over the outer ships towards the convoy ringed by the Hunts and cruisers. The fleets edged out away from the convoy to escape some punishment from badly set fuzes and faulty ammunition. The night turned into a holocaust of gunfire and roaring aircraft engines, climaxing into a violent explosion and sheets of rising flame, momentarily lighting up the shape of the *Arethusa*. The cruiser had been hit forward causing many casualties including her Captain, C.H. Cresswell DSO DSC RN, who was badly burned in the explosion; fires were raging below decks and could be seen through the broken plates in the bow and below the bridge. The stricken cruiser turned out of the wind and stopped with the stern up wind to help the firefighters struggling to control the outbreak, the damage control teams shoring up the buckled bulk-heads, and rescue teams recovering the wounded and the dead. The time of the torpedo hit was 1805, position 33 degrees 06 minutes north, and 20 degrees 44 minutes east.

CS 15 ordered two destroyers, fleets, to be detached to standby *Arethusa*, and help her return to base, while Convoy MW 13 proceeded on into the night, still under intermittent attack from the air. D12 and D14 detached *Petard* and *Javelin* respectively from the two wings of the screen, but as the two destroyers dropped astern to help the stricken ship, Mark Thornton as the senior officer of the pair, made a courageous decision involving considerable risk to his career if the cruiser had been lost because of it. He ordered *Javelin* to rejoin the convoy; his appreciation of the situation was that the convoy's arrival intact was vital to the besieged Malta, MW 13 had to take priority over the safety of the *Arethusa*. Days later the Commander-in-Chief endorsed Mark's decision as being both correct and courageous.

The destroyer in the dark moved round the stopped cruiser trying to give asdic cover against any submarine attracted to the area by the sound and sight of the torpedo attacks from the Ju 88s and the fires blazing in the *Arethusa*. Under the direction of David Dunbar Nasmith and the Gunner T, supply parties and men who could be spared from the guns and torpedo mountings, on the dark and spray covered iron deck prepared to take the cruiser in tow. A special flexible steel wire towing pennant had to be broken out of its stowage in the tiller flat, hauled up and round numerous upperdeck obstructions, and flaked down in large bights the full length of the iron and quarter decks, with the forward ends of each bight secured by spunyarn lashings to an iron bar fixed abaft the port whalers davits. Each bight could now be controlled and its immense weight prevented from taking charge as the pennant eased out over the stern, through two chain stoppers.

In both ships men were edgy with anxiety over the very real possibility of an attack on the stopped cruiser; somehow the damaged ship was left unmolested, and only in the receding distance, flares and gun flashes showed that the enemy was following the convoy away from the Arethusa. The ship had been struck on the port side, abreast 'B' turret flooding up to the waterline between bulkheads 20 and 61. The cruiser heeled over 15 degrees to port and 10 degrees down at the head. A serious fire fed by oil, paint and inflammable material enveloped the bridge super-structure which was evacuated and the ship controlled from aft.

Mark Thornton closed the cruiser, and over the loud hailer

discussed the situation with unseen owners of voices in the blacked out hull that towered over the plunging destroyer. The executive commander speaking on behalf of his wounded captain gave in brief terms a situation report; preliminary shoring of the bulkheads was well advanced, fires were coming under control, pumps were coping with the water entering the ship, armament electrics were functioning, and there was steam on the fo'c'sle capstans.

Out of the dark from the high fo'c'sle of *Arethusa* on *Petard*'s port quarter, came the sharp crack of a line throwing rifle, the cruiser's GI making an accurate first time shot, placed the light white line across the destroyer's 'X' gun deck, to be quickly found by the gun crew and passed down to the waiting party on the quarter deck. Gingerly led aft, then through the stern fairlead, it was carefully handed in to avoid parting the fragile cotton line. Successfully, first a series of joined stronger heaving lines were pulled in, followed by a stouter grassline that floated its weight on the sea and allowed all available hands to stamp out the hauling in on the dark unsteady and now wave lashed iron deck. After the grass line came a heavy hawser that began to strain the capacity of the hauling party on the destroyer's sea covered decks. The Captain did all that was possible to ease the task of the hauling party by allowing his ship to go astern as near as he dared in the dark, without putting his ship and men at risk under the crashing bows of the wallowing cruiser.

Without capstans to help, more men had to leave action stations at guns to join the hauling party; gradually with an agonising strain on bodies and tortured muscles, *Arethusa*'s $3\frac{1}{2}$ inch wire towing pennant was hauled inch by inch towards the destroyer's stern until the large thimble eye hove in to sight and within the reach of Petty Officer Rumsey on his stomach leaning out under the lower stern guard rail. Rumsey with the help of his quarter-deck hands and 'Y' gun crew finally guided the eye in through the stern fairlead and over the towing slip; only then the hauling party who for nearly an hour had struggled to get the tow inboard, could ease back on the hawser and allow the slip to take the weight of the tow. The cruiser's end of the towing pennant was secured to her port cable, now veering out slowly on her capstan in response to *Petard*'s winking blue light from a small heather signal light, informing the *Arethusa* of the destroyer's gradual move forward on her screws and the steady increase in engine revolutions working up the speed of advance through the water to three, four, five and over the next hour to 10 knots.

From *Arethusa* about two shackles of cable had been veered out to increase the weight and spring of the tow; the large and deep curve of the tow wire allowed for sudden jars and strains from the towing ship. The long struggle to reduce the 15 degree heel by transferring liquids and jettisoning upper-deck fittings had, after 6 hours, reduced the list to 5 degrees, and the steering of the cruiser began to improve, *Petard* had only to steer out a little to starboard to keep her heading on her course.

From the destroyer, where men were recovering from the long hard haul getting the tow connected, the cruiser's shape could be barely seen in the dark without binoculars; hot 'kye' prepared by the indefatigable galley staff was being drunk by tired men who had not stood down since action stations had been sounded 36 hours earlier.

More signal exchanges between the two ships to increase revolutions and speed to reduce the distance to base and to get inside adequate air cover before dawn: when with an unmistakeable jerk the tow parted as *Arethusa* yawed wildly to port, to broach-to across the path of the oncoming sea.

The long struggle to reconnect the tow started, made more difficult by the fact the narrow starboard iron-deck and waist of the destroyer had vital space covered by the massive coils of the grass and manila hawsers used to haul in the now parted towing pennant, the port side was already filled with the great bights of *Petard*'s own towing pennant lashed down ready for emergency use. These obstructions made the task more difficult for tired men stumbling in the almost total dark trying to keep their feet in a pitching rolling ship. The Captain again placed his ship close to the wallowing cruiser, and the long haul restarted, to take inboard a new towing pennant. The grinding battle was eventually ended, the two ships linked together and the destroyer slowly pulled the cruiser's bow round and back on course; dawn was breaking as the tow slowly and very cautiously worked up to 5 knots.

Signals were beginning to flow in from the C-in-C, first the *Arethusa* was to make for Tobruk, that only hours earlier had been recaptured by the Eighth Army. This was almost immediately cancelled, Tobruk harbour blocked by sunken shipping could not be cleared in time, and the worsening weather would make the tow across the wind and sea a near impossibility. The two ships were ordered to close the African coast and steer a course 30 miles off where air cover would be available; tugs would also meet the

Arethusa at the seaward end of the searched channel into Alexandria.

As the morning light of the 19th brightened, enemy reconnaissance planes found the tethered ships, as bleary eyed and exhausted men cleared decks of loose gear that might hinder the serving of the guns. Spirits rose when two Beaufighters appeared, exchanged recognition signals with the cruiser then bustled off to chase off the skulking German on the horizon. No one felt however that the Luftwaffe or the Regia Aeronautica would delay coming in force to deal a final blow to the crippled cruiser and the towing destroyer, sitting ducks for a determined torpedo or dive bomb attack; the ships were incapable of taking any form of avoiding action. All dreaded the possibility of a raid from one of the Stuka dive bomb squadrons that were reported to be still based on Crete and Greek mainland air bases.

During the morning two high level attacks developed; the first from three planes that were held off by the combined and accurate fire from the *Petard*'s 4 inch guns, supported by the battery of four twin 4 inch mountings on *Arethusa*'s boat deck. The gunfire forced the Ju 88s to release their bombs to fall well astern of the cruiser as the Beaufighters pounced, making them run for home before repeating the bomb run. The second attempt came not long afterwards, when two Savoias appeared out of the cloud ahead of *Petard*; before the ships opened fire the enemy sighted the patrolling fighters and turned back into the clouds and were not seen again. In the meanwhile it was clear from the signals being intercepted from CS 15, the ships and convoy of Operation Stoneage were having a grim time, they were under almost continuous air assault as they fought their way into the teeth of the gale that was punishing the tow.

The wind was approaching storm strength from the west, and things were going badly in the cruiser, the 5 knot tow started to cause serious strains on the plates and bulkheads as far aft as bulkhead 61 and something had to be done to ease the stresses on the mangled forepart of the ship. To save *Arethusa* it became clear that she would have to be turned and towed stern first. Preparations were quickly made to carry this out before the storm and ever worsening sea made the turning of the damaged ship impossible. The tow to the *Arethusa* was slipped by *Petard* and recovery started by the cruiser's fo'c'sle party using the capstans, while the ship fell off her course, broached to, rolling badly lying helpless across the heavy seaway.

Petard released from the tow turned and moved upwind to close the wallowing cruiser, moving in as close to her quarter-deck as Mark Thornton dare place his ship with decks now being continuously swept by deep seas and men clinging desperately to life lines as they prepared to pass out *Petard*'s towing gear. It was now the destroyers turn to fire a line to her charge and the large group of seamen and marines mustered on the wide but sloping *Arethusa*'s quarter-deck, ready to manhaul the tow across and through the sea that raged in the gap between the two ships. The delicate and dangerous manoeuvering of the destroyer, perilously close under the larger ships starboard quarter, with an ever present danger of lines or the wire towing hawser fouling his ship's screws, demonstrated Mark's superb skill as a seaman. He had been continuously on the bridge of his command for three days, conning the ship in action against enemy attack, playing his part in the defence of the convoy, and for the last eighteen hours handling his ship in heavy seas to save the crippled cruiser. He would only take very little food or drink from either his servant, Able Seaman Lofthouse or the wardroom steward, Petty Officer Steward Underwood, who struggled forward at intervals through the sea washed wire strewn iron deck, in the dark, to bring rations for the bridge and gun control crews.

The bridge staff were out on their feet, but Mark with a mixture of encouragement and brutal threats, drove the navigating and signal teams to achieve near impossible limits of mental and physical endurance. Below on the sea washed iron and quarter-decks the First Lieutenant, David Dunbar Nasmith, supported by 'Malaya' MacAllen, the gunner, had laboured for long hours to get the two tows in from the damaged ship; now they were organising the paying out of a third tow. They were without the assistance of the Chief Bosun's Mate or the Captains of the fo'c'sle and iron deck; with the fo'c'sle officer they had to remain closed up at their action station in the director to deal with any threat of surface or air attack. Miraculously none of the scratch parties that included off watch telegraphists, coders and radar specialists, who had wrestled in the storm-racked darkness with unfamiliar hemp and wire towing hawsers, were badly hurt by the frightening surges of wire writhing temporarily out of control along the confined pitch dark and heaving decks. Now in daylight the exhausted men could at least see the wires they were handling, the danger of death or hideous mutilation from the coils of the towing pennant running out over the *Petard*'s stern, was marginally less.

On the stern, while their Captain with screws and rudder held *Petard* into the wind under the lee of the cruiser as it drifted down onto her, Petty Officer Rumsey with 'Y' gun crew and some of his quarter-deckmen strained back on the lanyards of the chain stoppers, allowing the wire to slide out under the control of the choke brake, the weight of the wire increasing with each second as it was hauled out by the cruiser. Further forward along the iron deck under the charge of the Gunner, a party cut the ties that held the pennant in orderly bights, then saw that each loop slide aft, keeping the coiling wire from the many obstructions, any one of which could have caused disaster and fatalities.

The tow was passed without a hitch and quickly; *Arethusa* signalled that their end was on deck secured to a shackle of cable that had been manhandled down from the cruiser's fo'c'sle; *Petard*'s commanding officer began to slowly take the strain in the only direction that a tow line secured to the extreme stern limit of his ship would allow, down wind. Without a towing point near the centre of the destroyer on which to pivot, Mark Thornton was limited once the weight was on the tow, even with the use of the immense turning power of the twin screws, to something less than a 10 degree alteration of course, either to port or starboard; it was fortunate that the wind and storm sea remained in the direction that the tow had to proceed. Gradually the cruiser now down by the bows, by about 10 degrees, slowly using her screws going astern began to turn as *Petard* hauled her stern downwind and started again towards Alexandria. From the quarter deck of the destroyer, the cruiser's stern lifted up out of the sea by the fact that she was down forward, towered high above the destroyer, the great screws turning slowly, coming out of the water as the ship dipped and pitched in the following sea, menaced the towing ship. It was an awesome sight, the great stern and rotating propellers following the slow and straining destroyer, but a painful steady progress began to be achieved; 3 knots towards safety.

During the long afternoon only one attack was launched on the ships struggling painfully before the full gale raging down the Eastern Mediterranean; four Ju 88s broke through the protecting cover of the Beaufighters and made a determined attack in the face of the joint gun defence thrown up by the two ships. Bombs straddled the *Petard*, the closest only 15 yards off the starboard beam, causing the destroyer to lift and plunge at the end of her tow, but again the enemy failed to hit either ship. This turned out to be the last attempt to stop or cripple the tow, and the ships were left to fight only the gale which was proving to be a bigger threat than anything the enemy could lay on.

In the *Arethusa* the grim task of counting the casualties had gone on at the same time as the damage control teams shored up fractured bulkheads and restored power and light to the forepart of the ship. 157 dead from the explosion and fire that raged in the fo'c'sle messdecks and up through the bridge structure, was the heavy toll that had to be reported in the routine casualty signal to the Commander-in-Chief, with the Captain one of the many seriously wounded crowding the temporary and emergency dressing stations deep down in the cruiser. As the darkness of the second gale filled night of the tow closed in on the ships, men weary to the point of collapse were stood down from full action stations, to get a hot drink and something to eat, and in turn, two to three hours of uneasy sleep in the pitching straining ships. Even the iron man, Mark Thornton left his bridge for a short spell of rest when he felt that the tow was going to continue to hold without the danger of parting, caused by the cruiser yawing out of control. While the Captain rested briefly in his small box-like sea cabin below the open bridge, down on the messdecks men turned in fully clothed on mess tables, stools and odd corners for snatches of elusive sleep.

The painfully slow haul continued through the night with the officer of the watch constantly nursing the *Petard* forward, easing back on engine revolutions when necessary and avoiding large rudder movements that could put sudden strains on the towing hawser; his concentration and attention to the watchkeeper on the quarter deck, watching the straining tow, was so demanding that David arranged for the OOW to be relieved every two hours.

Dawn followed the long night that saw no easing of the gale, the seas were now grey mountains threatening to engulf the cruiser retreating backwards, stern first before the furious elements. Assisted by the *Arethusa*'s screws at slow astern, *Petard* succeeded in keeping the broken hull moving directly before the shrieking wind and breaking sea, without the storm causing fatal damage to the ship. During the first watch a signal from the Vice-Admiral 15th Cruiser Squadron addressed to the Commander in Chief was decyphered and the successful conclusion of Operation Stoneage became known to the two ships striving to ride out the gale.

The four ships of convoy MW 13 entered Malta Grand Harbour at 0031 hours, the first convoy from the east or west to be fought through to the island without loss of merchant ships for nearly two years. The convoy had fought its way against determined air assaults during the whole of the daylight hours of the 19th, the gunpower of the convoy and escorts had been reinforced by a squadron of Spitfires now based on Malta, who at the cost of three of the fighters being shot down by the enemy, made an important contribution to the convoy's safe arrival. Two of the pilots were picked up by the ships of MW 13.

From about noon there were signs that the gale would blow itself out, the barometer began to rise, but as the tow approached the end of the searched channel leading to the Great Pass into Alexandria, the seas were still too high and vicious for any attempt to turn the cruiser across the wind and sea to enter harbour. *Petard* was ordered by the Rear Admiral Alexandria to heave-to and await the arrival of two tugs who would take over the towing; for the present the beam sea was too bad for the tugs to steam out to the rendezvous, and in *Petard* there were those who began to wonder if the tow would finally finish up onto the lee shore of Palestine or the Sinai desert.

To the immense relief of the watchers in both ships two tugs *Brigand* and *Roysterer* were spotted forcing a way across the breaking seas from the direction of Alexandria, and in the fading evening light placed themselves either side of the cruiser's quarter-deck preparatory to taking over from the destroyer. One of the tugs at great risk to itself and to the Rear Admiral, managed to transfer the RA Alexandria, who was to take over from the critically burnt Captain Cresswell, and direct the final phase of the rescue operation. It was late into the night before the wind and sea had moderated sufficiently for the tugs to pass their tows to *Arethusa*; but this was done finally and *Petard* released from her charge; she remained in close proximity giving anti-submarine protection which became vital as the improving sea conditions made an underwater attack a serious threat.

She was joined by two sloops that had sailed from Haifa into the teeth of the gale and had suffered considerable damage to upperdeck fittings and boats before arriving to give additional asdic cover; soon after their arrival *Petard* was ordered into Alexandria and passed the boomgate vessel at 0600 going straight to berth on the oiler to refuel. Two hours later her ship's company having breakfasted and cleaned into the rig of the day stood by and reberthed onto the detached mole and waited for the barges to reammunition the ship.

While the weary crew embarked ammunition from the two barges, the crippled *Arethusa* with additional tugs secured longside still moving stern first, entered Alexandria, her ship's company manning the side to cheer the *Petard* as she prepared herself again for sea. The men in the *Petard* paused in their tasks and in their turn cheered the battered cruiser and her survivors. The successful rescue operation and Mark Thornton's feat of seamanship shared by the ship and crew, was recognised in the signal of congratulations received from the Commander-in-Chief Mediterranean fleet. The ship was profiting from the skills acquired in the working up period in distant Scapa Flow.

Next day the 22nd, the ship enjoyed a day in harbour; the first part spent on cleaning ship and essential maintenance, but after the pipes 'up spirits' and 'hands to dinner', David to the intense relief of the ship's company sent the quartermaster and bosun's mate round the ship again to pipe 'hands to make and mend'. Only a handful of the non-duty watch found the energy to clean into No 1 uniform and catch the first liberty-boat for No 50 gate landing in the dockyard; almost the entire ship's company excepting the watchkeepers turned in to recover a little of their lost sleep, before slipping ashore in one of the evening liberty boats to enjoy some of Alexandria's' many attractions, none more welcome than the opportunity to sleep ashore, in a bed, at one of the several hostels where servicemen could get a brief spell of quiet rest.

The following mid-morning, *Petard* led *Paladin* out of harbour to escort the armed merchant cruiser *Antwerp*, with troop reinforcements embarked, the familiar store ship with her companion petrol carrier still loaded with stores originally destined for Mersa Matruh, now bound for Tobruk.

As *Petard* cleared the boom-gate the fo'c'sle party raced with feverish anxious haste to secure anchors and cables for sea before the Captain increased speed and turned his ship up the Great Pass into the swell that moved perpetually down the approach to the Egyptian port. For some inexplicable reason Mark Thornton who was otherwise an exemplary and skilled seaman, found it difficult

THE EASTERN MEDITERRANEAN

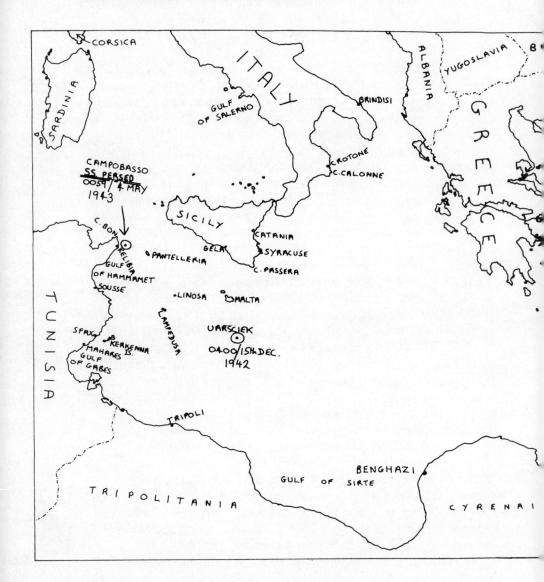

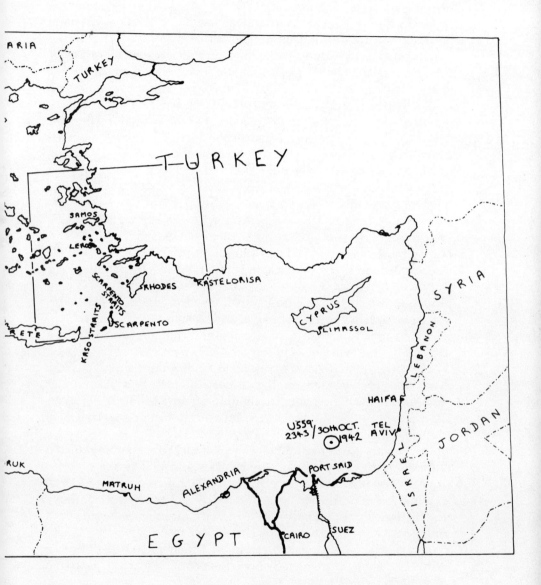

A larger scale map of the area indicated by the inset square appears on page 195.

to wait for the party on the fo'c'sle to complete their essential task, before driving the slim bow of the destroyer into the oncoming sea. If the cable party still struggled on the fo'c'sle tightening bottlescrew slips to bind home the self stowing anchors into the hawse pipes and lashing cables together to prevent vibration or movement of the anchor gear, which unless properly secured could lead to damage or at least noisy disturbance inside the ship, seas would roar in twin cascades up through the hawse pipes and bury the cable party under a foaming torrent. On the occasions when this happened, the sea retreated as the bow lifted, leaving the men sprawled and clinging desperately to cables and guardrails to stop themselves being drawn over the side.

This only happened once while Tony Fasson still lived, he very quickly made his views known to the Captain, he would not support this kind of stimulant to improve efficiency and let it be known that the evolution was not to be repeated. But the facts were, every time *Petard* left Alexandria despite protests from the fo'c'sle officer, the mad race by the cable party to avoid a heavy drenching was now often a grim evolution of speed against a real risk of being buried under a sea sweeping down the fo'c'sle. The Captain's impatient urgency to get out to sea, and his habit of driving the ship hard and over into tight turns earned him the nickname of 'Hard over Mark', but without animosity from his men.

The convoy under *Petard*'s command made an uneventful passage along the coastline using the swept channel that was under continuous check sweeping by the minesweeping flotilla; with the exception of the distant reconnaissance aircraft there was no sign of enemy activity.

The entrance and harbour of Tobruk, blocked with many sunken craft made the entry difficult to negotiate, but all five ships passed in safely, leaving many wondering how the ships would get away in a hurry should an air attack develop. There were so many obstructions in the anchorage, little room was available for .a destroyer to swing to her anchor, this caused both *Petard* and *Paladin* problems, but they were finally anchored at 1210 on the 24th. The *Antwerp* managed to berth on the shattered jetty and disembarked the troops.

The small town was a shambles, after changing hands five times since the start of the desert war two years before; the long siege of the isolated Australian garrison had ended only five months ago, in June, after the capture by Rommel's Afrika Korps. The last and latest change of ownership had taken place only a few days before *Petard* led in the sea-borne supplies. There were no civilians in the area, they had long since gone and before the town had been placed under siege; it was a scene of total destruction – no building remained intact, the waters of the harbour, town and surrounding desert contained little else other than old rusted hulks and the more recent debris of war. Over all hung the stink of death; there were still small groups and the single grotesque blackened decomposing corpses waiting for disposal by the clearing up parties.

Here was a place that the Captain could not resist visiting, leave was piped for the ship's company to go ashore in small parties for a brief two hours, and Mark Thornton accompanied by Robert de Pass at his side, stepped ashore for a conducted tour by the garrison commander.

In the late afternoon and before dark, the two destroyers slipped out past the sunken ships and underwater obstructions to sail direct to Port Said at 27 knots. Outside Port Said the following morning while *Paladin* carried on in, *Petard* collected a number of miscellaneous craft that were waiting for an escort to Alexandria, part of the return of the fleet base to the major Egyptian port. Sailing through the night of the 25th, the untidy group of ships and harbour craft neared the approach channel to Alexandria in the dawn of the 26th, to find that the channel was closed by mines, and sweepers were on the move up the Great Pass trying to clear the aircraft laid ground mines. *Petard* was ordered to turn her charges back to Port Said; while she was in the process of doing this, rather like a sheep dog racing round the bunch of shipping of all nationalities, the low profile of Alexandria and the desert mainland was beginning to show in the morning light, a group of Ju 88s fell upon the minesweepers and *Petard*'s convoy. The destroyer steamed through the centre of her alarmed and disorganised flock, firing everything she had at the rampaging German aircraft; with a tremendous explosion and sheet of flame one of the minesweepers blew up and disintegrated. The unfortunate overworked sweeper and her crew had disappeared when the flame, smoke and sea had subsided, only a handful of the men who had manned her were picked up by her flotilla companions; over three quarters of her ship's company had perished on the mine that she had activated. Whether it was because the Ju 88 squadron claimed the sinking of the minesweeper to their bombing, or wanted to get away before the fighters that would be inevitably scrambled, arrived on the scene, the bombers left suddenly, having only released a few bombs.

Taking advantage of the unexpected lull in the enemy air harassments and under the Allied fighter umbrella that had arrived, *Petard* shepherded the motley collection of craft eastwards and back to Port Said; this was completed without further alarms by the afternoon, and the ship found itself with an unscheduled two nights and a day in Port Said, able to give leave to both watches and to those who wished to renew acquaintance with the seedy entertainment on offer at the canal port.

Refreshed after two uninterrupted nights in, the ship was again at sea on the 28th, this time escorting the destroyer workshop depot ship, HMS *Woolwich* wearing the broad pennant of the Commodore Destroyers *Levant* on a short unmolested trip to Alexandria. The *Woolwich* was ushered up the now swept Great Pass with the destroyer carrying out an asdic sweep astern to discourage any submarine with ideas of achieving glory by sinking the rich prize. Luck that had for a long time been missing from the operations of the Mediterranean fleet, had over the last few weeks seemed to be returning to help the operational planners. The day after *Woolwich*'s safe arrival, the approaches to Alexandria were closed again; this time by several two man submarines that had obviously been deployed to catch the movement of the valuable fleet train ships, and were hopeful of repeating the successes achieved in 1941 when the battleships *Warspite* and *Queen Elizabeth* were put out of action for many long months by a brilliant feat of arms by the Italian manned underwater craft. The 2-man submarines were not able to repeat their performance, all their targets were safely in harbour protected by improved defences; Captain D12 in *Pakenham*. *Queen Olga* and four other fleets were outside the port waiting to deal with the threat. While *Petard* enjoyed yet another bonus day in, the 12th flotilla hunted the invaders throughout the 29th; although there were no sightings or conclusive evidence of submarines being destroyed, the enemy operation had been clearly dispersed.

On the last day of November 1942, *Pakenham* (D12), *Petard*, *Queen Olga* and four other fleets were outside the port waiting to rendezvous with the remainder of the flotilla, CS15 and the 14th DF from Port Said on the morning of 1st December at the start of Operation Portcullis committed to escorting Convoy MW 14 to Malta. The convoy was again to comprise of four merchant ships, general cargo carriers, and a tanker. The escort would be almost the same as the one that had fought convoy MW 13 into Malta, the 15th cruiser squadron, with the *Dido* replacing the damaged *Arethusa*, and the 12th and 14th destroyer flotillas with *Pakenham* and the *Jervis* leading their respective flotillas of fleet destroyers. Four Hunts would as for MW 13 form the convoy's close AA and anti-submarine cover.

The force set out to the west in high spirits, encouraged by their success in the almost identical operation that had started out from the same spot, a short fifteen days earlier. The prospects of heavy enemy air opposition were the same, but because of the advance of the Eighth Army, more and sustained fighter cover would be present. Force K of cruisers was now based on Malta and scheduled to reinforce the approaching convoy and its escorts two days out from the island. The familiar pattern of enemy reconnaisance aircraft constantly shadowing the force resumed, and on the first evening at dusk Ju 88 torpedo bombers delivered the first of many attacks. The combination of the escort's fire power and the harassing Beaufighters prevented the attack from being pressed home with determination, ships were able to comb the tracks of the approaching torpedo tracks without real difficulty so the force entered the first night of the operation intact, and had only a few scares during the dark hours, mainly from flares dropped by the prowling shadowers. The convoy proceeded west on a new course that brought the force close to the Cyrenaica bulge where the fighter cover from the freshly recaptured advance desert airfields reduced the time to reach convoy and prolonged the time they could remain over the fleet of escorts, and forced the enemy raiders to fly further to reach their targets.

On the second day out, there occurred a remarkable and fortunate coincidence at very nearly the same position as in Stoneage and on day two of that operation: the lookouts from *Petard*'s bridge sighted a raft to the north of the convoy course, when the ship closed the rubber raft, they again found RAF survivors, this time the crew of a Wellington bomber, shot down on the previous day. The airmen were rescued like their service colleagues in the earlier operation, because of the exceptional visual lookout standards maintained in the ship – something that had been drilled into the bridge watchkeeping staff, officers and ratings, ceaselessly by the Captain since his ship commissioned. The entire line of the starboard wing of the outer destroyer screen had passed the raft without it being seen, until, as in Stoneage, sighted by the *Petard*'s lookouts.

The cruisers and destroyers of Force K joined on the third day out, and although bombing and torpedo attacks continued intermittently by day and night, the convoy entered the Grand Harbour, Malta undamaged and with an additional ship, the fast minelayer *Welshman* full of stores. She had left Alexandria on the afternoon of the second day out, the 2nd, at thirty knots had overtaken and joined the convoy before dawn of the third day.

The battlements of the Grand Harbour were black with the population shouting and cheering in the second convoy to arrive intact; the ships of MW 13 were now unloaded and ready to return with the ships of MW 14 when their cargoes were discharged. The safe arrival of these two convoys and the discharge of their cargoes marked the turning point of the siege of Malta. The Maltese were sensing a victory that until recent events had seemed impossible, and they turned out in massive numbers to greet the ships without apparently fearing the repetition of the massive air bombardment of the island and harbour from the Regia Aeronautica which previously had overwhelmed the remnants of all convoys up to MW 13.

The protection from the reinforced and replenished Malta based fighter squadrons, enabled *Petard* with the other destroyers to berth in Sliema Creek, under the unbelieving eyes of the population who had given up hopes of seeing British destroyers in force again at the traditional fleet berths. There they remained for 36 hours only disturbed by several air raid warning Reds, but no bombers broke through the fighter cover, to exercise the waiting gun crews.

Leave was given on the two evenings that the destroyers were in Sliema, and men returned to the ships subdued by what they had seen. The islanders were in a bad way through the lack of food, many of the girls and children had ugly suppurating sores on their legs and arms due to diet deficiences; there was a bad and blatant black market, the town of Valletta including the narrow street 'the GUT' filled with bars and dives dedicated to the entertainment of the men who manned the ships of the fleet, was badly damaged; beer was rationed and food for the foraging libertymen unobtainable. The officers did find that the small club with its Edwardian furnishings, 'Aunties', had survived, the two elderly proprietresses were still there to welcome the officers who found their way ashore. To help ease the chronic civilian ration shortage, warships were ordered to discharge their entire stocks of frozen meat, this was done willingly by the men who had to fight their ships back eastward on short and very hard tack.

Convoy ME 11, as the final objective of Operation Portcullis, bound for Port Said, sailed at 0700 on the 7th, consisted of 9 merchant ships who had discharged their cargoes after surviving runs through the eastern and western Mediterranean seas. The ships had made their way to Malta either singly or in Convoy MW 13 and now empty they were to be taken eastward to the canal for redeployment, their names, well known to the men of the fleet; SS *Melbourne Star*, SS *Rochester Castle*, SS *Brisbane Star*, SS *Port Chalmers*, SS *Denbighshire*, SS *Robin Locksly* (USA), SS *Bantam* (Dutch), SS *Mormacmoon* (USA), SS *Yorbalinda* (Panama) Tanker.

As the island disappeared astern, the first of many air attacks commenced mainly from high level formations, bombing ineffectively as far as damage to ships was concerned. One merchant ship caught fire, but this was a self-inflicted wound, deck cargo ignited by a careless close range weapon gunner; the fire was put out without great difficulty and before the air attack terminated.

Between 1755 and 1855 a torpedo bomber attack developed, and *Petard* shot down her first aircraft seen to fall to the guns of the ship. A Ju 88 had released its torpedo towards the convoy ships, turned back to recross the outer destroyer screen, banked on its turn at about 400 feet above the ship; the pom-pom and oerlikons poured fire into the underbelly of the sitting duck, finishing off the aircraft already damaged by the ships own 4 inch barrage. The Ju 88 fell into the sea about a quarter of a mile off the port bow, cartwheeled twice and disappeared in a cloud of spray.

After a night of constant probing by flare dropping aircraft, attacks resumed in the morning, and for the *Petard* it seemed that she had been singled out for special attention, the ship was straddled twice during the morning by sticks of bombs, the nearest entering the water so close to the frantically speeding destroyer taking avoiding action, that water fell in solid weight over the midship action stations, and the ship leapt and plunged under the impact of the underwater explosions. A third near miss straddled the ship at 1220, when a stick of six crossed diagonally from the port bow to the starboard quarter, the ship passing between the third and fourth bomb.

The men below in the boiler-rooms, engine spaces, magazines with the ammunition supply parties could have only thought that the ship had met her end as the crashes immediately longside, knocked out lighting circuits, loosened deckhead and bulkhead fittings, leaving many of them in total darkness with damaged equipment running amuck in the confined spaces. The Yeoman-of-Signals, Petty Officer R. Chapman, later wrote in his diary, with simple understatement, that although 'he felt queer watching the bombs leaving the planes and falling towards the ship, he felt no real fear but only a desperate need to do something in retaliation', something more than having to keep a continuous watch on the flagship for light and flag signals.

In this attack the fighters downed two more of the enemy planes, both falling into the sea within sight of the convoy; *Petard*'s guns clearly damaged another that disappeared to the north emitting smoke, probably crashing before regaining its base.

During the whole of the 8th, 9th and 10th, Convoy ME 11 sailed within sight of the now recaptured north coast of Cyrenaica, receiving continuous fighter cover against the frequent day and night attacks; it was clear that the presence and threat of the fighters reduced the effectiveness and concentration of the German and Italian airmen. Finally at 1000 on the 11th, the crews of the escorting warships watched with some pride and satisfaction the last of the convoy ships pass the boom-gate and enter the canal at Port Said. Inside one month, two supply convoys to Malta and a return convoy of empty ships had been fought through the Eastern Mediterranean without loss, it seemed that the cruisers and destroyers with growing air support from the desert air command had the measure of the Axis air armadas; at the same time the cruiser squadron and two flotillas of fleet destroyers kept the Italian battle fleet cowering in its bases. — very short of fuel!

CHAPTER 5

The Italian Submarine
A Captain Departs

There was to be no break or rest for the *Petard* or her half section the *Queen Olga*; after the completion of routine refuelling and topping up depleted magazines, a barge moved longside the ships to embark urgent and vital stores required by the cruisers and destroyers that now remained based on Malta. Large quantities of small armament and engine room parts were stowed in all available spaces below and on the upper deck. The work went on for the entire afternoon and evening, making the granting of leave an impossibility, with the ship's company muttering that the Captain had volunteered for the immediate return run to Malta. Because Mark Thornton always showed his impatience to return to sea, he was suspected; the more probable truth was that the two ships were the juniors of the 12th Flotilla, and *Petard* was not yet very popular with the flotilla staff. The ships had to be content with a night in harbour at immediate notice for steam; they sailed next morning at 0700 on a special operation, Piker.

Proceeding at twenty knots for Benghazi where some mysterious packing cases had to be disembarked by *Petard*; the two ships were not long at sea before receiving a signal to close Tobruk at full speed to give support to a small convoy of two supply ships that had been under continuous air attack since leaving Alexandria. At thirty knots the destroyers overtook the merchantmen and their solitary escort the Hunt class destroyer *Dulverton*, as another torpedo attack developed from four Ju 88s. In the melée that followed, *Petard* shot down one of the aircraft as it closed to release its torpedo at the merchantmen. The plane received a broadside from the four 4″ gun battery under director control; raked also by the pom-pom and starboard oerlikons the aircraft disintegrated, debris churning the sea over a wide area. In the action, the unfortunate *Dulverton* which had been in almost continuous action since dawn, was smothered by the close range fire from one of the ships she was protecting. The merchantman engaged one of the low flying aircraft, but without the fire control and safety arcs drill that existed in the warships, her hard pressed gunners failed to see the *Dulverton* move into the line of fire.

Convoy ships desperately fighting off air attacks were liable to overlook the safety of the defending escorts. One officer and four ratings were killed in the gunfire that drenched the destroyer, tragic self inflicted casualties that only few escort ships escaped suffering in fleet and convoy actions.

The small convoy was eventually ushered into Tobruk, led by the *Dulverton*; *Queen Olga* and *Petard* bringing up the rear. A peaceful night followed, spent in the wreck crowded anchorage, without the customary flare dropping reconnaissance intruder to disturb the shipping. At 0643 next morning the 13th, the two fleet destroyers slipped out of Tobruk and set off at speed for Benghazi which they approached as dark began to fall over the tawny coloured desert coast and the low line of buildings of the recently captured port. The two ships picked their way with care up the roughly swept wreck strewn channel, unmarked by light buoys or shore navigation marks, as a heavy air attack started on the town and harbour installations. A tanker was hit and set on fire by the first flight of bombs; fire spread to other smaller craft while *Petard* nosed her way into the port and tried to place herself longside the harbour breakwater, every gun in the ship firing a blind barrage at the unseen planes that were bombing and firing cannon from above the forest of blinding flares falling onto the town, harbour and the two destroyers. The whole harbour became an inferno into which, from the night sky above the flares, there rained bombs; the two commanding officers somehow conned their ships into the breakwater berths, scrapping along the walls, despite the distractions of fire, blinding flares, gun and bomb blasts, berthed their ships.

A party of heroic Royal Army Service Corps soldiers took the destroyer's berthing wires and started at top speed to disembark the vital packing cases onto the stone jetty, ignoring the huge lumps of masonry that flew everywhere in a lethal shower as bombs hit the mole. Without waiting for the attack to ease off, another suicidal act was performed by transport drivers who backed two 3 ton lorries at speed the length of the stone jetty as far as the destroyers, still in action against the air marauders. The cases were quickly loaded and the whole party of phlegmatic soldiery drove into the town.

Nobody really knew what the packing cases contained that had been transported with so much urgency and for which so many risks had been taken; there was no time to indulge in speculation while the bombs continued to rain down.

Quite suddenly the roar of swooping diving aircraft coming at the ships out of the darkness stopped; surprisingly the ships were intact and free of serious damage or casualties. The fires in the town continued to burn fiercely, and for the destroyers the burning tanker and oil on the water remained to menace, until the shore based naval parties began to get the upper hand of the conflagration, with foam and water sprays. It was now approaching midnight, the searchlights and AA fire under army control in and around the town gradually died down and an uneasy peace settled over the battered Cyrenaican port; by 0200/14th, even the fire in the tanker was under control, flames only whimpered into flare-ups momentarily to light up the shattered harbour installations and shipping.

The destroyers relaxed and reverted to two watch defence stations, relying upon the army operated air raid warning system to bring them back to full action stations. As the night gave way to morning light everyone in the two ships was impatient and restless to leave, to get out into the open sea and room to take avoiding action should the enemy aircraft return; there seemed no reason to remain, now that the urgent stores had been landed. Late into the morning Mark Thornton eventually received his orders and permission to sail for Malta; preceded by *Queen Olga*, the destroyers slipped from their uncomfortable berths, stern first moving swiftly through the narrow gap in the partially blocked entrance, both ships clearing the harbour by 1400, turning into quarter-line formation, *Petard* leading with *Queen Olga* 45 degrees on her starboard quarter, distance 2 cables. The unit worked up to 25 knots, steering 300 degrees for Malta.

The job of the ship's cypher officer and mail censor was usually part of the doctor's duty in destroyers who carried one as part of the war complement. These particularly onerous duties were not considered to conflict with the doctors non-combatant status or the rules of the Geneva Convention, and so in *Petard* the doctor, sur-geon-Lieutenant William Finbar Prendergast RNVR from County Kerry, added these chores to his medical duties plus one or two oth-ers more to his liking, wardroom wine caterer for example.

This Irishman like so many of his countrymen was a paradox, a fierce patriot from the Republic, but at home and content in his role as a doctor in one of His Britannic Majesty's ships of war. Since joining the ship at Newcastle it was clear that he was a character and a personality that would be a match and foil to the Captain's tough and very physical approach to situations and problems.

Doc was a very unmilitary figure, his uniform on his short slight angular figure did little to disguise the fact that he was the most fiercely independent of non-combatants. His uniform cap sat always at a wild and uneasy angle on his mop of wiry copper coloured hair. Having a very pale complexion, the Mediterranean sun had a savage effect on his skin, like so many others of similar pigmentation, his white skin if it escaped being badly sunburnt, which was frequently his misfortune, was a mass of freckles. He cut a strange untidy, slightly grubby figure in white tropical shirts and too large shorts; white stockings clung desperately to his thin legs. Later when he grew a sparse ginger beard, it did nothing to improve the Irishman's appearance, the sun seaspray and often the lack of washing meant that the demon doctor looked out through a rather mangy, scruffy ginger fringe. Prendergast was a very good gynaecologist, a 'maternity doctor' the incredulous sailors called him, and it was some time before they trusted him with their ailments; his unsteady gait was attributed to drink instead of the fact that he never really acquired good sea legs, but in line with the other contradictions of his Irishness he was never sea-sick. Doctor proved very soon what a skilled and compassionate surgeon and humane individual he was, by the care he was able to give to grieviously wounded and dying enemy and ship's company alike.

A secret situation signal received earlier in the ship and decyphered by the doctor, gave details of allied ships and submarines in the area, including the estimated position of a British submarine *P-35* in the path of the speeding destroyers, so there was no immediate surprise when at the start of the first watch, 0405/15th in position 35 degrees 08 minutes north, 14 degrees 22 minutes east, *Petard*'s lookouts sighted in the dark moonless night, fine on the port bow, what at first appeared to be a surface vessel steering the same course as the destroyers.

The moving object, indistinct at first through powerful night binoculars, turned out to be a submarine on the surface; as the destroyers rapidly overhauled the unsuspecting underwater raider charging its batteries; the question to be answered, was it the *P-35*?

Mark Thornton ordered the challenge to be made; the reaction to the winking blue light from *Petard*'s signalman's heather lantern, suddenly spotted by the submariners coming from astern making an obvious code challenge signal, was immediate.

Both *Petard*'s asdic crew and the lookouts reported sound and sight indications of a crash dive, followed moments later by a shouted report from the bridge asdic hut that torpedoes could be heard approaching from a port bearing. Under heavy emergency helm, Mark turned his ship to port to comb the tracks of the advancing torpedoes, reacting also instantly to warn his Greek half section who was in real danger if the missiles missed *Petard*, by giving two prolonged whooping blasts on the ship's steam siren, simultaneously flashing on an unmasked aldis light, repeating by light the sound signal for an emergency turn to port, 10 degrees together. Both ships saw the phosphorescent tracks of the passing torpedoes; *Petard* reduced speed as the ship's company, the watch below shocked out of sleep by the alarm rattlers, tumbled out of hammocks and mess table top sleeping billets in the dim blue lit messdecks. Men forced their way out of the blackout canvas screens that blocked the openings to the upper deck, others dashed along narrow between deck spaces, down ladders to control positions, into magazines and their action stations.

The asdic crew on watch were in firm contact, passing ranges and bearings of the submarines movements to the action plot and the Captain standing at his action station by the illuminated bowl of the bridge polaris. The ship was now down to asdic attacking speed, moving in with a practised confidence; the water conditions were good and the sea calm and windless; without faltering a full pattern of depth charges was released as Brooksbank passed the firing position information to the Captain standing above him on the open bridge, his face just visible in the glow from the polaris bowl.

With the pattern released and fired from traps and throwers, the ship continued out of range of the depth charges, before turning slowly to starboard with everyone braced and tensed in the dark waiting for the underwater explosion, magnified many times by the darkness. *Queen Olga* had hauled out to port maintaining a back-up watch on the underwater target, ready to launch the next attack, but she lost contact at the vital moment; the water disturbance caused by the British ships exploding depth charges gave the Greeks problems. Brooksbank and his team regained contact quickly, with the depth charge crews aft on the quarter-deck working like maniacs to reload the throwers, Mark Thornton turned his ship on to another attack course. Ordering *Queen Olga* to keep clear, *Petard* delivered a second full depth charge pattern on the submarine frantically trying to escape from the avenging destroyer. *Queen Olga* was now in her turn in firm contact; a flickering barely discernible blue signal light told *Petard* that her Greek half section was going to attack. She could just be seen through night glasses crossing the senior ship's wake, and long seconds later the shock of her depth charges was felt.

A fourth pattern was not required, both ships reported to each other the unmistakeable sound of a submarine blowing its tanks; *Petard* spotted out on her starboard beam the water disturbance and phosphorescence that indicated the position of a large body breaking surface. Robert de Pass on the bridge control of the searchlight had the 36 inch beam ready for exposure; he switched on simultaneously with the Greek's searchlight; the two beams crossed on the conning tower of the Italian submarine *Uarsciek* riding high out of the sea. For a few moments the two destroyers, invisible behind the beams of their brilliant and blinding lights, watched the submarine for a move; the Italian was nearest to the *Petard*, about one cable distant. Suddenly a few figures were on the conning tower, then scurrying forward and aft along the casing, white toylike men, heads down and arms raised to shield eyes against the blinding glare. Those going forward may have been making a go at bringing their gun into action, not knowing the number and proximity of their adversaries.

As they ran, lurched and slithered, several quite naked, on the wet and slippery casing, a deluge of pom-pom and oerlikon fire poured out of the darkness down the two main searchlight beams, obliterating and tearing apart the small white exposed bodies, forms that had been living, breathing warm fellow men, were instantly smashed dead or dying into the sea or left as shapeless hunks of red torso and separated limbs on the casing under the unblinking merciless light.

In both ships, cease fire bells were ringing, stilling the murderous chatter of the close range weapons, and many stood in both destroyers appalled and numbed by what they had done, the results remaining in front of their shrinking eyes in the obscene searchlights. For a while there was a pause while nothing moved, then, more white figures, most naked, appeared out of the conning tower, cringed in the terrible blinding beams, stumbled through the awful bloody debris of their comrades. A few moved forward past the knocked out gun, others aft towards the dome of the hydrophone receiving equipment that stood out of the submarine casing.

By this time *Petard* had moved in closer to the *Uarsciek*, both vessels pointing the same way, *Petard* moving at slow speed; the voice of the Captain could be heard in the still air calling for fire to be reopened. The main armament and close range weapons remained silent, the guns could not be depressed sufficiently by the crews to hit the submarine, men also hesitated to obey, the director crew and everyone else overwhelmed by the slaughter. Seconds ticked away, more figures tumbled and fell from the conning tower onto the casing, as the Captain repeated his order. Then from the dark of the open bridge a strip lewis gun began its ghastly solo, directed on the men running aft. Bullets tore into the unprotected bodies below, three or four men fell before the firing stopped abruptly, the Captain found himself trying frantically to avoid a collision with the U-boat. He had failed to see that the submarine continued underway, with port helm, on a collision course.

The ship hit *Uarsciek*'s pressure hull with an unhealthy crunch, half riding over the submarine before sliding back clear under emergency full astern. It was not until the cries of Italian wounded and drowning men heard at the moment of impact confirmed the U-boat's nationality, that Mark Thornton's terrible doubt that it could have been the British *P-35*, was resolved.

Petard's second salvo of slaughter was probably justified, the men running aft towards the dome, may have set out on a suicide bid to activate an anti-capture or self destruction device, unlikely but possible; in war it was not possible to take chances, but the counter-action was still horrifying. The first round of gunfire had done what was intended, it put the submarine's gun out of action, and killed the Italian captain in the act of ditching his confidential books, they were later found by his body in a weighted sack.

The ship now lay close longside her helpless captive, the searchlights extinguished, while below Bertie Faunthorpe led the damage control party forward to investigate the damage caused by the collision. They found that the bow had been set back, flooding the chain locker but there seemed to be nothing that would prove immediately fatal to the ship; bulkheads had to be shored up and the work started right away. With the GCO, a number of the ship's company dropped down onto the casing to secure the submarine as a prize and to prepare for a tow into Malta. *Queen Olga* prowled round in the dark to fend off submarines and E-boats.

Immediate objectives were achieved by those led and ordered below by David Nasmith into the brightly lit interior of the submarine, all fearful with the recent memory of *U-559*'s sudden dive taking the entombed Tony Fasson and Colin Grazier to their deaths. The control room and adjacent compartments were rapidly searched, confidential books and charts passed up and out to be added to the blood soaked bag containing the secret books and operational orders found by the dead Italian Captain's body in the upper conning tower. As this was going on, 32 prisoners were being mustered on *Petard*'s iron deck, some wounded, two or three severely; these were taken to the enraged and disgusted Doctor in his sickbay for patching up, and a desperate fight to save the lives of the Italian seamen.

Doc Prendergast had witnessed the near massacre of the crew crowding out of the conning tower onto the casing, first to fight, then surrender their submarine; he was standing in his usual position at action stations, just outside the starboard entrance from the iron deck into the sickbay flat, in the dark he had been a noncombatant witness of the floodlit and surfaced submarine swept by gunfire at close range, and the butchering of half the crew. Prendergast's voice with its strong Irish accent could be heard condemning the bloodshed as he struggled to save the lives of the two men. His emotion was perhaps excusable and understandable, but he did not have the responsibility for fighting or the safety of the ship and her consort.

In the group of prisoners, were four officers including the engineer; no doubts about his actions diverted Mark Thornton from his efforts to secure the submarine as a prize, he ordered the Yeoman, Petty officer Chapman, the ship's only ex-submariner, to board the *Uarsieck*, taking the Italian engineer officer with him, to assist the securing of the vessel against premature sinking. The press-ganged engineer was able to stop the auxiliary machinery that continued running, confirm that no sea-cocks were open or that scuttling charges were armed, and he was to remain on board the vessel that he had so recently abandoned to guarantee the safety of the prize crew. All the water-tight doors were then closed.

David Dunbar Nasmith had by first light got a tow passed out to the men working on the forecasing, a prize crew detailed off and

The prize *Uarsciek* sinking on end of tow

Midshipman Goddard and some of his prize-crew return to the ship

Christmas 1942, the captain entertains his messdeck escort of disguised junior officers and ratings

Christmas at the bottom of Gabbari Dock, Alexandria. The miscellaneous mess

Penelope with *Petard* retire followed by Pantellaria's coastal batteries' 11 inch shells

Petard at speed

The Wardroom chef records his BBC message
to the family

Rupert Egan introduces the ship's company
BBC broadcast to families

(*Right*) Husky D+1, General Eisenhower **in**
Petard

(*Below*) Screening *Rodney* bombarding the
Italian mainland in the Straits of Messenia

embarked under the command of a midshipman, Peter Goddard, who had only very recently joined from the cruiser *Orion* for his destroyer training. His prize crew included Yeoman Chapman, Leading Telegraphist James Porteous, known as Rattler to his messmates, signalman Kenneth Hannay RNVR, four seamen, a stoker and the captive Italian engineer officer; they were transferred via the whaler that had been lowered into the flat glassy sea to help pass the tow across from *Petard*'s stern. The whaler brought back the GCO and the party who had secured the wire tow and cleared up the worst of the human remains in the conning tower and casing.

Quite suddenly, while the transfer was in progress, out of the low overcast sky dived two Regia Aeronautica Fiat fighters. The planes swept low over the two destroyers and the submarine without opening fire. In *Petard* the gun crews were caught flat footed, no gun engaged the fighters, from *Queen Olga* nothing stirred; the planes banked in tight formation and again for some inexplicable reason the ship's guns remained silent, they flew at almost zero height so that the people on the bridge could clearly see the pilots in the cockpits. The Fiats passed over the *Uarsieck* again, then up into the clouds and disappeared. It is possible that a rendezvous had been previously arranged with the submarine, and the Greek and British destroyers had been mistaken for friendly forces.

At 0630 with the whaler rehoisted, the ship moved slowly ahead to take the weight of the tow, but immediately the submarine sheered away to port under what was clearly 30 to 40 degrees of port helm. The ship struggled for a time to adjust speed and towing angle to accommodate the port helm left on the submarine when abandoned. There was nothing that the prize party could do to centre the rudder as all power had failed on the steering controls, except to open up the water-tight bulkheads, to get aft to the rudder head and by hand restore the helm to midships. While the risks entailed in the opening up of the water tight compartments were still being debated in the towing ship, the tow parted, deciding the issue for the Captain. The risk of heavy air attack was too great to await the arrival of tugs from Malta, so while the destroyer prepared to pass another tow, the prize crew were ordered to get the Italian engineer aft again to direct and assist in the manual operation of centring up the submarine's rudder.

The nervous prizemen opened up the bulkhead doors, releasing an outrush of air that indicated pressure had built up from sea entering the hull, confirming the fears that a loss of buoyancy would accompany the watertight zone being opened up aft. The adjustment of the steering gear gave very little trouble and was completed quickly and bulkhead doors closed again, but the flooding caused by the operation was to prove fatal to the submarine. Meanwhile *Petard* was having problems, the tow that terminated on a shackle of ships cable transferred aft, now hung down vertically from the towing slip, the dead weight of wire and cable proved to be beyond the capacity of the ship's company, cleared from lower-deck and action stations, to haul back inboard; it had to be slipped and abandoned after a long and fruitless struggle. After this delay a new tow was passed and the prize under way by 0800, now moving quietly and steadily in *Petard*'s wake with the white ensign flying from the periscope above the Italian flag. It seemed for a time that the tow would succeed, especially when recognition signals were exchanged with two destroyers appearing over the horizon from the direction of Malta at high speed, ordered by the Vice-Admiral Malta to reinforce the escort.

By 1000 the submarine could be seen to be settling down by her stern, making it necessary to order the prize crew out of the interior, closing down the conning tower hatches in a last effort to save the *Uarsciek*. Midshipman Goddard and his party had found a small plywood dinghy stowed in the conning tower structure; into this they were stowing items that seemed vital to salvage, plus some articles that could not be classified into this category; the ship's funds in many thousands of lire, that were exchanged at a later date for fresh provisions and wine in the newly captured towns of Italy's north African colonies.

The bow continued to lift while the stern and after casing sank lower in the sea; at 1100 the tow had to slow to a stop, Peter Goddard and his men were forced to evacuate the conning tower, and launch the dinghy. Only four could join the loot piled in the small boat, the remainder having to swim in the mirror like sea. At 1133 the *Uarsciek*'s bow reared up vertical and with both ensigns still flying, she slid stern first with barely a ripple out of sight to the bottom of the Mediterranean, the tow parting as the sinking hull sank beyond the limits of the wire hawser.

The small dinghy moved alongside, followed by the swimmers including the enemy engineer, Peter sat in the bow, a seaman with Porteous at the oars and the Yeoman crouched in the stern hugging a large fretwork fronted radio receiving set that would have

appeared more at home in the parlour of a suburban house than in
the complicated machinery filled interior of a submarine. The prize
crew were quickly recovered; proceeding at 20 knots, *Petard*'s bows
standing up to the speed in the smooth sea, the unit of four
destroyers closed Malta during the afternoon, arriving off the
Grand Harbour at about 1700/15th.

News had spread through the island that two destroyers were
bringing in a captured submarine of the detested Italian Navy,
hundreds of Maltese were crowding the ramparts of the ancient
fortifications built by the Knights of St John, and other vantage
points. The fact that the *Uarsciek* had sunk, had not been made
known to the waiting crowds as the destroyers approached with
dusk and entered harbour. When the silent expectant watchers
realised that the submarine was not with them, the disappointment
of the waiting dark clad throng could be felt in the ships passing
below. Suddenly Mark Thornton reacted, displaying his flare for
showmanship, he ordered Signalman Hannay to stand up on the
bridge windbreaker, to wave over his head the ornate gold fringed
ceremonial Italian colours that had been removed from the
submarine. As Hannay waved the colours on the gilt stave carrying
long gold tassels, the assembled population spotted it, and
recognising what it was, erupted into a frenzy of cheering and
waving. The two destroyers reacted to the emotion of the crowds by
waving back from the ranks lining the ship's rails and stations for
entering harbour. For a brief interlude the scene resembled a regatta
instead of the end of an action with a submarine that resulted in the
loss of half her crew.

The watching Flag Officer Malta was reported later to have not
been impressed by the break from the formal routine and ceremony
of one of His Majesty's ships returning to harbour. *Petard* was
ordered into a quiet secluded corner of the dockyard, away from the
emotional crowds, to disembark her prisoners and then to dock for
a quick examination and first aid treatment to the bow.

Later when making his personal report to the Vice-Admiral
Malta, Mark Thornton received a mild rebuke for his flamboyant
gesture, but this did not depress *Petard*'s commanding officer
unduly or for very long, when he became aware of the signal that
was actually in transit while the interview was underway:

From the Commander in Chief Mediterranean, my 1358/16th.
1. If   Vice-Admiral   Malta   considers   circumstances   justify

recommendation for immediate award of decorations to the Commanding Officers of both *Petard* (senior officer) and *Queen Olga*, request he will signal views to Admiralty and C-in-C Med.

2. An early award to the Captain of one of His Hellenic Majesty's ships for the destruction of an enemy submarine in the Eastern Mediterranean would have a very good effect on the Greek Navy here.

3. Recommendation for awarding a decoration to the Commanding Officer – *Petard* for his prominent part in the destruction of German U-boat on the 30th October, in transit to Admiralty under cover Med 4525/0171 dated 9th December 1942. (C-in-C Med's 2120B/16 to Admty, VA Malta (R), FO (D) Med.)

The awards were published in the *London Gazette* a few months later, DSOs for Lieutenant Commander Mark Thornton RN and Lieutenant Commander George Blessas of the Royal Hellenic Navy. DSC to Lieutenant David Dunbar Nasmith RN. There were DSMs for Petty Officer Yeoman of Signals R. Chapman and Leading Seaman Trevor Tipping Captain of the pom-pom; other officers and ratings were mentioned in despatches, and the Greek King made his own awards to his subjects, and to Mark Thornton, the Greek Military Cross Third Class.

Petard undocked next morning, the 17th, after Bertie and his team with the dockyard shipwrights had confirmed that the hull would stand up to the return to Alexandria. Later in the afternoon the cruiser *Orion*, followed six 'Hunts', *Exmoor, Croome, Belvoir, Hursley, Hurworth* and *Aldenham*, the two Fleets *Queen Olga* and *Petard*, to deploy outside the Grand Harbour entrance for the start of Operation Quadrangle 'C', to escort a convoy of empty supply ships for Port Said, Convoy ME 12. At 1930 the convoy emerged, there were ships from Convoy MW 14 and others that individually or in pairs had found their separate ways to Malta hugging the Cyrenican coast, following the current C-in-C Med's policy to route ships in small groups under the air cover now available from the desert air fields, groups that would be too small to attract the attention of the major Italian Fleet units.

After a day of prolonged and vicious air attacks, mainly at high level from German Ju 88s and Heinkel 111s, the 18th terminated without damage to any ship, and warships' companies reverted to defence watches as the night closed in, confident that the concentrated gunfire from the escorts backed up by the steadily increasing number of Beaufighters, now had the upperhand. The remainder of the operation was relatively uneventful with only a few minor ineffectual air assaults and no submarine attacks.

On the 20th, *Petard* was detached at 1930 to proceed alone into Alexandria, arriving there soon after dawn on the 21st. For the next two days she disembarked ammunition and oil fuel, moved longside the *Woolwich* for some armament repairs and maintenance, then on Christmas Eve, tugs moved her into Gabbari dock. On Christmas Day the ship reverted into the traditional naval Christmas routine of units on active service; overnight almost magically under the direction of the veterans, the messdecks were transformed into decorated grottos, the yeoman's flag lockers had been raided to provide colour and flags to disguise deckhead ventilation trunking, cable channeling, steam, water and fuel pipes; with materials to hand mess caterers and cooks laboured to produce instant and 'near' Christmas puddings, and stuffing for the pork that the supply petty officer and Jack Dusty had scrounged out of the depot ship for issue to the mess caterers.

David Dunbar Nasmith after seeing that the minimum of essential shipboard chores had been done, dismissed the ship's company for a normal harbour Sunday routine. At 1130 after the rum issue, a strange party of junior members of the ship's company, officers and ratings, the ratings dressed in borrowed officer's uniforms, and the officers as clowns or in captured Italian ratings gear, waited on the Captain for Christmas messdeck rounds. Mark Thornton entered into the spirit of the occasion, accepting endless offers of sippers and gulpers from messes, drinking to the good health and fortune of the occupants, drinking also proffered glasses of beer, closing his eyes to the fact that it had been smuggled aboard illicitly from the Arabs trading under cover and out of sight in the ship's company heads ashore on the dockside.

Mark's massive constitution coped with the variety and quantities of food and drink pressed on him and his motley entourage. After his ordeal he was able to invite his escort down to the wardroom to partake of the Captain's hospitality. He was by nature an abstemious man, but on this day he demonstrated that he could survive the dangers of having to accept, to avoid giving offence, the hospitality of the many messes of his ship's company.

Doctor, Bertie and some of the junior members of the wardroom found that the day only bearable with the numbing of the senses that came from the plentiful flow of drink, Christmas Day at the bottom of the stinking dock at Gabbari after the events of the last few weeks, terminating in the slaughter of the *Uarsciek*'s crew, was approaching the limit of endurance for more than one in the group that tried to celebrate the greatest event in Christendom. For some it was the fourth on active service away from family and friends, and for one it was the second to be spent in this dock. The GCO had been a member of the *Coventry* when she docked in 1940 to have her torpedoed bow repaired.

The ship's repaint routine was repeated during the three days 28th, 29th, 30th, and this time a new and lighter grey colour adopted by the Mediterranean fleet gave the ship a fresh and handsome appearance. The undocking took place on the 29th, and the next day as the finishing touches were being made to the repaint the ship was placed under three hours' notice for steam, with orders to sail on the 31st for Haifa escorting a slow convoy. On New Year's Eve, Mark Thornton as senior officer of the escort, steamed *Petard* out of Alexandria harbour, through the boom, turned hard a starboard into the swell of the Grand Pass, cracked on speed and nearly swept his cable party off the fo'c'sle.

This time Doc Prendergast was on the bridge and witnessed the scene of an officer and eight ratings spreadeagled on the iron foredeck, buried deep under the sea that covered the cables and capstan, frantically wrapping arms and legs round cable and deck fittings to prevent being carried overboard on the receding tide as the ship lifted her bow clear of the swell. The Doctor with no inhibitions caused by fear of the Captain or personal career prospects in the service, troubled still by what he regarded as the unnecessary bloodshed in the recent submarine action, raised his voice in protest at the spectacle on the fo'c'sle. He swore that it would not happen again and declared that the Commanding Officer would have to have a medical check-up and a rest; this proved to be the last operation with Mark Thornton in command.

Setting out from Haifa on the return trip to Alexandria, escorting three merchantmen, the asdic crews confirmed that the repairs to the bow had not been a success, there was still so much distortion to the underwater flow past the bow that the asdic detection gear was useless; Mark Thornton had to signal a request for a return to dry dock and a further examination. At sea during the 3rd and 4th January the ships ploughed their way back to Alexandria through a dense sand storm, a storm that drove the Buffer frantic as the sea spray mixed with the flying sand, coated the newly painted superstructure, mast, funnel and gunshields.

On the 5th *Petard* entered the fleet floating dock, sharing it with the sloop *Flamingo* that had been hit by a bomb through the quarter deck, passing without exploding out by the keel. It was a strange experience to stand on the bottom of the dock, to look up through the hole and see the sky above.

The inspection in the floating dock confirmed that a more permanent repair was required to the destroyer's bow if her asdic effectiveness was to be restored, so a return to Gabbari dock had to be arranged. The ship re-entered the small graving dock at the remote and seediest end of Alexandria's dockyard on the 8th.

On the 9th, Mark Thornton departed from the ship, without ceremony or the usual courtesies that included the opportunity for the wardroom members to 'Dine Out' their Captain. Except for the First Lieutenant, David Dunbar Nasmith and Doc Prendergast, no one was forewarned of the departure; so, suddenly after a brief stilted pre-lunch session of drinks, followed by the meal, he was piped over the side for the last time. The officers were barely able to comprehend that the formidable, apparently indestructible commanding officer who had dominated their lives, had gone. Two days later the officers received 'flimsies' from Mark; practically all were surprised, some with a feeling of guilt for privately held opinions of the Captain's more controversial actions, at the generosity and quality of the written brief assessment of their ability and service in *Petard*.

The ship's company were equally surprised by the suddenness of the commanding officer's departure; although most had immense confidence in his seamanship and ability as a fighting captain, many felt that he volunteered for operations and viewed the future with considerable apprehension; there was a general feeling of relief when the news flashed round the lower deck that he had left and was no longer in command.

Before he left, Mark Thornton who had not forgotten his promise to Walkers' Navy Yard, arranged for the despatch of the ceremonial colours captured from the luckless *Uarsciek*; the same colours that he had ordered to be waved to the waiting crowds when the ship had entered Grand Harbour, Malta. This was to be the last trophy sent to the builders, the ship's future kills were to remain anonymous.

POSTSCRIPT
by
Rear Admiral G.C. Leslie, CB, OBE, MA

I have been asked to add a postscript to the first five chapters of this book to put certain incidents in perspective. My qualifications for so doing are that I served for a year with Mark Thornton in HMS *Harvester*, his previous command, first as navigator and then as First Lieutenant.

Mark was a very experienced destroyer officer who started and finished the war in command of destroyers. Fortunately for Britain he was one of a large number of destroyer commanders who had been very highly trained between the wars and whose courage and experience were instrumental in defeating the enemy at sea. It is important for the reader to realise the strain that these dedicated professionals were under during these five years of war at sea. Every moment waking or sleeping they had to be fully responsible and ready for instant action. They were cooped up in tiny sea cabins below exposed open bridges. They were lonely men, and there were few who went through the whole war without a breakdown. It is in this context that Mark Thornton requested to be relieved of his command when the strain became too great to bear. After a rest ashore, he went on to command a further fleet destroyer in his usual inimitable manner.

This book paints a very good portrait of him as seen from the point of view of an inexperienced junior officer who has been generous with both praise and implied criticism. There is no doubt that Mark was a very strong character who could at times be ruthless, but it was just these characteristics which enabled him to weld together a superb fighting machine.

Working up a destroyer to the pitch of efficiency achieved in *Petard* is always a traumatic experience and there are bound to be periods of tension, exhaustion, anger and elation. *Petard*'s work up was very similar to that carried out in innumerable other ships in the Allied fleets except that it was conducted by a master trainer and was therefore better than most. The incident of the exercise in the stokers' mess deck is a good example. Mark deliberately timed this for when his ship's company were near the end of their tether. The realism of the exercise was of vital importance. One of the main ingredients of battle training is to simulate the real thing as closely as possible so that men may discover that they can cope with situations beyond their imagination. Those readers who have been through battle training in the Army will understand what I mean.

Another of Mark's notable qualities as mentioned by the author was his ability to decentralise his responsibility and give complete trust to his officers. I know from my own experience how rewarding was this trust and how much it added to the efficiency of the ship.

The sinking of enemy submarines was one of the most important tasks of any fleet destroyer and in this *Petard* was conspicuously successful; but a far greater prize lay in the capture of a submarine intact. Not only could the capture of code books and charts lead on to further successes against other enemy submarines, but also might give the Admiralty decoding branch the chance to break secret enemy signals with the probability of saving countless lives.

Every destroyer Captain had his plans and orders ready for an operation to capture a submarine, and it was normally the First Lieutenant who was designated as the boarding officer. *Petard*'s Captain and First Lieutenant had discussed this plan before the ship commissioned in Newcastle, and decided that it was essential to try and prevent the submarine's crew scuttling her. This was to be done by keeping the crew in the submarine by small arms fire on the conning tower and casing until it was possible to board her. The narrative has described most vividly the two attempts to capture first a U-boat and then an Italian submarine. The first ended in tragedy when the First Lieutenant and Able Seaman Grazier were lost. The second was a success because the plan worked out long before was carried out to its conclusion. Ruthless it may have been but then war is ruthless. The reader may spare a thought for the courage shown by the First Lieutenant leading the party down into the Italian submarine with his predecessor's fate in identical circumstances fresh in his mind.

One of my abiding memories of Mark Thornton in HMS *Harvester* was his fanatical insistence on a proper lookout being kept at all times, and it is clear that he had again insisted on this in *Petard*. A number of men owe their lives to him in consequence.

In conclusion these first five chapters of the story of *Petard* leave

me with an enhanced respect for her Commanding Officer and a
great admiration for the ship's company that supported him
through such stirring times. It must have been a heartbreaking
decision for Mark Thornton when he felt it his duty to relinquish
his Command, but at least he could feel that his labours had been
crowned with outstanding success.

PART TWO

10th January 1943 – 16th August 1944

THE SECOND COMMANDING OFFICER

CHAPTER 6

Club runs out of Malta
The end of the 12th Destroyer Flotilla

Lieutenant Commander Rupert Egan RN joined *Petard* direct from his previous command, the *Croome*. He had been driving the 'Hunt' class destroyer for about one year, after a spell on the staff of Commander-in-Chief Mediterranean at Ras el Tin, Alexandria. Junior to Mark Thornton, he came from the same professional background, starting first at a nautical primary school, then as a cadet at the Royal Naval College, Dartmouth. He was an excellent seaman, less spectacular and physical than Mark Thornton, a sophisticated man, a *bon viveur*, and sought and enjoyed female company; he was unmarried. During his time on the C-in-C's staff he developed numerous social contacts among the Greek, Lebanese and French expatriate communities, many of these he had retained.

Rupert assumed his new command while the ship lay at the bottom of Gabbari dock where her temporary and unsuccessful bow had been removed prior to a permanent repair that would take about three weeks to complete. He rather characteristically did not find the living conditions to his taste, so after formally taking over his command responsibilities, decided to live ashore in accommodation that he had continued to lease after leaving the staff job at Ras el Tin, taking with him Mark Thornton's old servant, Able Seaman Lofthouse, a 'stripey' of fourteen years service. The new captain appeared on board daily to pressure the dockyard repair team and to arrange with the flotilla and base staff, refresher courses for the gun, torpedo and asdic crews. He made sure that all the ship's company not immediately employed on maintenance or repair work, were kept out of the ship and away from the depressing and demoralising berth at the bottom of the dry dock. The Port followed by the Starboard watch in succession were sent back to Cairo for seven days' leave.

By the 26th January all leave and training parties had returned to the ship, refreshed physically and mentally, but totally broke. None were anxious to return to sea, to the daily round of antisubmarine activity and the constant threat of bombardment from the air.

The weary process of re-ammunitioning, storing and refuelling went on through the 27th and 28th, followed by a day of successful sea trials to prove the asdic fitness of the ship. Unbelievably *Petard*'s run of luck continued to hold, causing the ship's circle of permanent pessimists, to predict a series of horrors that would catch up on the ship and her company; a just retribution for the soft numbers that continued to come *Petard*'s way since the sinking of the *Uarsciek*. Immediately after Rupert Egan had signalled to Captain D, 12th Flotilla, reporting successful asdic trials, D12 ordered *Petard* to join *Pakenham* with *Queen Olga* hurrying eastward to Port Said. The three destroyers entered the canal without pausing, sailing south to spend one night at Port Tewfick before moving on into the Red Sea.

The passage down the sea was one of searing heat; the lack of adequate washing facilities caused many to suffer torments of prickly heat, but no one seriously grumbled while the formation steamed at high speed for Aden with rumours of a possible release from the Mediterranean station begetting buzzes of an early return to the United Kingdom. On 4th February after a fast refuelling evolution at Aden that began to kill off the homeward bound rumour, the ships sailed immediately for a rendezvous off Perim. The destroyers raced in line abreast across a flat indigo blue sea; the ships that they had been ordered south to find, appeared like great grey steel islands moving as one through a shimmering heat haze; Convoy Pomphlett made up of the ocean giants, SS *Queen Mary*, SS *Aquitania*, SS *New Amsterdam*, SS *Queen of Bermuda* and the SS *Ile de France* bound empty for Colombo, Ceylon, after discharging thousands of troop reinforcements for the westward surging Eighth Army and the Middle East land forces.

The three destroyers joined others familiar in the Mediterranean, *Isis, Derwent* and *Hero*, to form an escort that for three days steamed at 20 knots with the convoy south and east until on the 8th new escorts from the Eastern fleet approached over the horizon ahead. Four immaculate 'Q' class destroyers from the 4th flotilla, lead by their leader *Quilliam*, looked sleek, elegant and free from stains acquired only by long days at sea and action against the enemy. In response to well drilled flag hoists, with spectacular peacetime precision they took over escort screening positions at high speed. After only a very brief delay while the two destroyer flotilla Captains exchanged courtesies, *Pakenham* led away a disconsolate shabby mixed bag of six ships, back on a reverse course to the Mediterranean war theatre. As the destroyers moved past the new Colombo bound escort and the great convoy ships, shouted obscenities from the departing ship companies could not be heard, but there were few doubts about the meaning of the gestures flung towards the fortunates of the 4th flotilla.

Following a refuel in the inferno that was Aden, the rapid return passage north up the Red Sea continued, with Captain D 12 exercising his sun blistered charges all the way. One day out from Port Tewfick the speeding destroyers passed the cruiser *Arethusa* limping her crippled way south at the start of a long journey to the USA for permanent repairs.

Following three days back in Alexandria, *Petard* sailed at 1730 on 17th February as part of an escort of a large 24 ship supply convoy bound for Tripoli; the port had just been entered by the Eighth Army continuing their pursuit westward after the retreating German and Italian desert forces. The convoy of stores and troop reinforcements arrived without incident on the 21st, to find the harbour mouth was still partially blocked by many wrecks and block ships, forcing the convoy to anchor in the roads outside, with the escorts prowling round the ships to ward off air and submarine attack. Troops offloaded into lighters and landing craft were ferried quickly ashore into both the harbour and beaches to the east of Tripoli, while the store ships waited to be called forward and piloted cautiously through a gap blown and being rapidly widened by explosives of the naval port clearance team, continuing in the intervals between ships squeezing into the port to offload and returning to the anchorage outside.

That same evening *Petard* and *Isis* sailed with the troop carrier *Princess Kathleen* for Tobruk, and for the next six days ran a shuttle service bringing troops forward to the new front, west of Tripoli. At Tobruk men from the escorts were able to stretch their legs for an hour or two between runs while *Princess Kathleen* embarked the troops who had been transported over the reopened desert road leading right back to the great base camps in the Nile Delta.

Petard's men added to their souvenir stocks, and Doc replenished his sick bay from captured German medical stores. A rumour that the eccentric doctor could not decipher the German drug descriptions, for a time reduced the numbers reporting to the sickbay for attention, fuelled also fears of being poisoned or rendered impotent at the hands of the doctor, especially after a lunchtime gin session had reduced his powers of observation.

Much captured Italian tinned food became available to the ships calling at Tobruk, but as most tins had lost their labels, the task of mess caterers and cooks became very much of a lottery. Tins of turnips or carrots could be opened in endless succession when looking for meats or fruit; however the *Petard*'s luck still stayed with her for a while. Jack Dusty and some of the seamen ran across a group of soldiers sitting on a great cache of tinned peaches, they were completely out of cigarettes and the *Petard*'s men had a huge stock of Victory V cigarettes that none but the hardiest and most desperate seaman smoker could stomach, but were keeping by for an opportunity to trade. A deal was quickly settled, and before *Princess Kathleen* had finished embarking the battalion that was to make the latest run back to Tripoli, the cases of peaches were inboard the destroyer and stowed, leaving the late owners to cough their way through a dreadful brand of smokes.

On 2nd March, *Orion*, *Isis* and *Princess Kathleen*, with *Petard* arrived back at Alexandria, the last visit for six months; three days of enjoying the familiar relaxations, the most popular as usual being the chance taken by the lower deck to sleep ashore for one night away from the crowded hammock congested messdecks and machinery noises. On the 6th, *Pakenham*, *Queen Olga*, *Isis*, *Paladin* and *Petard* waited outside the harbour in the Great Pass for three merchantmen loaded with war stores and the *Princess Kathleen* with more reinforcements embarked; the convoy bound as usual for Tripoli. From now on, all the destroyers of the 12th Flotilla were to be based on Malta, joining the 14th Flotilla, 15th Cruiser Squadron and Force K that collectively would spearhead Operation Retribution; the operation designed to cut off reinforcements to the German and Italian armies retreating into Tunisia and being compressed by the 1st Army Corps and the Eighth Army towards the Keliba peninsular and destruction.

The sea forces at the same time would deny the defeated armies any chance of evacuation and escape into Sicily or into the mainland of Italy.

Princess Kathleen and the accompanying merchantmen arrived unopposed off Tripoli at 1200 on the 9th, the destroyer escort departing after a short pause in the anchorage for Malta, arriving there next day at 0700. For the following four days *Queen Olga* and *Petard* worked out of Malta escorting tankers to and from Tripoli. The lack of enemy air interference made life deceptively peaceful;

other ships were subject to desultory attacks but it was clear that for a while the Luftwaffe and Regia Aeronautica had not completed reorganisation after the rapid advance of the Allied desert armies had driven them from their air bases in Tripolitania and Tunisia. They were now to operate from airfields in Sicily.

On the 16th at 2300 *Pakenham* led *Queen Olga* and *Petard* out of the Grand Harbour, Malta, for one of the first offensive sweeps that were to form the keystone of Operation Retribution. The three destroyers headed out in line ahead into the darkness; $1\frac{1}{2}$ cables apart line astern, steaming at 20 knots down channels through Italian minefields, using copies of the information obtained from the charts removed from the captured submarine *Uarsciek* to navigate by. The offensive patrol took the ships round and close to the island fortresses of Linosa and Lampedusa.

The destroyers and cruisers that sallied forth every night, sweeping as far west as Bizerta sinking the supply and evacuation ships, bombarding the islands of the Sicilian channel into submission and surrender, were soon to call the nightly and deadly sweeps out of Malta, with typical under-statement, 'The Club Runs'.

The first club run for the *Petard* was uneventful, searchlights from the two islands, dimly seen as black lumps looming against the night sky, swept fitfully and nervously across the sea surface, once or twice licking momentarily across the line of speeding grey ships. The lights did not 'fix' onto the destroyers so they could not have been seen, but it did indicate that the garrisons knew that they were there. The ships, closed up at action stations, followed *Pakenham* on patrol round and between the islands looking for supply ships, reported in the afternoon by air reconnaisance, heading towards Lampedusa. The night bitterly cold, with a south wind blowing off the Tripolitanian mainland, made the sea short and uncomfortable, and the task of sighting or hearing E-boats known to be based on the larger island, a near impossibility.

As dawn approached, the destroyers moved away to the south to meet a small convoy out of Tripoli bound for Malta. By noon the escorts and convoy were under heavy attack from six Ju 87 dive bombers escorted by Me 109 fighters. The Stukas came screaming out of the sun into a barrage of 4 inch AA fire put up by *Pakenham* and *Petard*. The almost unbroken crash of the two 'P's firing at a rate of 22 rounds a minute from each gun of the main armament, backed up by the sharper staccato crack from the close range oerlikon and pom-pom weapons in all three destroyers and the merchant ships, made an unholy ear crushing din.

Rupert Egan distinguished himself in the eyes of the ship's company of his new command, by demonstrating his style of handling the ship to meet dive bombing attacks. Lying back in his bridge chair at a spine cracking angle, bending the trunk of his body horizontal to the deck, and wearing smoked glasses, he sighted the near vertical diving Stukas coming out of the sun. As the bombs were released he called out helm and speed alterations to avoid those aimed at the ship. The first barrage destroyed two of the Stukas who plunged straight into the sea without any attempt to pull out of their dives. They had obviously received fatal direct hits passing through the concentrated 4 inch barrage.

All bombs missed their targets, only two store ships suffered near misses that wounded a few seamen and strained the plates of one ship. While the four surviving Stukas pulled out and away from the attack a third was shot down into the sea by Beaufighters that had arrived on the scene, the crashing plane narrowly missed a speeding and indignant *Queen Olga*. In the late afternoon the convoy entered Malta without further incident. That night while destroyers of the 14th Flotilla and the cruiser *Orion* carried out a club run; prowling off the coast of Sicily near Cape Granitola looking for a reported supply convoy; ships of the 12th Flotilla had a night in harbour, a few libertymen ashore, sampled the rationed and frugal offerings in bomb battered Valletta.

A larger convoy than usual, ME 20, left Malta bound for Tripoli at 1900 on the 19th, but before dawn the next day *Queen Olga* and *Petard* were detached from the escort and headed back to Malta with a tanker having engine-room problems. At 2300 *Petard* was again at sea with *Pakenham* bound for Tripoli to reinforce the escort of yet another short haul supply convoy. On arrival at 0900/20th both ships entered the harbour for the first time, berthing onto damaged and burnt out hulks of Italian transports that still occupied many of the longside berths. Short leave of four hours piped for part of a watch, released a quarter of the ship's company ashore for a first look at the handsome Italian colonial city. Away from the harbour, the city had suffered little damage, the Afrika Korps and Italian Army had retreated leaving the civilian population spared from bitter hand to hand fighting through the urban area.

Petard's men hurried ashore, some supplied with lire that had come from the *Uarsciek* and anxious to exchange the captured currency for fresh vegetables, fruit and wine, to improve the limited fare available to the Malta based ships. Libertymen from the two 'P's had very little time to gain impressions from the first captured populated enemy city, when with a deafening roar, a mixed force of Ju 88s and Heinkels attacked the harbour area that they had only left minutes before. Aircraft also assaulted shipping lying outside in the anchorage; the planes came in from the sea, having travelled from bases in Sicily, low at zero height to avoid the army and ship borne radar warning sets.

In addition to carrying bombs, the planes were introducing a new form of weaponry, circling torpedoes. *Pakenham, Petard, Derwent* and the shore based AA artillery managed to open fire as the first flight of aircraft swarmed in from the anchorage over the harbour, but were unable to prevent a tanker longside and discharging being hit, causing a vast eruption of flame and smoke which quickly spread to vehicles on the jetty and moved on with lightning speed to ignite the fuel tanks of the wrecks sharing the same berth as the unfortunate tanker. *Derwent* underway in the harbour turning with all guns in action, to pass out through the partially blocked harbour entrance, received hits by two bombs from the second flight of raiders; the bombs entered aft and blew out her starboard side.

Listing badly, but with her steering gear still operating and under way, the commanding officer managed to beach his ship in a corner of the harbour formed by one of the main moles. While damage control parties fought flames caused by the explosion, her gunners continued to engage the aircraft circling the harbour and anchorage.

Several torpedoes were dropped outside amongst the ships at anchor where the alarmed helpless and near hypnotised crews watched the lethal tin fish rampaging in circles amongst the ships frantically trying to weigh anchors; none were hit, the torpedoes finally expired at the end of their runs, most sank, one or two remained afloat with their armed heads bobbing like phallic symbols out of the calm sea. These were quickly sunk by close range weapons, one exploding spectacularly and harmlessly.

In the harbour, four torpedoes were dropped, one straight into a wreck where later it was found and recovered, two plunged direct into the mud and silt of the inner harbour, remaining impotent and harmless; the last took off circling at high speed, miraculously keeping to the centre of the crowded harbour away from the ships that cringed against the dockside berths. Gun crews in *Petard* found it hard to concentrate on serving the guns while the torpedo circled viciously and erratically, making passes at the stationary ships. After what seemed an interminable time the compressed air propellent ran out and the torpedo sank without hitting any craft.

Petard's 50 odd libertymen raced back to rejoin their ship and action stations, through a dockyard filled with flame and smoke from the burning tanker and wrecks; recently purchased vegetables, fruit and the occasional broken wine bottle marked their headlong rush through the debris strewn dockyard. The arrival of the fighters from the desert air force ended the attack without further damage being caused to ships or the installations ashore, and *Pakenham* led *Petard* out of Tripoli harbour to escort the thoroughly alarmed merchantmen in convoy to Malta, clearing the anchorage at 1600; a great column of black smoke plumed into the still air from the harbour, remaining astern until lost in the falling night.

Soon after arrival at Malta next day, following routine refuelling, *Pakenham* led the 12th Flotilla to join the 14th Flotilla and the 15th Cruiser Squadron for fleet engagement exercises. The Italian fleet kept close to their home ports, cowed and reluctant to seek action with the British fleet, still inferior in terms of heavy ships. While the Italians had battleships and heavy cruisers within easy steaming distance of Malta and the North African ports, it was essential for the British ships to pause in their escorting and offensive 'club runs' to exercise tactics and strategy against the possibility of the Italian fleet emerging in force to cover the evacuation of the defeated remnants of the German and Italian armies out of Africa.

During the following four days *Petard* carried out a self boiler clean in Malta dockyard, with 48 hours leave given to each watch at a rest camp now set up for the ships based on the island fortress. The conditions were spartan: accommodation with no pretensions of comfort consisted of standard pre-fabricated huts with two tier iron bunks and little else; food limited to basics as fresh meat and vegetables were still almost unobtainable. No one refused the opportunity of a brief break from ship board life and routine; all benefited from the chance to relax, laze in the sun and swim off the flat smooth rocks of St Paul's bay. The ration of one bottle of beer frustrated the thirsts of the luckless libertymen, but enforced abstention returned men to the ship who were rested and free from hangovers.

On the 30th *Pakenham* with *Petard* following close astern, steamed out of Grand Harbour into the evening darkness to carry out a 'club run' offensive sweep into the enemy-held Gulf of Hammammet. The Axis armies stood at bay along the coast of the gulf, waiting nightly for reinforcements and supplies to be brought into Sousse and Keliba by sea from Sicily and the Italian mainland. The Afrika Korps and its Italian allies were trapped within the northern third of Tunisia and the north east corner of Algeria. The major ports of Bone and Bizerta were still in enemy hands, the smaller ports of Sousse in the gulf and Sfax further south and opposite the Kirkenna islands had not as yet been captured by the rampaging and victorious Eighth Army.

Fall of the latter ports was imminent, for all four harbours were receiving continuous attention by day and night from the desert air force, with additional harassment from bombardments coming out of the night darkness of the sea, initiated by the marauding cruisers and destroyers on 'club run' operations out of Malta.

Captain D12 with *Petard* following, west north west to round Pantelleria Island leaving it to port, then south west down into the Gulf of Hammamet, to intercept shipping moving north and south round the western tip of Sicily into the Gulf under the cover of darkness, bound for Kelibia, Sousse and Sfax. The two destroyers tore westward at thirty knots into a black rain showered night and a sea sprinkled with unseen mines, torn from moorings to appear in daylight as black menacing half spheres that could be seen everywhere in the seas between Sicily and North Africa. The crews of the 'club run' ships on their nightly runs prayed that the mines were all dearmed by the severance from their moorings, and for those that still remained alive and armed all hoped that bow wave and wash from the speeding hull would force the mines in the line of advance, away from the stem and ship sides.

Petard's bridge and flag deck teams moved quietly about their familiar tasks; the officer of the watch and Yeoman Chapman kept constant watch on *Pakenham*, $1\frac{1}{2}$ cables ahead, seen only as a vague shape above and ahead of a turmoil of white foam and wake from the mighty thrust of her screws and passage through the sea. A tiny shaded blue light on the stern of the leading ship helped the 00W astern to maintain contact and correct station. Few signals were passed or were necessary, radio and radar silence was complete, the practised techniques of operating at speed at night in close formation with well understood reactions to situations reduced the necessity of passing signals to a minimum, rehearsed drills covered most eventualities; those that did not were left to the almost unique British armed services strength, use of the commanding officer's initiative. Only the very occasional flicker of blue light from *Pakenham* brought a brief one or two lettered code signal to the attention of *Petard*'s Yeoman Chapman and his action team.

Brooky, the navigator, worked constantly to check the position of the ship using a combination of accurate plotting, dead reckoning and check bearings on any identifiable land that could be seen by the bridge team and lookouts. Action lookouts scanned the night horizon within their 90 degree sectors, moving slowly with care and concentration from ahead to aft and back again sitting in the steel seats of rotating lookout positions, binoculars clamped to the moving structure but free to elevate or depress allowing the lookout to compensate for the pitch and roll of the ship. Above the bridge team and lookouts, the gun control director trained slowly and continually through 360 degrees, with layer, trainer, range taker and GCO scanning the dimly seen or sensed horizon and sea through powerful optical instruments.

In the sickbay, Doc with his Tiffy, tried to read or doze, waiting ready to exercise their skills to save lives and repair torn, mutilated, burnt limbs and bodies. Doc from time to time had moments of intense activity deciphering signals received by the listening watch in Petty Officer Telegraphist Shove's W/T receiving office, adjoining the sick bay.

In his Captain's chair, starboard side of the bridge, with his head showing just above the wind-break, Rupert Egan sat hunched in his duffle coat, cap jammed down hard on his ears, frequently lifting his binoculars to his eyes to check the bearing and distance of his senior officer's ship, followed by a careful scan of the dark horizon. Then, leaning over to his left for a short look down the spy optics to the red-lit plot in the chart room below the bridge. Rupert sat confident and ready as his 1540 ton command followed in the wake of the *Pakenham*, his men were refreshed and on their toes after four days in Malta and 48 hour break at the St Paul rest camp. In contrast, the *Pakenham* was on her fourth successive night 'club run' with only brief daylight moments of rest after refuelling and storing in Malta.

The destroyers sped past the great bulk of Pantellaria, leaving it three miles to port, then turning to port on a course down towards the approach channel to Sousse through the enemy mine barrier laid across the Gulf of Hammamet. An increase of tense expectancy surged through the ships as first to port on the western tip of Pantellaria and starboard on Cape Bon, navigation light marks were sighted, switched on at intervals and reduced brilliancy as a clear indication that shipping was on the move into or out of the Gulf. It also indicated to the *Pakenham* and *Petard* that they had not been located; radar and radio silence was giving results and confirmed that reconnaissance aircraft had not sighted them heading westward, before darkness hid the sally from Malta.

Approaching the minefield guarding the route to Sousse, a brief flicker from *Pakenham*'s heather lantern, reduced speed first to twenty knots, ten minutes later to 15 knots. It was clear as the ships moved into the Gulf that something was expected at Sousse; navigation shore lights at low power were spotted by the raiders closing in from the sea.

It was a restless uneasy night; inland to the south and east of Sousse the occasional Star shell and Very light pierced the dark sky where the Eighth Army continued to probe the enemy rearguard. Closer at hand, now that the noise of the wind and sea had been reduced by the reduction in speed from the 340 knot dash, engine noises could be heard coming down on the wind and from ahead. First with a great roar, three great heavily loaded Ju 52s lumbered overhead, the transports flying low over the sea to escape radar detection passed in a straggling line over the startled and surprised destroyers; the noise of their struggling engines had hardly faded astern before the unmistakeable sound of E-boats could be heard from more than one bearing. A number were in close vicinity probably standing by as escorts for the expected supply ships from Italy. One of the E-boats sighted the incoming British ships, challenged not being sure whether the vaguely seen vessel was friend or foe; as the two destroyers stood to their guns ready to open fire with a broadside, a second E-boat sighted astern of the two destroyers, who must have passed without spotting the intruders, replied to the challenge mistaken as intended for itself, instead of the unseen *Pakenham* and *Petard*; this apparently satisfied the more alert but obviously confused challenger, the two destroyers stole away deeper into the Gulf unmolested.

Closing Sousse blacked out and indistinguishable against the backdrop of restless desert night skirmishing which continued to light up the sky with intermittent flashes and the infrequent slow falling flares and star shell, it was possible to pin-point the exact position of the small coastal town. The flashing light that marked the end of the mole that gave Sousse a semblance of a port, enabled the navigators in the two ships to check their positions with unexpected exactness; the characteristics of the navigation lights and their positions marked on the charts removed from the *Uarsciek* had obviously not been altered.

A plan quickly evolved by Captain D12 based itself on the assumption that the shipping from Sicily had not arrived, but could be close astern of the British destroyers. Using the light marking Sousse as a ranging point, the ships in line astern steaming at 15 knots would steer parallel to the coast and bombard the town, turn and repeat the performance before dashing at speed away from the area on a return course through the minefield and fall upon the incoming enemy shipping.

The first part went according to plan, eight four gun salvoes were delivered into the unfortunate township, using the flashing harbour light for ranging with the optic range finders in the ships' directors; reversing course the ships delivered a second deliberate bombardment using flashless ammunition to confuse the defenders. The shore light continued to blink for some time until no doubt the sound of the gunfire coming from the sea alerted the shore to what was happening. A further six salvoes went shrieking in before the light was doused. Increasing speed to 20 knots *Pakenham* led the way towards the route back, to round Pantellaria hopefully to find the shipping for which all the navigation lights had been switched on for; expectations were high that they would intercept important transports and supply ships; but the E-boats had to be dealt with first, and they were not long coming. Radar now switched on as the enemy knew of their presence, but the relatively primitive equipment did not detect the small E-boats coming in fast towards the two destroyers. The boats were now thoroughly roused, no doubt informed of the bombardment, they were ordered back to engage the destroyers.

Pakenham altered course suddenly to port, and as *Petard* followed round in her wake, it became apparent the reason for the violent change from the course to Pantellaria; three or four E-boats in line abreast attacking from the port bow could be heard, their white bow waves just seen; the two 'Ps' conned possible torpedo tracks and at the same time counter attacked by passing through the line of motor torpedo boats firing to port and starboard with tracer ammunition at the dimly seen speeding craft, the destroyers laid smoke as they passed, and for the next half hour the E-boats and the two larger ships played a murderous tag game with each other.

Petard clung grimly in the wake of the flotilla leader following every alteration of course, $1\frac{1}{2}$ cables astern, the two ships as one, dived into and out of the smoke frustrating the largely uncoordinated attacks from the smaller but speedier craft. The situation became more alarming when at least two aircraft began dropping flares; for long moments the destroyers were blinded and then raked by small calibre fire from the E-boats, but the fact that these craft never got organised the damage inflicted was slight and without casualties. From time to time the destroyers caught the E-boats silhouetted against the falling flares and obtained hits with Pom-pom and oerlikon; one fire started in a boat flared brightly for a while until the conflagration disappeared from sight in the smoke barrier still being laid by the destroyers. The E-boats retired towards the coast of the gulf without either *Pakenham* or *Petard* confirming that any had been sunk, and much delayed, the destroyers were able to turn at speed steering to the north and start the search down the route towards the western tip of Sicily and the straits of Marittimo, looking for the shipping suspected to be abroad that night.

As the latitude of Pantellaria was reached hopes faded, the bombardment and the E-boat fracas had frightened them off; whatever had been steaming down towards the Gulf of Hammamet had obviously turned back and now probably sheltered under the eleven and six inch gun batteries guarding the small fortified island port. It was now 0200, the morning of the 31st March and the destroyers had some 150 nautical miles to cover back to base although the temptation was strong to close Pantellaria and shell the ships if they were in fact sheltering there. If the air cover from Malta was to be reached by first light, this could not be done; reluctantly Captain D12 turned his small raiding force east, increased speed to 28 knots and retired to base with weary ships' companies grimly anticipating the inevitable refuelling evolution followed by the reammunition barges to replace the impact action shells expended in the bombardment, and close range projectiles used in the E-boat action that followed. The ships returned and entered harbour at 1130; from noon *Petard* was duty and emergency destroyer at immediate notice for steam!

For the next ten nights *Petard* sailed out on club runs, the first alone to Marittimo island to intercept a convoy that had been sighted in the early afternoon by American reconnaissance aircraft, but not unexpectantly the sweep proved abortive, either because of faulty reporting by the still inexperienced allies from the other side of the Atlantic, or because the enemy ships laid up during the night.

Other 'club runs' by ships of the 14th Flotilla and the cruisers were producing results, several small transports and supply ships had been intercepted and sunk; the submarines operating out of Malta sank a number of enemy ships north of Sicily, the approaches to the Straits of Messina, and in Tyrrhenian, Adriatic and Ionian seas.

During the next few days, *Petard* carried out a variety of escorting jobs, these included giving a fast minelayer extra AA and anti-submarine cover as far as Tobruk on the *Abdiels* return to Alexandria. Into Tobruk on the 11th to refuel and then as far as Tripoli, *Petard* escorted a regular convoy that should have been joined by the *Queen Olga*. The Greek ship was however unable to rendezvous, she had lost one of her propellers negotiating the hazards of the wreck strewn entrance of Benghazi. *Queen Olga* had to limp back to Alexandria for a welcome break of leave while a new screw was fitted.

Meanwhile after seeing the convoy safely into Tripoli, *Petard* escorted two supply ships on to the now captured Sfax, sinking floating mines all the way. The mine sinking continued during the daylight hours of the 14th/15th while the ship returned to Malta so she could collect more supply shipping for Sfax. The sea as far as the horizon within the Gulf of Gabes and out into the open water surrounding the islands of Pantellaria, Limosa and Lampedusa remained thick with sinister horned black half spheres of released moored mines. It was a continuous wonder that there was no wholesale loss of shipping, particularly at night when the floating mines were unseen and avoiding action impossible to take.

At 0500/16th, *Petard* on her return trip, approached the channel to Sfax with her convoy of supply craft, threaded her way up the still partially swept path through the minefield adjoining the Kerkenna Islands when Doc appeared on the bridge more dishevelled than usual after his early 'shake' to decypher an operational IMMEDIATE signal addressed to *Petard*. The signal ordered Rupert Egan to leave his group of supply ships, to proceed at full speed and assist *Pakenham* and *Paladin*, who had been in action, a little to the north and east of Pantellaria, with two large enemy destroyers.

The 'Ps' had sunk with gunfire and torpedoes one Italian war-ship in a short high speed action, in the dark, but D12's ship had been damaged and suffered a number of casualties. Soon after 0800, *Pakenham* with engine and steam systems damaged beyond repair, had to be sunk by *Paladin*'s torpedoes to avoid further casualties. *Paladin* crowded with a doubling of her normal complement by the crew of the sunken flotilla leader, steamed at 30 knots back to Malta under a protective umbrella of fighters, as *Petard* arrived from the south west too late to help or save the stricken *Pakenham*.

Given very little time to ponder on the consequences of losing their flotilla leader, and the fact that Captain D12 with his staff were ashore, without a ship, *Paladin* and *Petard* followed *Nubian* to sea at 1030/19th for the next turn in the 'club run' series, ordered to sweep as far west as Cape Bon. They were to return passing close to the north of Pantellaria, seeking shipping entering or leaving the small island harbour; then north for a quick sweep along part of the Sicilian coast before returning to Malta.

The run proved uneventful until the leg north approaching the coast of Sicily when the force sighted at 0200, an enemy destroyer. The sighting appeared to be mutual, for the enemy ship that had been steering a course south, towards **Pantellaria**, turned and at high speed retired inshore pursued by the three British destroyers in whom alarm rattlers were bringing the action closed up ships' companies to instant readiness. *Nubian* leading the column of three in line astern, fired star-shell from her twin 4.7 'B' mounting, illuminating the target fleeing like a startled hare before three coursing greyhounds. The prey slipped in close under a headland protected by heavy coast batteries and into waters known to be heavily minded but not accurately plotted on the charts held in the British destroyers.

The Italian destroyer became difficult to see against the steep cliffs of the headland, and back echoes confused the gunnery radar; star-shells fired by all three ships also failed to show up the outline of the quarry. Time began to run out, the raiding force prowling just south of the limits of the protecting minefield, could not risk a stay to be caught in daylight so close to enemy airfields; as each ship turned in succession to starboard, to a course of 120 degrees for Malta, released in turn a salvo at the indistinct fugitive, more as a gesture of warning than a serious intent to maim.

Signals from C-in-C Mediterranean formally disbanding the 12th Destroyer Flotilla arrived in the ships during the 21st. During its short existence, perhaps because of the fact that it rarely operated as a complete flotilla, the miscellaneous group of destroyers never fully achieved the feeling of a close knit identity; *Petard* especially, through her ship's company, officers and ratings, did not make close personal contact with its flotilla companions or in particular the Captain D and his staff and the ship's company of the *Pakenham*. The exception to this was the very close companionship the ship felt for its half section, the Greek *Queen Olga*. Nevertheless it was with feelings akin to a suddenly orphaned family, albeit the deceased parent was distant, stern, respected but not greatly loved, the miscellaneous group of destroyers now received orders to disperse and join other flotillas.

Paladin, Queen Olga and *Petard* as a group were deployed to join the 14th Flotilla, led by the distinguished and formidable Captain A.L. Poland DSC., in *Jervis*.

The three ex-12th Flotilla ships were formed into a sub-unit within their new flotilla's organisation.

With *Queen Olga* and *Petard* able to continue their close association *Petard*'s next 'club run' was again with *Paladin* and *Nubian*, Commander D.E. Holland Martin DSC, leading the raiding group. The ships cleared Malta Grand Harbour during the late morning of the 24th, taking up the normal formation for passing down the channels through enemy minefields at 1600; *Nubian* leading, followed by *Paladin* and *Petard* last, each ship 1½ cables astern of the next ahead; moving west at 20 knots in the growing dusk, gun crews now at action stations, checked instruments and circuits with the gunnery transmission stations and director controls.

Out of the growing gloom astern and from the east a plane swept in low, unsighted by lookouts or detected by radar, raked *Petard* from stern to bridge and flag deck with a cannon and machine gun fire deluge. The surprise was complete, later no one seemed able with certainty, to identify the type or nationality of the attacker, it was variously reported as a Ju 88, a Savoia and a Me 109. Even *Paladin* the next ahead who saw the ship astern enveloped in sudden smoke and flashes, failed to positively identify the aircraft as it passed overhead, banking steeply to starboard before disappearing to the north.

The pain and casualties were grievous, while material damage was slight. The whole of 'Y' gun crew on the unprotected quarter deck and part of the ammunition supply party were wiped out, three of the guns crew killed instantly; the Captain of the gun, Leading Seaman Rafton critically wounded, a Leading Stoker in charge of the supply party also killed; seven, the entire remainder of the gun crews were also wounded, four very badly. Two more, members of the supply party were also casualties. Forward in the director, the GCO received a deep furrow in his skull from a bullet that then shattered his binoculars, and below on the flag deck, Yeoman Chapman had a narrow escape from a cannon shell that exploded on impact with the armoured door into the transmitting station.

Racing aft along the iron deck, Doc Prendergast and his first aid party joined David Dunbar Nasmith, whose action station was aft, on the quarter-deck working in the closing darkness to get the dead, dying and wounded of the shattered gun crew and supply party off the upper deck, in through the canvas darken ship screens that masked the after door of the X gun superstructure, into the wardroom galley flat. Here under dim blue lighting, the casualties requiring immediate emergency attention could be identified, the badly congested space and poor lighting allowed only the most elementary and cursory examination, sufficient just to separate the tragically obvious dead from those still living. Five requiring crisis surgery were lowered down the steep ladder to the wardroom and pantry flat, leaving long ugly trails of blood, to be laid on the deck under bright wardroom lights with the bearers striving to stem life ebbing away in a pumping spreading crimson blood flood. Doctor now backed up by the wardroom stewards and chef turned the dining table into an emergency operating table, instruments spread along the wine sideboard, passed into the pantry via the serving hatch to be sterilised in the electric boiler.

Outside the dusk turned into a dark night, the moon masked by thick low cloud, allowed the three hunting destroyers to slip unseen, but not undetected, west in the nightly hunt for supply or evacuating enemy shipping. Radar sets were being jammed by transmissions that came from Pantellaria indicating that the Italian garrison knew that raiders were out. Below in *Petard*'s wardroom Doc with his helpers fought to save the lives that still flickered in bodies that had been grotesquely mutilated by bullet and cannon shell. Fortunately the night and sea remained calm to help Prendergast and the desperately wounded men in their isolated compartment of pain; one by one the men were lifted onto the table now covered by blood soaked blankets and sheets so that Doc could carry out emergency surgery, his bizarre appearance did nothing to disguise his superb skill as a surgeon. Clad only in blood stained collarless shirt and shorts, his skinny legs and feet bare to grip the cortosene covered deck as the ship rolled and pitched to the slight swell; smoking in an endless chain, he stemmed the flow from torn arteries and dealt with the shocked and damaged life support systems.

Eventually he had done all that could be done, each of the wounded was laid on folding camp beds that David had organised and arranged in whatever space could be found in the wardroom, pantry and cabin flats for men that could not be accommodated in the officers' bunks. By the side of the worst of the badly wounded and shocked men Prendergast organised a rota of messmates to give courage and the will to fight their injuries and shock, to help their determination to live.

The destroyers reached the limit of the patrol area without sighting any surface vessel; numerous low flying aircraft were about, by the sound of their engines they were mostly transports, but none blundered close enough for the unseen destroyers to engage. The ships turned back to the east and commenced the return run to Malta, still with nothing to show for yet another night in the mine infested sea between North Africa and Sicily.

As dawn began in the east the shape of the indefatigable doctor could be seen, still in his half clad state, climbing the ladder at the rear of the bridge from the flag deck on his way up into the director to inspect the GCO's wound. His scruffy bearded face as it appeared over the edge of the open director was both startling and welcome to the cramped and chilled inmates, the stream of Irish obscenities and general comment on the interminable Club Runs went on endlessly as he gave first aid to the scored skull, and with surgical spirit freed a blood soaked beard that had become dried and part of the collar of a fur flying jacket which the GCO wore on night watches and prolonged action stations.

Later when the ships moved under the fighter cover from Malta, Doc returned to supervise the hoisting out of the GCO from his seat in the director and the lowering down to the upper deck. With his usual gift of the unorthodox, he had the officer placed fully clothed into a full bath of warm water, and with a large double scotch at hand for himself and one for his patient, soaked and then cut him free from the blood stiffened clothing.

Before the ships reached Grand Harbour, when still 10 miles out, the unit of three ships slowed to ten knots; *Petard* with her starboard screw stopped committed her dead to the Mediterranean. Rupert Egan standing aft still in his duffle coat, muffled against the early morning chill and uniform cap under his arm read the funeral service over four still shapes, laid in a row, sewn into their hammocks, each covered by a white ensign. In turn, the inert bodies were lifted by their messmates onto a board prepared by the Buffer, then at a signal from Chief Petty Officer Haustead the weighted bodies were tilted to slide quickly into the sea and from sight, as Rupert read the committal prayers. It was a scene of considerable poignancy and sadness, the ship still at action stations, the First Lieutenant, David Dunbar Nasmith on the bridge conning the ship for his commanding officer now aft on the quarter-deck, conducting a brief funeral service for men who had shared the crowded community life of the ship since the commissioning in the Tyne; the only sound to be heard other than Rupert's voice was the hushed sea noises and the muted roar of the engine room and boiler room forced draught fans; sailors and officers stood silent and bareheaded at their action stations while messmates committed their friends to the blue Mediterranean.

Twenty minutes later the ships entered Grand Harbour still flying ensigns at half mast, to refuel and prepare for the next sweep towards Cape Bon. *Petard* moved longside the dockyard jetty where ambulances were waiting to take the wounded to hospital; ten stretcher cases were disembarked, and with two, Doc insisted that they should be accompanied with friends who had been working and sharing the struggle to overcome the effects of shock. His fury was difficult to control when the hospital refused to retain the volunteers and made them return to the ship. The day was Easter Sunday, 25th April, and the three ships had a night in.

On the 26th *Petard* sailed at 1500 alone for a sweep along the coast of Sicily and back past **Pantellaria**. Before she sailed news arrived on board of Leading Seaman Rafton's death; he was buried ashore while his friends and shipmates were away on the sweeps that were part of Operation Retribution. The ship sailed with fourteen replacements, seamen and stokers to fill the places left by the casualties suffered by 'Y' gun and the supply party. The new men had no time to shake down before the ship sailed, David and the GI had to reconstruct the gun crew with a mixture of experienced hands from the other three 4 inch gun teams and the new draft; the new and old crews with replacements were carrying out strenuous drill as the ship sailed.

The night passed uneventfully until the return back to base; as men, stiff with cold and weary from a long night at action stations, began to anticipate a hot drink immediately following the dawn stand-to, alarm rattlers brought everyone scrambling to full alert, the bridge lookouts could be heard shouting that a submarine had surfaced ahead and a little out to starboard.

The submarine sighted the destroyer coming in fast; it could be seen blowing its tanks for a crash dive as the pom-pom opened up. Cannon shell churned the sea round the fast disappearing conning tower, with the ship heeling over to port under full starboard helm Rupert Egan conned the track of an approaching torpedo, the phosphorescence of its track passing uncomfortably close in the slip stream on the starboard quarter. The ship's company with a mixture of surprise and relief found their ship resuming course and at high speed retired to Malta. The operational orders were precise, no submarine was to be attacked in the Sicilian straits unless positively identified as enemy, *Petard* could not confirm the sighting.

The next night *Petard* had a night in, *Paladin* and *Nubian* out on the normal run encountered a medium sized Italian merchantman which they sank without difficulty or harassment from escorts that fled at the raider's approach.

May Day heralded the start of a month of increased activity, little rest but a share in many successful actions and a part in a historic victory, it also found *Petard* again at sea in company with her new Captain D14 in *Jervis* and *Nubian*, in the usual line ahead formation; this time *Petard* very much the junior ship between the two destroyers commanded by Captain Poland and Commander Holland-Martin.

The patrol between Marittimo and North Africa was uneventful, no doubt because of the very bad wind and sea conditions. The seas were the roughest encountered since the start of Operation Retribution, and forced enemy evacuation craft to shelter in whatever havens remained in Axis hands. The three destroyers returned to Malta after an extremely uncomfortable night in the turbulent seas of the narrows between Cape Bon and Marittimo. After a night in, *Nubian* lead *Paladin* and *Petard* out again, clearing the boom at 1800, to follow the familiar route NE of Pantellaria up to Marittimo, then SE passing to the north of Pantellaria, closing Cape Bon.

The three ships arrived at Cape Bon shortly before midnight steering south and east, prowling close inshore, listening and watching to the sounds and flashes of the conflict ashore that was nearing its inevitable end, as the British and American armies closed in on the last toe-hold of the Axis in North Africa.

Off Ras al Milhr the raiders caught up with a large supply ship and its escort a short distance from their destination, having successfully crossed the narrows after a voyage from Naples where vehicles, bombs, ammunition and land mines had been embarked for the desperate and defeated armies. The supply operation was within an ace of success; until at 0059 on 4th May, just 20 miles off Keliba, a short murderous action annihilated first the escort and then the 7000 merchant supply ship.

Laying a heavy smoke screen, a Cassipeo Class destroyer, the *Campobasso*, frantically tried to break away to the east and escape at speed towards Pantellaria, perhaps to find shelter under the islands massive coastal batteries. Led by *Nubian* firing star shell, the three pursuing destroyers plunged through dense smoke and a sea suddenly filled with screaming, drowning Italian sailors who were jumping from their fleeing ship to escape the holocaust that was about to eliminate the *Campobasso*. The hunted destroyer turned desperately to port, like a terrified stricken and doomed animal, and there under the combined searchlights of the hunters the remnants of her crew could be seen to emerge fearfully from deck hatches and doors in the superstructure to make a last scrambling struggle in the pitiless glare, to abandon ship, as the combined broadsides from the destroyers hit her.

Nubian fired only one salvo from her six 4.7 guns, her 'B' gun mounting continued to fire star shell to keep the merchantman SS *Perseo* under surveillance while the escort was being destroyed. The rapid fire from the *Paladin* and *Petard*'s 4 inch guns poured into the *Campobasso*'s hull and superstructure as she still made way through the water out of control; ammunition lockers began to explode on the upper deck, the destroyer started to heel to port. Then with a lurch the ship capsized, her keel, bilge plates and screws showing briefly in the searchlight beams before the torn hull slipped in a swirl of foam below the sea surface.

Searchlights now switched to the undefended *Perseo*, followed by broadsides fired at a high salvo rate; flash and flame from inside the ship could be seen through shell entry holes. The destroyers were still firing when the entire cargo of explosives blew up; a gigantic ball of flame and an ear-rendering detonation threatened to overwhelm the destroyers, a great blast of heat, smoke and debris plastered the ships. The *Perseo* had vanished, parts of her continued to fall and rain out of the night for long seconds into the sea and on to open decks; the immensity of the explosion could only have further depressed the witnesses ashore from the doomed army within the Kelibia peninsula.

Nubian led her line of three away from the area, a light sighted further south and west from the direction of Korba or Nabeul drew her and the two 'Ps'. Closing the source of the light, it was quickly recognised to be an outward bound hospital ship, brilliantly lit and marked, its white hull painted with huge red crosses, the converted liner loaded to capacity with wounded seemed vulnerable and nakedly alone in the dark night. Three destroyers appearing suddenly from out of the night into the circumference of light that radiated from the hospital ship's floodlights, can only have terrified the master and his crew; *Nubian* reassured the Red Cross ship by calling up by light, using international code and ordered the Italian master to follow the destroyers and prepare to pick up survivors from the sea.

Night began to give way to a dawn moving in from the east as the British ships leading the hospital ship, arrived back off Cape Ras al Milhr and the area of the sinkings. Much to the surprise and to the relief of some in the destroyers there were signs of many survivors from the *Campobasso* and *Perseo*. The destroyers paused only briefly to pick up a few men as the hospital ship lowered her boats; *Petard* draped her sides with scrambling nets, three Italians and a similar number of Germans decided to climb inboard, rather than wait to be recovered by the hospital ship, before *Nubian* ordered her two consorts to follow away at high speed back to Malta. The three destroyers steered a course direct and to the south of Pantellaria harried by six Ju 88s trying to avenge the ships that had been sunk. *Nubian*, *Paladin* and *Petard* jinking at full speed firing their main armament in the AA role, with an ease born from experience and confidence, held off the bombers until the arrival of the air escort from Malta.

Nubian as she led her group back through the harbour boom, had completed 22 sorties against enemy shipping since her return from home waters after Christmas. On seven of the night 'club runs' she had been present at the destruction of one or more supply ships and their escorts.

Twelve hours later at 0800/5th *Petard* was again at sea in command of a group, *Queen Olga* and *Isis* patrolling down to Sousse still blocked by fresh mines dropped by enemy aircraft; and for the following six nights the ship was out in company with her Greek half section and the *Isis*, part of the blockading force of destroyers working out of Malta, Sfax and Tripoli, sealing off the escape of the Axis army from Cape Bon. By day the escape craft and air transports were sunk and shot down by the Allied desert air command squadrons swarming over Cape Bon, Kelibia, the sea beyond up to the Sicilian coast, and at night the prowling destroyers assigned in groups to planned patrol areas between Sousse and the Cape with the submarines caught and sank nearly everything that set out from the African coast. In addition the submarines and cruisers with destroyer support, stopped any intention or attempt of a rescue operation from the Italian mainland.

Only hospital ships moved out into the menacing darkness with any hope of getting through, even these were from time to time ordered to heave to and boarded by search parties to check that no fighting troops were embarked and evacuated with the wounded; *Petard* stopped two on the 7th and a third on the 10th. The destroyers frequently were the spectators of air attacks on enemy targets ashore, and when possible added their own gunfire if the targets could be seen. In their turn the ships were frequently under attack, mainly now from Me 109s that sighted the ships when either flying in to help their ground troops or on return to base in Sicily; these airmen helping the rearguard troops inflicted some damage and casualties to the ships in the narrows, but many paid the penalty from accurate shipborne AA fire.

A strange mid-sea drama was interrupted on the 9th by *Petard* steaming alone south from the Patrol area off Cape Bon to Sousse. 30 miles out from Kelibia the ship came up to a large launch containing 12 men towing a rubber dinghy in which there were two men threatening the occupants of the launch with tommy guns. The aggressive pair, Italians ditched their guns with some reluctance and considerable despondency as the ship moved alongside ordering the occupants of both craft to climb the scrambling nets onto the iron deck. When the 14 men were checked, *Petard* found that it had a mixed bag – 2 RAF pilots, 10 Germans and 2 Italians.

The RAF officers had a story of treachery to tell. They had been shot down the evening before by Me 109s and had ditched successfully in the Beaufighter, roughly in the middle of the Gulf of Hammamet. A dinghy was inflated and launched before the aircraft sank, they then spent the night floating in a moderate sea with a drogue out hoping to be picked up by the destroyers that they knew were on patrol. A little before first light an engine of a boat had been heard approaching from the south and shortly afterwards they were nearly run down by a launch manned by German and Italian soldiers escaping from the land fighting. The escapees ordered the airmen into the launch and taking the dinghy in tow, continued to proceed in the general direction of Sicily. It was soon obvious to the airmen that the Italians were afraid of their allies, and that something was about to happen.

They did not have to wait long; after a conference amongst the Germans who were all Panzermen, the Italians by sign language were ordered to get into the dinghy that had been hauled alongside. The Italians refused to budge, if the RAF officers had not been there, it is probable that they would have been shot, instead a struggle ensued, which finished when the Germans forced the Italians bodily into the dinghy. The strange aspect of the menacing episode was the fact that the Germans wanted to get rid of their companions when escaping to Italian territory where the Italians would be expected to be of vital assistance; the other odd factor, the men now in the rubber dinghy had not been disarmed, they were both in possession of tommy guns. The dinghy was about to be cast off, when one of the Italians sighted *Petard* closing fast and apparently hoping it was a destroyer manned by his own countrymen, immediately cocked his gun and threatened to shoot the Germans unless they stopped the launch. It seemed clear that the two Italians had expectations of turning tables on the Germans, and their disappointment was profound when an order in English came through *Petard*'s loud hailer for the launch to heave to and take a rope. There was no time to interrogate the captives after they had been embarked and the launch cast adrift, to be sunk by oerlikon fire. By 1000 the ship had arrived off Sousse and transferred the prisoners and the British airmen to a Hunt class destroyer that had to return to Malta for refuelling. The reasons for the strange and near fatal altercation did not, because of language difficulties, become known to the *Petard* in the limited time available; it may have had its origins in the probability that the launch had been taken by force from the late owners, Italian colonials, who had been butchered by the escaping Panzermen and the two Italian commandos.

The patrols continued, the ships at sea learned that Bizerta had been captured and that Commodore G.N. Oliver RN had hoisted his broad pennant in Fort Foudiat and was now in business as naval officer-in-charge.

Petard intercepted a sailing craft and removed four Germans, again Panzermen who seemed pleased to be taken from their craft. These were discharged next day when the ship entered Malta for fuel and ammunition, arriving 0530 on the 12th. By the late evening she was returning out through the boom led by the familiar *Nubian* and followed by *Isis* this time followed in turn by the cruiser *Orion*, all bound for Pantellaria.

The final stand by the enemy on Cape Bon was being enacted in a last vicious and bloody battle, the trapped armies were subjected to day and night bombardment from allied artillery and air force squadrons, watched by the prowling destroyers lying five miles out from the coast to give the British and American airmen a free hand over land and the immediate coast approaches to possible embarkation points. Temporary jetties and ramps had been photographed by reconnaissance patrols, freshly constructed in several areas round the cape; there remained still a faint possibility that some sort of evacuation effort would be attempted. The destroyers and other patrolling craft were now to close the trap by day as well as night and a fiercely worded signal sent by Admiral A.B. Cunningham, who had returned again to the post of C-in-C Mediterranean, to his small grey and battered ships, ended with, 'Sink, Burn and Destroy let nothing pass'. Most of his destroyer captains and very many of their crews had endured the agony of the evacuation from Greece and then Crete, two years before. Operation Retribution was well named.

So that the still largely raw and brash American airmen could be helped to identify the Allied ships that now dominated the seas between Sicily and Tunisia to the total exclusion of any enemy shipping, the ships at sea during the night that preceded the first of the day saturation patrols leading up to the now inevitable surrender of the Afrika Korps, were forced to paint their bridge structures a lurid red. This turned out to be an appalling and messy job, the cursing ship's companies toiled through the night as a breeze freshened into a strong wind that blew paint over the ships, plastered bridge crews, OOW's, lookouts, signalmen, asdic and director crews, as well as driving the commanding officers to near apoplexy.

The dawn of 11th May revealed ships with red lead paint spread in varying degrees of effectiveness, and with large numbers of the crews looking if they had been stricken with a sudden and violent plague that manifested itself in brilliant red spots. The ships plunging into the short white capped seas looked ghastly, but everyone accepted it as a small price if it would defend them from the dangerous Americans. This proved to be a forlorn hope, for as the sun rose, two wretched Hunts thrusting their way into the breaking short seas of the straits, outside the five mile free bombing zone were suddenly attacked out of the sun by American manned Spitfire fighter bombers. Fortunately there were no casualties in either the *Zetland* or *Bicester*. The latter was hit by a bomb in the wardroom that came to rest and lodged without exploding on top of a fuel tank.

Petard like nearly all the ships in the great line across the Sicilian Channel, with those covering the Gulf of Hammamet against any attempted escape to the islands of **Pantellaria** and Lampedusa, tuned into the maniac Americans Spitfire operational R/T network. To their delight all eavesdropped into the *Bicester*'s commanding officer's comments. Lieutenant Commander S.W.F. Bennett RN famed for his extensive grasp of contemporary and historical English and in particular seafarers' oaths was in full spate. The R/T channel recoiled under the impact of the enraged destroyer captain's vehement and colourful command of profanity, even the Americans were impressed, the listening ships heard one drawl, 'Say, I guess this guy's friendly!' Bennett's retort was unforgettable, but unprintable.

The cruiser *Orion* closing **Pantellaria** found herself escorted by three destroyers that were still disfigured by bridge structures crudely dabbed with red paint, and who had little time to do more than make tentative starts to clean up the mess. The ships in bright moonlight approached the area where large coastal gun batteries guarded the small town and harbour to the island. The great lump of land mass loomed over the ships as they neared the bombarding position, destroyers in extended line ahead, with *Petard* in the centre station, manoeuvred so as to be between the 6 inch gun cruiser and the island; at 0200 *Orion* opened fire on the main and largest shore battery housing 11 inch coastal artillery, using star shell to illuminate the target area. The enemy who must have seen the ships approaching over the sea that sparkled under a full moon, had until that moment held their fire, probably hoping that the ships were only on patrol, looking for supply ships, answered immediately, and to *Petard*'s great discomfort and alarm, she was straddled twice by six gun salvoes from the batteries.

The ship reacted, replying with four rapid salvoes, knowing that her Direct Action (DA) shells would do little more than spray the immensely strong coastal gun positions with shrapnel, but might make the Italian gunners keep their heads down. As the destroyers fired at the gun flashes ashore, *Nubian* ordered smoke to be made to screen *Orion* now receiving attention from accurate fire returned by the Italian gunners. Black smoke poured out of the three destroyers masking the *Orion* who continued to fire four full broadsides through the screen. As *Petard* turned with her consorts away from the island into the smoke, a third salvo fell very close to her retreating stern, so close that plates were strained by the exploding shells and the sea entered the tiller flat. The after damage control party led by the 1st Lieutenant David Dunbar Nasmith and Bertie were on the scene within minutes, found that the damage was not serious and the leak within the capacity of the bilge pumps. A portable pump as a precautionary back-up, should the leak worsen, was lowered into the space shortly afterwards while the bombarding force broke off the engagement at 0245 and retired under the cover of the smoke screen. The larger coastal battery guns continued to fire after the ships, but caused no further damage or concern to the task group.

The ships entered Malta at 1300; after a brief inspection by the dockyard shipwrights, *Petard* entered dry dock so that her stern leak could be sealed. Night leave was given to one watch. During the afternoon news was broadcast that the remaining enemy forces in North Africa, a quarter of a million men compressed into the Cape Bon area, had surrendered: Field Marshal Meese and General von Arnim had accepted the Allied terms for cessation of hostilities. All that remained now to conclude the objectives of Operation Retribution was to force the surrender of the island garrisons in Pantellaria, Linosa, Lampion, Lampedusa and an islet called Zembra, but it would be another month before the Governor of

Pantellaria finally conceded defeat.

Petard undocked at 1300/14th and then gave night leave to the other watch. This was an opportune and necessary break for men who had been pushed hard, all were under considerable mental and physical strain, a result of operating most nights in thickly mined waters and subject to many air attacks. A handful had cracked and were discharged after Doc Prendergast had confirmed that he was satisfied that there was little chance of recovery within the crowded confines of a working destroyer.

The number that failed were very few, and perhaps paradoxically the fact that so few failed was due to the continuous and insistent demands made by David Dunbar Nasmith backed by his commanding officer, Rupert Egan. He allowed no concessions or departure from standard naval routine or protocol, the ship always entered harbour with her ship's company manning the sides and fallen in dressed in the correct rig of the day; no matter that the ship may have been pursued to the very portals of Malta by enemy aircraft, the ship's company cursing the name and origins of the First Lieutenant, would be piped to clean out of action stations and sea rig into No 3 dress or tropical rig, depending on the time of the year and the station orders. In harbour, unless stores or ammunition were being embarked, men on the upper deck and duty men always had to be in the dress laid down in the Malta and flotilla standing orders. If the ship was in harbour on a Sunday, the Captain's rounds of mess-decks and flats were carried out, with particular attention to the standards of cleanliness of all living spaces; at regular intervals David saw that Rupert carried out the routine commanding officer inspections of the armament and upper-deck, magazines, stores, engine-room and boiler-rooms.

The chore of changing into and out of working/action rig and into the No 3 blue uniform eased a little for *Petard*'s men when on 13th May, station orders not only carried the news of the North African surrender but also the welcome fact that tropical rig, white shirts and shorts would be the dress for the ships of the fleet and shore stations. The dedicated emphasis on good order and naval discipline was a constant source of tooth sucking by the ship's company, but the First Lieutenant's insistence on maintaining a strict and pusser naval routine, nevertheless kept the ship that was under maximum pressure, in a high state of fighting effectiveness and morale.

Saturday 15th found *Petard* with *Isis* and *Queen Olga* back on patrol between Cape Bon and Pantellaria to scoop up any escapees that may still be trying to get back to Sicily and to stop reinforcements to the islands, at the same time relieving off patrol, the *Miaoulis*, a Greek manned 'Hunt' class destroyer, and two other 'Hunts', *Dulverton* and *Exmoor*. On Sunday *Petard* picked up four half-dead Germans who were floating in a raft of metal buoyancy containers. One of the frail scraps of barely living humanity was later discovered to have been a crewman in the merchant ship *Perseo* that his rescuers had helped to sink 12 days earlier. After surviving the sinking of his ship, the Italian hospital ship brought to the scene by the *Nubian* and the two 'Ps', had failed to pick him up. Two days later, days spent clinging to wreckage, a Sicilian caique found him.

The caique had been sunk a day later by the cannon fire from an Allied plane, and he with six companions, three Germans and three of the Sicilians manning the craft had launched and scrambled onto a raft. For seven days it had drifted in the Sicilian channel its occupants able to see many patrolling vessels and scores of low flying aircraft without in turn being spotted. As day succeeded day, three of the men on the raft died.

Doc Prendergast somehow salvaged the lives of the four who were lifted out of the raft, each was so weak that they had not been able to fend off the sea birds that had started to treat them as dead flotsom; where flesh was exposed, the birds had pecked away at the still living bodies. The little merchantman had suffered most, his mouth and face had been badly mutilated by the beaks of the sea birds, but even he was slowly weaned back from the brink of death by the tender care of the doctor and his sickbay attendant; nourishment fed by using a glass fountain pen filler helped Prendergast to keep his patient alive.

On Monday a landing party of twenty armed men went ashore at Zembra, the party leaving *Petard* in the motor cutter towing the port whaler. There was no sign of life on the small island, it had been vacated some days earlier by the men who had manned the enemy signal installation, leaving abandoned large quantities of food and stores. The day following, still on patrol, the three ships sighted smoke to the east, and closing at high speed intercepted and stopped a large German hospital ship on course for Pantellaria. *Petard* sent across the usual search party of ten men including a signalman, commanded by Robert de Pass. While the motor cutter covered the distance between the destroyer and the white painted hull of the ex-liner, the *Isis* and *Queen Olga* prowled round the area to discourage any adventurous enemy submarine from intervening.

Small indications in the behaviour of those on board the hospital ship warned that perhaps all was not as it should be in the vessel flying the Red Cross flag. Activity on the bridge caused suspicion in *Petard*, messengers could be seen to arrive and depart in rapid turn to all parts of the ship, there was also some considerable delay in providing the boarding party facilities to board the ship. No gangway ladder had been lowered, or entry port opened, and it required a threatening gesture from the destroyer training her armament onto the hospital ship before a chain jumping ladder was finally lowered for Robert to lead his party climbing the towering side of the stopped ship. Once in the hospital ship a signal came quickly from the boarding party which caused little surprise; a number of men who were clearly not seamen, dressed in make-shift civilian clothes had been found and were suspected to be members of the armed services, as they were not wounded. Rupert Egan ordered Robert to get the hospital ship under way immediately to proceed to Malta for detailed interrogation; this after some delay and difficulty was carried out, without the boarding party having to use force.

Underway and realising that the game was up with no possible chance of escape from the guns and torpedoes of the three destroyers, the nature of the illegal operation of the ship masquerading under the Red Cross flag became revealed; before the ship entered Malta at 2300/18th a complete company of uniformed German infantrymen supported by numbers of technical support troops emerged from their hiding places between decks. A considerable amount of ammunition and automatic weapons as well as demolition explosives were also later found when the ship search had been completed in St Paul's Bay.

The day and night battering of the Pantellarian defences continued unabated; daylight bombing from British and American aircraft only rarely disturbed in their missions by enemy fighters from Sicily, continued the unrelenting destruction of the life support for the garrison and island population. Accurate fire from the Italian manned AA gun batteries that greeted the first of the mass raids soon declined as the sites were gradually one by one, as day succeeded day, reduced and then eliminated. By night, every night, a cruiser with destroyer support pounded the coastal battery positions, town and harbour installations and defences; the islanders' ordeal of days and nights without respite spent in deep tunnels used as shelters, was similar to the long torment endured by the Maltese which only ended with the lifting of the siege after the arrival of convoys MW 13 and 14.

Petard's next turn on the bombarding club runs, came after she had returned from an unexpected and uneventful offensive sweep north up the east coast of Sicily as far as Catania, in company with her new flotilla master, Captain D14 in *Jervis*.

Troubridge with *Petard* sailed as escort for the cruiser *Orion* during the afternoon of 30th May to carry out a joint operation with aircraft dropping flares to illuminate the target area, the town and protecting gun batteries. The time for the rendezvous with the Albacores was 0100/31st with the bombarding ships to be in position 10,000 yards from the harbour entrance. Precisely on 0100 the first flare exploded in the dark sky 2000 feet above the town, drifting slowly down preceded by a long tail of falling bright star like sparks. From this first flare a long line quickly appeared at 150 yard intervals, of other flares parallel to the sea, lighting up the town, the steep hillsides and cliffs with a hard harsh brilliant white light. The positions of the coastal batteries could be seen as black slits in the near vertical white bare cliff slopes. Bursts of anti-aircraft shells appeared in the sky to deter the Albacores and tracer streams mounted towards the flares as the defenders tried to douse them.

At 0110 on 1st June *Orion* opened up with a full broadside of eight 6 inch guns from her four turrets and until 0200 fired 150 salvoes into the island and harbour defences as planes flew back and across the target area dropping a continuous series of flares, bathing the town and harbour in an intense white light.

Petard inshore from the bombarding cruiser added her own contribution to the battering of the shore installations and coastal gun sites; she patrolled across the harbour entrance, deafened by the roar of *Orion*'s broadsides and the double echoes coming back off the steep terrain. The destroyer was so close that the director gun control through their optical instruments could see in the windows that still remained intact in the town, reflection of the ships gun flashes. Many of *Petard*'s rapidly fired salvoes of semi-armour piercing (SAP) shells, because of the flat trajectory of the high velocity naval ammunition, ricocheted off the harbour and town targets to bound up the steep hillside and valley to explode among the distant rocks and buildings. Some crashed and exploded in the white square flat roofed houses that crowded down to the harbour to cause the destroyers gun control team agonising fears for any civilians who may not be sheltering in the deep hillside galleries.

The opposition fired only a few salvoes in retaliation, most wild and none straddled the bombarding vessels. At 0200 the flare dropping ceased, with the return of darkness over the town and harbour, the ships retired leaving a few fires burning ashore.

The force entered Malta at 0600 to fuel and reammunition, and for *Petard* a brief pause before sailing at Noon as the only escort for the cruiser *Penelope*. The two ships approached the gun batteries that had been attacked earlier that day, *Petard* finding herself back and approaching the same main gun batteries but this time in broad daylight, while the island defences were being distracted by a heavy attack from a mixed force of twenty American and British bombers, who in turn were being harassed by about six Me 109s flown in from Sicily. Great clouds of dust and smoke rose from the bomb explosions in the town and harbour, while the islands few AA guns still in service added to the general uproar that came down the wind to the ships closing in to renew the bombarding of the coastal guns.

Shortly before reaching the turning point on a pre-planned course for bombarding, *Petard* took station ahead of *Penelope*, 3 cables; the guns of 1,4,5 and 6 batteries who had spotted the ships closing in with guns and turrets obviously trained for engaging the shore targets, opened fire with uncomfortably accurate 3.7″ and 6″ fire. At 1830 *Penelope* returned the fire from her forward turrets sending 6 inch four gun salvoes directed at the barracks and No 2 battery area, scoring immediate hits. This battery returned two salvoes then went silent; the other batteries high up in the cliff face and some behind and above the town continued to fire with considerable determination, straddling both the ships as they turned in succession to fire full broadsides.

At a range of 6000 yards much to the relief of the gun crews, who were getting anxious while the ship held her fire as the range shortened, *Petard* joined in with her smaller 4 inch gun power, but with a higher rate of salvoes. From this point, the nearest to the targets, the two ships commenced to lay heavy smoke screens to retire behind just as the heaviest of the island guns 11 inch No 5 battery began to get the range of the *Penelope*. The cruiser and destroyer broke off the engagement still pouring out a dense barrier of smoke to mask their retirement towards Malta as one 11 inch shell plunged in without exploding through *Penelope*'s quarter-deck. The shell drove through compartments aft, and out of the ship's side without causing serious damage or affecting speed or manoeuvrability; the mighty shells continued to follow the ships out to 16,000 yards, falling to port and starboard, sudden narrow pillars of spray rose up from the sea to mark where the shells fell, some ahead after passing over the fleeing ships with a roaring scream. The exhilarating pursuit finished without further damage.

Petard left *Penelope* at the beginning of the swept channel into Malta Grand Harbour and joined with *Paladin* to escort the troop assault ships *Princess Beatrice* and *Royal Ulsterman* ordered to rendezvous with a command ship *Largs*. The group of ships moved between Sfax and Sousse for the next three days, the 3rd, 4th and 5th, and the sight of large numbers of landing craft exercising the embarkation and landing of troops convinced the ship's company that they were taking part in rehearsals for a final assault on the islands of the Sicilian Channel. The facts were still unknown to the men and ships taking part, the type of terrain should have given the clue; the low desert and Tunisian coast was being used to prepare for a much greater enterprise, Operation Husky, the invasion of Sicily.

On the evening of the 5th, *Petard* and *Paladin* were ordered to return to Malta, leaving as the assembled shipping exercising off Sfax was attacked by eleven Me 109s, a hurried half-hearted attack causing little damage, but one of the Mes was shot down. The two ships arrived back into Malta at 1700 hoping to give leave only to find that this could not be, the ships had to remain at one hour's notice for steam. 1300/7th the two 'Ps' sailed for intensive patrolling round Pantellaria and out to Cape Bon and Marittimo. The patrols during the 8th produced nothing; although there were several reports from air reconnaissance sightings of some shipping moving along the north coast of Sicily towards the Marittimo area, but none appeared to venture round the western tip of the Sicilian mainland.

The number of floating mines in the seas surrounding Pantellaria seemed to grow daily, almost hourly, the entire stretch of water between North Africa and Sicily was thickly covered, many were equipped with antennae, a particular threat with the long tentacle like antennae floating on the sea around and attached to the parent mine, as if groping for the passing ship. During the day unless the sea was rough and broken the mines were fairly easy to spot, but at night there could only be hope and a trust in luck.

After another daylight search that produced no enemy shipping on the night of the 9th, *Paladin* and *Petard* stood in close to Pantellaria harbour looking for craft that air reconnaissance had reported longside after successfully giving the Sicilian Channel patrol and the blockading ships the slip. *Petard* with torpedo tubes trained outboard moved in to the entrance of the small harbour, with her guns engaging the now reduced coastal batteries who tried to oppose her approach; the ship's pom-pom smothered one attempt by a small searchlight to illuminate the destroyer. No worthwhile target could be seen in the harbour, the reported craft had gone; *Petard* withdrew without firing a torpedo and rejoined *Paladin* who had been covering her from attack from seaward. The two destroyers linked up as a small force of E-boats, probably not more than four, roared in from the north to attack the blockaders. A confused running action developed with the few guns that still remained serviceable in the coastal batteries lobbing in the random shell at the melée taking place in the mine-littered waters some two to three miles out, to menace friend and foe alike. The location was marked by streams of tracer fire exchanged between the E-boats and destroyers; much ammunition was expended but without damage having been suffered by the 'Ps', the E-boats broke off the engagement retiring to the north without any seen to have been sunk or badly damaged.

Moving west, continuing their patrol between Cape Bon and Marittimo the destroyers located a Walrus flying boat down on the sea, forced down just before dark through problems with its single thrust propeller engine. The crew had streamed a sea anchor and the small amphibian had ridden out a moderate night sea without serious difficulty. By 0630/10th *Petard* had the flying boat in tow and on course for Bizerta with *Paladin* still in company as additional AA and AS cover.

The tow completed successfully and the Walrus handed over to a harbour launch the two destroyers returned at speed to be on station again by nightfall, remaining on patrol round the island until 1130 when both ships with the aid of flare dropping Albacores were ordered to commence a long nuisance series of bombardment on the harbour defences and coastal battery positions still remaining active. Through the middle watch until 0430 the ships discharged at intervals four gun salvos at a wide range of targets ashore, starting a few small fires and perhaps putting one or two defence posts out of action, but achieving the main objective, denying rest to the hard pressed garrison. The 'Ps' withdrew to the west without encountering any effective opposition and were rounding Cape Bon bound for Bizerta as an invasion task force, under the command of Vice-Admiral Roderick McGrigor flying his flag in *Orion* appeared off Pantellaria.

Operation Corkscrew started with a massive final bombardment from the four cruisers of the 15th Cruiser Squadron and the eight escorting destroyers. The bombardment supported by attacks from the desert air force bombing force commenced at first light, while from accompanying assault boats a strong mixed force of Royal Marines and Army units swarmed ashore. They were met at first by strong and spirited resistance from prepared defences, but by 1137 a large number of white flags began to appear in the town, harbour and defence positions; at 1211 the governor, an Italian Admiral signalled, 'Beg to surrender through lack of water.' Shortly afterwards Admiral McGrigor accepted the formal surrender from the Governor and Garrison Commander. There were 21,000 people on the island, and for the last three days, under the baking June sun of the Mediterranean, the islanders and garrison had been without food or water.

The task force moved on, at 2245 the ships of the 15th Cruiser Squadron were in position off Lampedusa Island and commenced to bombard. The assault from the sea, joined as soon as daylight returned, by the desert bombing force, continued as the last overwhelming bombardment until 1800/12 when the garrison asked to be allowed to surrender.

Earlier *Nubian* with *Troubridge* arrived off Linosa, to find the garrison of 150 men in poor shape, they were dirty, poorly disciplined, with low morale and eager to surrender. The garrison commander had apparently given up long ago and retired to his bed he needed a great deal of persuasion to emerge and surrender his command.

The four destroyers of the late 12th Destroyer Flotilla, who with the *Nubian*, *Jervis* and others, had shared the continuous patrolling of the heavily mined Sicilian Straits to deny the escape of the Axis Armies from North Africa, the final actions of Operation Retribution, the weeks of island bombardments, were not present at the surrender. Their ships' companies were angry and frustrated when press releases failed to mention their ships, only the names of the recent arrivals from the UK who appeared in time for the last assault made the headlines.

Queen Olga and *Isis* were at Sousse rehearsing for Husky; *Paladin* and *Petard* fuelling and replenishing depleted magazines after the last of the night bombardments, were in Bizerta.

CHAPTER 7

Husky, Avalanche and more Club Runs

Men of the two 'Ps' still in Bizerta, were disappointed and angry that their ships had not been mentioned in the BBC overseas broadcasts announcing the successful conclusion of Operations Retribution and Corkscrew. It was not a simple issue of not being granted a share in the victory, but a missed and rare opportunity for friends and relatives to know where the ships were operating. The strict censorship of letters home prevented giving this information to anxious families.

It was ironic that once the moment of glory had gone, the ships who had helped carry out the long advance softening up operations, returned to the scene to clear up. On the day following the surrender of the Pantellaria garrison, *Petard* with *Paladin* and an armed trawler departed from Bizerta escorting a large merchantman loaded with supplies for the starving islanders. Arriving off the harbour in worsening weather, the merchantman found it impossible to enter because of damage caused by bombing and the long naval bombardment. The port clearance party found great difficulty working with the seas outside causing a bad swell inside the harbour which impeded work on the obstructions blocking the small port.

The supply ship, trawler and destroyers as AS and AA guard ships, lay off waiting for a signal calling in the merchantman to discharge her cargo of urgently needed food and other supplies. Hove to, in brilliant sunshine, plunging into white capped seas getting steadily rougher with a wind increasing in strength from the west, the four ships waited under the guns of the now silent coastal batteries high up in the cliffs and brown barren hills steeply rising up and away from the small town and harbour.

The delay lengthened into the night through into the following day, when an air attack by six Ju 88s developed. The attackers came from airfields less than 100 miles away on the Sicilian mainland; approaching from the east the planes flying in tight formation came in to deliver a high level and deliberate attack on the merchantman.

The two 'Ps' moved in close to their protégé and countered with controlled high angle fire that effectively broke up the formation causing the planes to release bombs in uncoordinated sticks. Great mounds of white brown eruptions of water and spray, several times the mast height of the pitching, rolling ships, filled the sea surrounding the small group. The formation broke up and for the next quarter of an hour the planes made individual shallow dives, dropping sticks of two to three bombs without effect. The destroyers fired an intense short barrage from their 4 inch main armament, backed by the close range weapons, supported by the trawlers and merchantman's smaller guns, holding off the German aircraft without great difficulty. The Ju 88s seemed almost furtive in their attacks, as if expecting a sudden fighter counter attack from over the mountain that dominated the small harbour and sea threshold, but this did not materialise until the bombers had broken off the abortive attack, and had started back to base.

The obstructions in the harbour obstinately resisted efforts of the clearance teams, hampered by the worsening swell, it seemed certain that the ships would have to ride out the storm for a further night. Minefields round the island prevented the ships taking shelter under the lee of the land mass, the mines also limited the area in which they could steam or lie heaved to. Supplies were now so critical to the island that the supply ship had to remain on station ready to enter the harbour as soon as it was feasible to do so.

The ships continued to wait for the signal summoning the supply carrier, but with dwindling hopes that they would be released from the vigil, the evening wore on, and with darkness hope died. At 0600/16th, the Germans returned, this time a squadron of eight Ju 87 Stukas had taken over from the Ju 88s. In the short sharp engagement that followed *Petard* was near missed twice aft by two successive direct attacks on the ship. Only Rupert Egan's skill in taking avoiding action in particularly difficult circumstances when his movements were restricted by the need to keep close to the supply ship, saved the ship being hit. The misses were close enough to cause leaks from strained plates and rivets, and for bomb splinters to tear holes in the ship side.

The tiller flat and steering gear became flooded, which spread into the spirit room and clothing store; the flooding aft was serious only because of the now gale force wind and very rough sea conditions. The Stukas continued to try to break through the destroyer gun defences and may well have succeeded, the pitching violence of the ships made highly unstable and wet platforms for the sailors to fight their guns, but for the timely arrival of Spitfires from Cape Bon area who put the dive bombers to flight.

Petard's bilge pumps and emergency pumping equipment just coped with the sea inflow aft, but a run to Malta for repairs downwind with a following sea, would be a risky undertaking. Rupert Egan reported the damage to VA Malta and received orders to proceed westward to the captured former French Fleet base at Bizerta for emergency repairs.

The weather continued gale force winds and very rough seas, but Rupert was able to head his ship almost directly into the weather, without the weakened stern receiving further damage from the elements, and made good progress for Cape Blanc leaving *Paladin* on station outside **Pantellaria**. The ship arrived at Bizerta at 1830 that evening, with a ship's company relieved to get into calm waters, while the gale blew itself out later that night.

Early, soon after first light, the port naval repair party appeared longside in a launch with equipment to help Bertie, with his artificers and shipwrights, to seal plates and rivets, and to weld patches over some ten holes in the plating. Good progress continued through the day, and by evening Rupert reported that his ship was fit to sail as soon as the sea had moderated.

Bizerta still received raids from the enemy who had retreated from the African mainland, these came mainly at night while the sky was clear and the moon bright; on these nights the shore AA defences and ships in harbour remained alert at defence stations. *Petard* at two watch defence stations settled down hopefully for a quiet night in harbour, with those on watch wary as the moon climbed into another clear sky. The middle watch had nearly run its course, and the bosun's mate on his rounds of the darkened hammock festooned messdecks piping to call the sleeping watch below into reluctant wakeful reality, to turn out and relieve the watch on deck, engine, boiler rooms; radar and w/t offices now in their turn anxious and ready for their hammocks.

A wild shout up the voice pipe to the bridge had the officer of the watch instantly listening with a finger on the action stations alarm rattler button, another on the Captain's call bell; while the radar watchkeeper tried to make a fast coherent report of aircraft echos close, and coming in fast; sirens wailed ashore, at the moment that the OOW pressed the alarm button, dive bombers screamed down onto the harbour.

The rattlers sounded their harsh frightening URGENT alarm as two bombs in rapid succession near missed *Petard*'s stern, throwing the ship aft into the air with a terrifying lurch, spraying the quarter deck and iron deck with a hail of steel splinters, at the same time driving through the ship's side a little forward of the patches covering the holes made by the near misses off Pantellaria. Splinters punctured fuel tanks, stores and the port magazine aft, also ripping to shreds the bunk in the First Lieutenant's cabin vacated seconds earlier by David Dunbar Nasmith.

The ship started to take on a list to port and below decks lighting failed as the generators came off the power control board. Forward in the watchkeeper's mess, the small messdeck below the main seamen's mess on the main deck and immediately aft of the chain locker and paint stores, there was some confusion but no panic in the dim glimmer of the emergency lighting. Some of the off watch, signal, telegraphist, radar and asdic members of the mess had been sleeping on mess tables that collapsed with the wild leap of the ship, onto messmates sleeping on small ship camp beds underneath. At the same time several hammocks tipped the occupants out into semi-darkness, and the debris of broken tables and tangled bedding. The men in the shambles of the wrecked, crowded and dark compartment now heeling over at 10 degrees, with the crash of recoiling 4 inch 'B' gun overhead, without any trace of panic, with speed and the almost casual discipline of the action experienced and hardenèd seamen, found their way up the emergency ladder and away to their action stations.

Two men had been wounded by the splinters that swept the decks, as they ran along the iron deck to man 'Y' gun on the quarter deck; the fact that the ship only manned 'B' and 'X' guns at defence stations prevented a second slaughter of the quarterdeck's gun crew in the hail of bomb shrapnel. The Royal Fleet auxiliary *Agatha* had been hit and now on fire, the flames exposed the ships in harbour to the plunging Stukas; in spite of the bad list, *Petard*'s main and close range weapons were now pouring out a furious barrage in her own defence and in support of the shore based AA gun batteries engaging the Ju 87s picked out in the ranging beams of the massed searchlights.

While the guns were fought from decks that continued to list further to port, damage control parties struggled to seal flooding spaces, and to organise counter flooding to stop the steady and worsening settle down by the stern and heel to port. 'Malaya'

MacAllen's torpedo-men had restored power to the gun control equipment that now helped the defence of the ship. The raiders withdrew quickly without inflicting further damage, leaving *Agatha* and *Petard* to gain control of their respective fires and flooding.

With the cease fire of the AA defences, the gun crews and torpedo men began to shift upper deck weights to help the counter flooding. The starboard whaler and motor cutter were turned outboard on the davits as additional counterweight, ammunition in the upper-deck ready use lockers transferred from port to the starboard side, fuel tanks on the port side had fuel pumped across to fill the opposite tanks. All hands remained on watch and work, proceeded in departments to clean up below decks, repairing at the same time much of the equipment damaged by splinters and the ship's violent leap. The ship's company breakfasted, and at 0800 the ship weighed anchor, still with a 5 degree list to port and moved under her own power up the Bizerta canal to the inland lagoon behind the city. Here with the assistance of the base staff, the flooded compartments were pumped out and a reverse list simulated.

A fresh crop of splinter holes and strained plates below the waterline were exposed, allowing Bertie and his hard pressed team to get to work with the base party to make the hull sufficiently watertight for a return to Malta dockyard. The counter-list to starboard put the ship out of action for some hours, and except for the port side close range weapons it was impossible to man the armament; while the ship depended on the port's AA defence, parties of 20-30 men were allowed ashore to stretch their legs round the perimeter of the lagoon or to swim in its clear warm water.

One party skylarking in the shallows with a couple of fighter bomber, torpedo shaped, long range fuel tanks, using them as floats and substitutes for beach toys, spotted Rupert's slightly hunched and stocky figure walking along the beach. He stopped, standing leaning on his walking stick, the uniform cap with slightly larger than regulation peak that he always wore, jammed down on his short necked head, watched his men relaxing. One or two of the bolder extroverts called out to him to join them; with a light hearted wave from his walking stick Rupert acknowledged the invitation before resuming alone, his short break from the crushing pressure that was the lot of an officer commanding a fleet destroyer at war.

The two men who had been hurt in the raid, had both received painful but not serious flesh wounds, they had been landed before moving up the canal, for treatment in an Army base hospital in Algeria. All were sorry to see the popular Tanky go, he had the misfortune of having a large piece of his buttock sliced off by a bomb splinter that caught him while assisting the Buffer reeling up the falls of the port whaler, when the Stukas jumped the ship.

Later on the evening of 19th June at 2000 hours after Bertie had reported that the ship was again seaworthy, *Petard* sailed for Malta for more permanent repairs arriving next day at 1100 to find the entire base on its toes, HM King George VI was on the island. At 1600 the ship entered dry dock for plate repairs and replacement of damaged pipe and cable runs that had been severed or temporarily repaired after the series of near misses aft; remaining there until the 25th then continuing a self refit until the 30th.

During this spell everyone had 48 hours at the rest camp, and despite the fact that beer, food and above all else female company was scarce, all took the opportunity of relaxing for a few hours away from the ship. Even those who remained on board working to restore *Petard*'s fighting efficiency, found that a few air-raids did not prevent the enjoyment of small diversions, including swimming naked in the clear water of Hospital Creek, creating interest for the off duty nurses resting and sunbathing on the cliff top; this rated high in Telegraphist Neil Allen's and other members of the watchkeepers' mess off duty occupations.

While enjoying the brief break at the rest camp and Malta dockyard, all the ship's company were aware and affected by the general uplift in morale and optimism following the complete defeat of the Axis armies in North Africa and the collapse of the 'impregnable' island fortresses in the Sicilian straits. The grinding day and night air attacks at sea and in harbour had eased; the ascending effectiveness of shipborne AA gunfire and the support of the now dominent allied air power was an accepted fact. The purpose of the embarkation and landing exercises that the ship had shared at Sousse and Sfax began to make sense, and now that at Malta, specialist shipping began to appear in considerable numbers, headquarter ships, troop and tank landing craft, quantities of assault ships of many shapes and sizes, they created rumours and speculation on the probable location of an Allied invasion into Europe. Speculations ranged almost the length of the Mediterranean, Corsica, Sardinia, Sicily, Italy and even Greece, but a decision had already been made some time ago, the planning for Operation Husky was well advanced.

Petard's part in the detailed plan was in a minor role, perhaps because of the succession of near miss damage she was considered as a doubtful starter for nomination as an escort at the invasion beaches and left out, so with no one except perhaps Rupert Egan aware of imminence of D-Day, the ship passed out through the boom from Malta at 1900/1st July bound for Gibraltar, it was almost as if the ship had been ordered home, the ship's company were jubilant. Steaming westward through smooth warm seas with a colour that matched the vivid blue of the sky, at 25 knots and alone, the ship creamed a straight path through an area free from the serious threat of air or surface attack; again buzzes of an escort job back to the UK and a major refit lifted the hearts of the married men in particular, and were not dispelled until after the arrival at the Rock. The ship entered Gibraltar at 1600/3rd and berthed onto the battleship *King George V*, and leave was given to one watch.

For one libertyman, telegraphist Neil 'Darby' Allen it was an opportunity to see his father Chief Petty Officer Allen stationed at the naval radio station; they had not seen each other since before the outbreak of hostilities in 1939. Neil telephoned from the battleship's w/t office and received a happy and surprised invitation from his father to join him in the Chief's mess ashore and to help the mess sample part of a recently arrived consignment of crated beer, Whitbreads. Before seeing his father, and because he was also a regular, ex-Greenwich school and boy telegraphist entrant, son of a CPO Telegraphist RN, Neil called into a barber shop to have his hair trimmed. This had barely started, he had been in the chair for a few minutes only when the town patrol entered calling for all *Petard* libertymen to return to the ship immediately. He returned to the ship to find that she was under orders to sail at one hour's notice; a fresh call to the Rock's radio station brought CPO Allen down to the *Petard* for the only occasion that father and son were together for the entire war.

Although the ship remained under orders to sail she did not leave until noon next day, then proceeded towards the Atlantic to escort an incoming convoy of troop ships back to a position off Gibraltar where the ship waited for the battleships *Howe* and *King George V*. When the two great ships moved out they were preceded by three 'Ps' meeting for the first time their destroyer sister, *Petard*. *Pathfinder*, *Penn* and *Panther* with *Jervis*, *Tyrian* and *Arrow* made up the seven fleet destroyer escort for the first division of Force H capital ships moving east to rendezvous off Algiers with the remainder of the force, battleships *Nelson* and *Rodney*, the aircraft carrier *Indomitable* and attendant fleets linked up with the division from Gibraltar at 0800/6th; the complete Force H continued eastward, moving past Cape Bon down towards the area off Sousse.

The fleet surrounded by 16 destroyers turned east from Sousse keeping clear of the great convoys moving towards Sicily on a precise and complicated time schedule. These convoys were converging from the east and west as well as moving up from the south, the anchorages off the captured Tunisian and Tripolitanian coast. *Formidable* provided the air cover and reconnaissance probes for the fleet while it moved in wide sweeps north into the Ionian sea to interpose between possible moves from the Italian fleet towards the invasion convoys.

In pairs and singly the destroyers detached to fuel; *Petard*'s turn came on 8th when she entered Malta to refuel, leaving as soon as completed to rejoin the battle fleet. It now became possible to tell the ship's company that an invasion was to take place in the SE corner of Sicily and that D-Day was to be the 10th. Under the direction of the Supreme Allied Commander, General Dwight Eisenhower, the American 7th Army was to land along the coast between Licata and Scoglitti centred on GELA and drive through the centre of the island to the north coast, while the British Eighth Army had to land each side of the cape forming the SE corner of the island, Cape Passero, with the premier task of capturing Syracuse, Augusta, Catania and then drive on to Messina completing the capture of Sicily.

The men manning *Petard* knew little of the details of the Husky invasion plans, nothing about the objectives, timetable of landings or the composition of the sea, land and air forces taking part. There was no policy then of briefing men manning the ships of the fleet, and it is doubtful whether Rupert Egan or any of the subordinate commanders of ships and units knew much beyond their immediate objectives. *Petard* had a chance that was denied to the remainder of the fleet; after pushing north during the night of the 10th to ward off any move the Italian Fleet may have contemplated to disrupt the invasion convoys moving towards the landing beaches, then turning south again during the daylight of the 11th, the ship received orders at 1600 to leave the fleet and proceed to Malta with all despatch, fuel and stand by for a special job.

The ship arrived, refuelled and stood by ready at immediate notice to sail at 1000 after landing four exhausted German airmen who had been picked up out of the sea during the middle watch. At midnight led by a Staff Captain representing the Commander in Chief Mediterranean a small mixed party of American and British Army and Air Officers embarked, and the ship went to action stations with hands at stations to leave harbour. The ship stood by with wires singled up ready to slip for the next two hours, then at 0200, Vice-Admiral Malta's barge swept in longside the Mediterranean ladder and the Supreme Commander, General Dwight Eisenhower climbed onto the iron deck following by his naval, air and army aides; the ship slipped and sailed direct to the invasion beaches to the west of Cape Passero.

Steaming north the ship passed through waters where hundreds of British airborne soldiers had drowned in their gliders 48 hours earlier, cut adrift from the towing air tugs by inexperienced, confused and mainly American pilots. On the evening of the 9th, 144 glider tugs left a number of airfields in North Africa, 109 American C47's and 35 British Albemarles towing Horsa and Waco gliders packed with highly trained élite British airborne soldiers. As dusk closed in over the sea a gale began to blow that tested and strained the airmanship of the tug pilots; by the time the great air fleet reached Cape Passero, some pilots had lost their way, others buffeted by the high wind were confused and lost contact with their squadrons, and turned back to Africa.

In the darkness over the land, almost all the pilots failed to identify the glider release points. Unbelievably in a situation of almost utter confusion 115 gliders were released blindly; 1200 men in the prime of their manhood were abandoned by the towing craft, half the gliders fell into a night angry foam covered sea, all but a handful perished. Just 54 gliders out of the 144 that set out, landed on Sicily, and only 12 near the planned landing zone; instead of 1200 men, less than 100 made their way to the objective of the airborne operation, a bridge south of Syracuse called Ponte Grande.

A hint of the disaster, but with none of the details, which were then still only suspected, leaked from some of General Eisenhower's entourage, to the crew of the *Petard*, filling almost all with an angry horrified gloom, so it was with a sense of relief to find on arrival at the first main British beach Pachino at 0600 signs of a successful landing. The sight and sound of battle was slight, what there was came from inland well away from the beachhead. In the light of a beautiful morning, the crowded bay was full of the ordered movement of support troops and stores out of the anchored transports to the beach. The attendant warships fired only occasionally in response to requests of distant forward observation officers with the advancing troops, to dislodge pockets of enemy still holding out.

Petard did not anchor, an assault craft moved longside embarked the Supreme Commander and his staff, leaving quickly to transport the party to the headquarters ship *Largs* to confer with General Montgomery and the Naval Commander Force B, Rear Admiral McGrigor. Meanwhile *Petard*, moving slowly through the shipping in the anchorage waiting for a recall to take the General to other parts of the British Sector, gave her crew a unique chance to watch the working of an invasion fleet, without being committed to a specific task. The conference in the *Largs* lasted only for an hour; shortly after the conclusion General Eisenhower returned to *Petard* for a high speed passage up the eastern side of Cape Passero into the Gulf of Noto and Porto Palo Bay, the beach area of the British 13th Corps and General Dempsey's headquarters ship *Hilary* at anchor off Avola. Here the same routine repeated itself, the Supreme Commander in Chief, leaving his destroyer transport to be briefed by his subordinate Field Commander and the Naval Commander Force V, Rear-Admiral Sir Philip Vian in his floating headquarters.

The sea around was crowded with about 1000 of the 3500 invasion ships that had carried the American and British Armies, and in the very calm waters of this assault area *Petard* watched the remarkable performance of the amphibian vehicle the DUKW. It was the first time that these vehicles had been seen by many of the ships and men of the East Mediterranean fleet, the sailors were impressed by the seamanship skills of the soldier crews.

General Eisenhower re-embarked and soon after 1200, he was on his way back to Malta. These were the first Americans seen at close hand by the *Petard*'s ship's company, they were almost to a man prejudiced by their limited contact with an ally whose airmen always seemed to make mistakes and were considered to be highly dangerous to have around. The obvious brash abundance of material and technical know-how fed the resentment felt because of the Americans' late entry into the war and the opinion that they had as a nation held off deliberately until the Britain had exhausted her Empire and mortgaged her worldwide assets, repeating the tactics of the 1914-18.

Eisenhower and his American staff during their brief visit did something to change the *Petard*'s attitude, the relaxed and seemingly casual manner of these senior officers, particularly with junior officers and ratings, made a considerable impression. Speech and methods of address were in complete contrast to that used by many senior and regular members of the Royal Navy. When General Eisenhower asked a member of the bridge staff to assist him adjust the focus of binoculars lent to him, and explained, 'I guess I got bum eyesight', the Allied Supreme Commander did much towards getting his countrymen accepted and it became the ship's catch phrase for a very long time afterwards.

The destroyer entered Grand Harbour in the early evening, after landing the General, had a night in, leaving again next day to rejoin the battle fleet in the Ionian Sea. As she left, *Eskimo* the tribal class destroyer limped in with damage in her gearing room from German dive bomb attacks. The battle fleet received attention several times during the 13th from German bombing and torpedo aircraft; the attacks were carried out by small groups, that early on in the day fled before the counter attacks from fighters flown off from the aircraft carrier *Formidable*. During the afternoon while the ships of the fleet again held off further attacks, *Formidable* suffered a torpedo hit from a submarine which undetected had placed itself in a position to strike at the capital ships. The carrier's airborne reconnaissance and fighter aircraft were ordered to make for Malta, while the *Formidable* was able to follow and made harbour safely.

That same evening, Captain D14 in *Jervis*, taking *Penn* and *Petard*, received orders to leave the battle fleet screen, to close the coast and bombard the coastal road between Catania and Misterbianco. Two other destroyers, the *Echo* and *Ilex* not at that time with the main fleet, were ordered to join the group, but on the way came across an Italian submarine which they sank after a short engagement; 32 of the crew being picked up by *Echo* who was then ordered to land her prisoners at Malta, leaving only *Ilex* to join Captain D14 and the two 'Ps'.

The attack on the highway commenced soon after first light, at a point where the road ran along the edge of the coast for several miles. The road carried a fairly heavy flow of traffic in both directions, most of it military but some that seemed to be civilian lorry transport, when the four destroyers approached in line ahead, led by *Jervis* from the east at 90 degrees to the road.

Turning to starboard each destroyer opened fire in turn as they took up a course roughly parallel to the highway until all four ships were saturating the road and its verges for a distance of about a mile. In a few moments the vehicles were in a shambles, a few were hit and on fire, others abandoned by the crews and passengers now running to take cover in the fields away from the sea; many others turned into the roadside ditch, while at the portions of the road back to Catania and to Misterbianco not yet receiving attention from the naval guns lorries, tanks and cars were trying frantically to turn back away from the area under attack.

Before *Jervis* turned away back to the east, at least two of the tanks had opened up on the ships less than two miles out, firing solid shot that they carried for anti-tank fighting. One shell hit *Petard* above the water line, forward of the boiler room, passing out of the starboard side of the ship after drilling a neat hole through intervening bulkheads but without causing any casualty or damage to equipment and ship services.

The tanks had retired when Captain D14 turned the destroyers back for a second run at the highway, this time at the congestion point nearest Catania and a number of heavy military vehicles received hits, several catching fire.

This action on road communications from the sea was the first of many bombarding tasks that *Petard* now found herself engaged in over the next few weeks, either on her own or part of a small or larger task force. That evening of 15th July, *Jervis* led the same group in to bombard the airfield south of Catania shortly before British airborne troops captured the airbase. While the destroyers lobbed shells inland, *Petard* received attention from a lone Ju 88 torpedo bomber that approached from the dark side, from the east as dusk closed in. *Petard* the last ship in the line like the others concentrated on the task of firing at the target in the Catania plain, only received a brief warning from the radar watch that an identified target, that could only be a single plane was closing in a little abaft the starboard beam. Rupert Egan took no chances, under emergency helm he turned the ship 90 degrees to starboard towards the closing aircraft and escaped a torpedo whose track could be seen to miss the port side moments after the releasing plane flew out of the gloom over the ship.

It was a very narrow and fortunate escape from an almost certain hit if the ship had remained on her original bombarding course.

In the dark the destroyers rejoined the fleet still manoeuvering as a shield between the Italian fleet bases and the invasion beaches, but during the early part of the morning *Petard* again left, one of the destroyer screen detached to escort the battle ship *Warspite* out of Malta to bombard the city of Catania. *Warspite* wearing the flag of Rear-Admiral Force H, emerged from Grand Harbour Malta at 1329/17th to be joined by the waiting destroyer escort outside, *Faulknor, Fury, Eclipse, Inglefield, Raider, Queen Olga* and *Petard*, the last two the only East Mediterranean veterans in the operation.

The attack on the city commenced in the evening, the bombarding force operating under a massive Allied fighter umbrella. The damaged caused by the 15 inch shells from the *Warspite* was extensive, and could be seen at close range from the *Petard* who formed part of the screen close inshore, between *Warspite* and the targets in *Catania*.

At 1840 *Warspite* was in position 180 degrees Cape Molini light 10.45 miles, steering north 15 knots, closing the target, the northern half of Catania clear of the port area and railway station. The area was a triangle 1000 x 800 yards centred on the military barracks, with other military quarters on the NE and NW corners. The battleship opened fire at 1844, position 141 degrees Sciara Biscari light 13000 yards, salvoes fired at minute intervals. After A and B turrets fired eight 2 gun salvoes, *Warspite* altered course at 1850 to 020 degrees to allow 'X' and 'Y' turrets to fire six 2 gun salvoes from each turret. The bombarding finished at 1903. Yeoman Chapman described the attack in his diary:

> It was a terrific occurrence. The town is something like Portsmouth and we .were so close that we could see large buildings collapsing as the huge projectiles tore their way through them. Large hotels went up in dust, theatres were laid in complete ruin. We in *Petard* were heavily shelled from the shore but no damage was inflicted. Our CO must be after a medal, we went right inshore and as we approached the deadly screaming of shells tormented our ears – we got right in, blazing away with everything we had, then turned round and spewed a white and black smoke screen in order to prevent the shore batteries from hitting the *Warspite* who had finished and was belting away. She had fired about 100 tons of shell. We got rid of 40 broadsides, but

the slaughter of innocent people must have been awful; however that's war.

Petard's smoke screen as she retired from the harbour entrance where Rupert had placed his ship, caused the broadcaster from the German radio station reading a communique in English, to announce that a British destroyer had been hit several times at the harbour entrance to Catania, and was seen retiring on fire with dense smoke pouring from the ship prior to sinking.

The ship returned to Malta with *Warspite*, entering Sliema Creek during the last minutes of the 17th, to find that she had been detailed for emergency destroyer; no shore leave could be granted and the ship's company denied from discovering for themselves if there existed any truth in the buzz that beer supplies had improved. While at the emergency destroyer berth at short notice for steam, two more patches were welded on the ship's side over the entry and exit holes made by the German tank shell. The ship now had begun to gain a small reputation for the number of patches that were being earned from bomb and shell hits and near misses.

The next morning the ship returned to the scene of the bombardment carried out 48 hours earlier, this time one of four destroyers escorting the cruiser *Newfoundland* with orders to shell the railway station. Again *Petard* found herself on the inside berth, a hot position where shells from the bombarding force passed low overhead and the defending batteries tended to concentrate their fire. From this inshore station *Petard* found it possible to add her quota of destruction to the railway station, shells could be seen going in through the roof and soon flames appeared with the smoke that rose from in and around the station and rail junction. All the ships returned to Malta without suffering any damage, entering harbour at 1700 for a long evening refuelling and topping up magazines then to standby at short notice for steam.

It turned out to be a night of little rest, the enemy shattered all hopes of sleep by turning on the heaviest night air raid for several months, and succeeded in dropping a large number of bombs into the harbour area wrecking and damaging several stores and workshops in the dockyard, recently restored to service after destruction during the siege period. Some auxiliary craft were sunk and others damaged, but none of the warships in the harbour and creeks received direct hits, only a few had superficial damage from splinters and near misses.

The 15th Cruiser Squadron ships, *Aurora* and *Penelope*, with six destroyers *Troubridge*, Captain D24, *Piorun, Quilliam, Tumult, Offa* and *Petard* sailed from Malta at 0915/20th, to hug the Sicilian coast, then along the toe of Italy to bombard Cotrone on the heel of Italy at the south west entrance to the Gulf of Taranto.

CROTONL

During the fast passage north very many antennae mines were sighted causing the individual ships in the speeding formation to alter course and jink to avoid the deadly tentacles. By 2200 the squadron was passing six miles off Cape Spartivento and proceeding NE along the Calabrian coast. At 2300 a powerful searchlight•from *Locri* swept the sea and down the length of the squadron. The fact that the ships had been located was confirmed by a signal light on Cape Rizzuto challenging several times by flashing the letter CR.

At 0153 the *Aurora*, the flagship, passed through position 085 degrees Crotone, Group Flashing light, 6 miles, on a course of 330 degrees, steaming at 25 knots leading *Penelope* and the six destroyers in line astern and prepared to bombard. In the operation orders targets were allocated to ships as follows:—

Aurora	The chemical works north of the town.
Penelope	Harbour area to the west of the breakwater to a depth of 600 yards.
Troubridge *Piorun* }	North of *Penelope*'s area.
Quilliam *Tumult* }	South of *Penelope*'s area.
Offa *Petard* }	The battery on Cape Colonne until silenced, then the harbour.

Action started when the cruisers fired six salvoes of star shells to illuminate target areas and the town. Response ashore was immediate, anti-aircraft artillery opened fire at the falling flares perhaps mistaking them for flares dropped from aircraft to precede a bombing raid. *Offa* and *Petard* closed the shore battery positioned on the Cape, and having established the range by sighting salvoes pounded the coastal guns with devastating effect, the battery did not reply. The remainder of the squadron saturated the target areas starting large fires. Soon after, the squadron started the bombardment, Royal Air Force bombers attacked the air station close to the town, and this probably stopped any attempt to molest the ships. The engagement ceased without any opposition from shore guns or air attack, and only as the Vice-Admiral 15th Cruiser Squadron broke off the bombardment to retire back along the Calabrian coast that E-boats appeared briefly to follow the squadron without attacking.

The ships returned back to the Malta base without incident arriving at the boom at 1600 hrs; *Petard* had to replace 160 rounds of 4 inch ammunition fired into shore batteries and Crotone harbour.

While the ships rested during the following day, the cruiser *Newfoundland* entered slowly and listing, damaged by torpedo submarine attack; shortly afterwards *Petard* sailed to reinforce the destroyers carrying out anti-submarine sweeps off Syracuse where, the cruiser had been hit. For 36 hours the ships quartered the sea but found nothing, and early on the 24th *Petard* returned to Malta to give a night's leave to each watch.

In perfect hot Mediterranean weather the ship's company relaxed, swam and lazed in the sun, and played water polo against the ship's half section *Queen Olga* sharing the same 48 hour break. This short break spent with their Greek brothers-in-arms proved to be almost the last occasion the two ships would share time together; except meeting up at sea along the Sicilian coast and one or two short pauses longside the same tanker to fuel, the partnership was soon to be broken.

For the next few days, *Petard* joined Captain D24 in *Troubridge, Offa* and the Polish destroyer *Piorun* carrying out anti-submarine sweeps off Cape Mudra di Porco, Augusta and Syracuse. She rejoined the battleship fleet off Malta for exercises on the 30th, but had to retire back into Malta almost immediately with a hole in her bow and the sea flooding into the port forward magazine. *Petard* damaged herself while closing the fleet flagship *Warspite* to pass over despatches. As Rupert Egan approached from astern to place the port bow of his ship close to the Battleship's starboard quarter to allow the bag containing despatches to be transferred by line from the fo'c'sle of the destroyer to the flagship's quarterdeck, *Warspite* under a sudden and large amount of helm turned to port, driving her great armoured quarter into *Petard*'s slender and lightly plated bow. She entered Malta at 1600 wearing her new hole like a badge and moved into the now familiar dry dock for repairs. The bonus for the ship's company was a four day boiler clean giving each watch a break at the St Paul's Bay rest camp where things had improved.

By this time the *Petard*'s men had found that the rumour about increased beer stocks was true, the food had changed, there was more of it and the variety extended beyond the monotony of a corned beef, rice diet that had sustained the destroyers and cruisers based on Malta since the start of Operation Retribution. The arrival of the ships of the battle fleet, the Anglo-American Operation Husky planning and operational staffs, brought great convoys through from the west to restock the island and support the new arrivals. Above all else there were now members of the WRNS and many more nurses on the island; after many months *Petard*'s men found a rare chance to see and talk to an English speaking girl. The ship's Lotharios, long silent or reduced to reminiscences, frayed and dulled with retelling, now were again to be heard in the ship, claiming actual or imaginary conquests; life ashore had improved.

When *Petard* undocked on 5th August the British Eighth Army had finally driven the Hermann Göring Division out of Catania and the tough fighting to break the Italian/German Etna defence had succeeded. The American 7th Army following the northern road and coast line was now racing the British Eighth Army to capture Messina. The destroyers of the fleet were deployed to assist the desert army to achieve this objective; in sub-divisions of two ships, they operated a leap frog system along the coast northwards from Catania into the straits of Messina, straffing troops and vehicles whenever they could be seen on the coastal highway or landing special services troops behind the enemy lines.

Despite air and sea superiority the Allies failed to break the retiring enemy land formations, who behind well organised rearguard formations gradually moved into the final enclave west of Messina, saving most of their armour and transport from falling into either the British or American hands. The American airforce continued to frighten its friends as much as the enemy; bombing Canadian formations after they had succeeded in capturing Troina in the centre of the island following a hard and bloody battle; General Bradley commanding the American 7th Army received a forcible request to keep his airmen away from the British Army.

In stabbing assaults from the sea, *Petard* and *Queen Olga* were together for only one night raid, the last they were to share before the Greek received orders to return to Alexandria to refit.

The raid took place a little to the south of Taormina with the red glow from the volcano, Mount Etna, dominating the night enshrouded land as the ships cautiously closed the landing place where troops were to be landed from assault craft towed by the destroyers. The troops quickly left the two destroyers in a series of ferry trips made in powered landing craft, disappearing towards the black unseen shore, while *Petard* and *Queen Olga* stood by ready to lend fire support if called for by the naval forward observation officers who landed with the first troops. All remained quiet with only a brief confirmation about an hour later that all was well over the landing forces radio net.

Leaving the night raiders to penetrate inland to blow bridges and roads, slowing down the orderly retirement of the German divisions, the destroyers moved away from close proximity to the coast, *Petard* to remain on patrol while *Queen Olga* returned to Malta thence on to Alexandria. Later that same morning the Polish destroyer *Piorun* arrived to take *Petard* under her orders for a succession of sudden gun raids against any shore target that seemed worthwhile. The Pole was commanded by a Commander of tenacity and a ruthless determination to destroy the German enemy wherever he could be found. It was rumoured that the Polish commander had been a cavalry colonel of great distinction at the time of the German invasion of his country.

He commanded a ship of large silent taciturn men, few could speak any sort of English, all were consumed by an obvious and rather frightening hatred of the enemy who had raped their homeland and in many cases butchered families and friends. The crew of the *Piorun* were almost to a man older than *Petard*'s ship's company, and on the few occasions that ships berthed on each other during the short association working out of Syracuse, later Augusta and Catania, *Petard* found her allies unable to relax; men worked endlessly on ship maintenance and weapon overhaul, discipline also seemed unbending and rather grim. They contrasted sharply with the relaxed rather casual discipline and gaiety of the Greeks in *Queen Olga*, who despite their sufferings at the hands of both German and Italian invaders somehow found it possible to find laughter a way to ease their sorrow.

Piorun took *Petard* on a series of attacks at close quarters against troop transport and armoured vehicles as well as coastal defences; *Petard* following astern, behind the new senior officer, found herself often being straddled by enemy artillery with alarming accuracy after *Piorun* had pounced at targets, firing her six 4.7 guns on the three twin mountings, closing the range until the ship was endangered by grounding, only giving way at the last possible minute, turning away while *Petard* grimly holding station at $1\frac{1}{2}$ cables astern found when it came to her turn to turn away, the battered targets had often recovered sufficiently to range the turning point and straddle 'tail end Charlie' with retaliatory gunfire. The dangerous targets that were calculated to cause *Piorun*'s most determined efforts to destroy, were Tiger tanks of the Panzer Regiments, despite the fact that her 4.7 shells could do little more than give the tank crews a bad headache, even when direct hits were registered. Quite often *Petard* found the tanks firing back at almost point blank range when it came her turn to fire, only the high rate of fire from her smaller and less effective main armament in terms of destructive power, plastering the front and sides of the powerful land destroyers made the tank gunlayers falter with their aim at the lightly armoured fleet destroyer.

Piorun and her somewhat reluctant British half section scored a number of notable successes when troop and supply convoys were caught on cliff roads with little chance of escape into open country and large numbers of vehicles received hits and were set on fire. Freight trains also came under fire from the sea raiders along the coast north of Taormina, one carrying ammunition exploded with tremendous effect, spilling freight cars down the short cliff onto the foreshore. Other trains moving along the coastal line of the toe of Italy found themselves being shelled at close range from the two destroyers emerging out of the disappearing night.

Along this track that dived in and out of short and long tunnels the destroyers played a bizarre cat and mouse game as frantic train crews tried to hide in the tunnels, many of which were not long enough to take the entire train. Engine drivers would get the locomotive and first few cars into a tunnel leaving the remainder, like some great unprotected tail, exposed to the merciless attention of the avenging *Piorun*. Parts of the track along the length of the spectacular Calabrian coast clung to ledges cut out of sheer cliff faces; here the naval gunfire blasted away rock and masonry buttresses supporting the permanent way, stopping trains that then were destroyed by the bombarding ships. On one occasion the Polish gunners brought down the tunnel exit trapping a locomotive inside, and before the crew could back the train away from the danger zone, the destroyers wrecked the tail of the long line of freight cars that remained outside of the opposite end of the tunnel.

Petard had a break from her Polish senior ship on the 11th, sailing from Augusta with *Offa* and *Raider* at 2000 for a raid into the Straits of Messina, where searchlights were encountered that probed the dark surface of the sea looking for the destroyers; the light crews received for their inquisitiveness a massive saturation of gunfire from out of the dark night that quickly doused the lights and silenced the guns that tried to stop the ships. The destroyers had hardly ceased fire when a signal recalling them to intercept E-boats reported off Augusta was received. After a headlong dash through the night the ships arrived to find that the high speed enemy craft had given them the slip.

On 17th August the port of Messina was occupied by the Allied armies, the Americans winning the race to the last city in Sicily by arriving a few hours ahead of the 8th Army; but the enemy had succeeded in escaping with a large part of their forces intact after conducting a masterly withdrawal in the face of superior land forces that were supported by complete air and sea dominance; the relatively weak Axis army of 50,000 Germans and 145,000 Italians had held off a joint allied force of 200,000 Americans and 250,000 British. The Axis were able to withdraw though Messina and ferry into the mainland of Italy 115,000 men and 10,100 vehicles, 200 artillery pieces. 47 tanks, 1,000 tons of ammunition, 970 tons of fuel and 15,700 tons of miscellaneous equipment.

Mopping up processes kept all ships busy, also escorting stores and reinforcements from Malta to Augusta and Catania, as well as all the usual submarine and E-boat patrols. Fleet exercises took up two whole days finishing on the 29th when the capital ships returned to Malta. The following day late at 1900 the giant battleships *Nelson* and *Rodney*, departed from Malta with *Petard* one of the escort of six fleets, to bombard the Italian coast defences in the Straits of Messina. From 1000/31st the two great ships manoeuvred in the narrows of the straits bombarding gun sites and forts on the Italian mainland. The triple gun turrets discharged a massive tonnage of 18″ shells into the installations ashore without any serious opposition from the enemy. The destroyers took no part in the cannonade, concentrating on protecting the battleships from submarine attack, and cringed under the blast of the mighty guns and the shells that screamed overhead. The attack finished at 1200 leaving large columns of smoke and dust rising from the target areas and silent shore defence positions; the task group arrived back without incident at Malta at 2000, 25 hours after leaving.

Queen Olga had returned without her expected refit, only a short boiler clean of four days had been substituted for the two week break that the disappointed Greeks had hoped for. To add to their general gloom and angry frustration, following *Petard* out of Malta at 2200/2nd September the port screw became entangled in the boom net. *Petard* continued on alone bound for Benghazi while the Greeks struggled to clear their ship, finally succeeding at 0330 and at full speed proceeded after *Petard*, whom she rejoined returning to Malta escorting a convoy out of the north African port. The two chummy ships shared a strong submarine contact not far from where they had sunk the *Uarsciek* nine months earlier; but after an hour of careful stalking both destroyers lost contact, and raced after the convoy that had continued on course for Malta, arriving late on the evening of the 5th.

The two ships left Malta on the 7th at 1530 with 23 other destroyers, the fleet destroyer screen for two aircraft carriers, *Illustrious* and *Formidable*, four battleships *Nelson* (Flag ship force H), *Rodney*, *Warspite* and *Valiant*; the massive fleet moved into the Ionian sea to cover invasion forces assaulting the mainland of Italy scheduled for the 9th September in two main attack formations, one in the Gulf of Taranto and the second Avalanche in the Gulf of Salerno.

During most of the 8th, the fleet came under heavy air attack from the remaining air squadrons available to the German command in southern Italy, but the combined defence from the carrier borne fighters and the ships' AA gunfire prevented the fleet being damaged in any way. Two Ju 88s trying to launch a torpedo attack at dusk received hits from the battleships' barrage inside the destroyer screen and crashed into the sea together; shortly afterwards *Petard* closed two rubber dinghies and picked up the crews, eight German airmen. The fleet continued the offensive patrol off the Eighth Army landing areas without further attempts to interfere with its passage. Then when it seemed clear that the Italian fleet was trying to extricate its units from German control to surrender to the Allies, returned to Malta, entering the base at 2000/12th.

The combined American/British Operation Avalanche was in bad trouble, after the initial landing in the Gulf of Salerno on the 9th, little progress had been made against immensely strong German resistance put up by Panzer divisions. These forces had been deployed against the probability of an advance by the Eighth Army up Italy, linking with a sea borne thrust somewhere between the Bay of Naples and the Gulf of Policastro. The fact that details of the Italian surrender had not been published until 1830 on 8th September had not caught the Germans off balance. Between 10th and 13th September a crisis developed on the invasion beaches; nowhere had the Allied armies penetrated more than an average of 6 miles, and only in the face of extremely heavy and savage resistance from the Germans. Both British and American forces were pinned down on congested beach heads and subjected to constant artillery fire pouring down from the surrounding hills dominating the Bay.

Enemy air attacks had assumed dangerous proportions, a new menacing air weapon was being used for the first time, remote control bombs directed from a discharging plane standing off from the targets, began to cause heavy casualties amongst the shipping supporting the landings.

On the evening of the 13th, the Germans who had by now identified the dividing line between the British and American beach heads mounted a counter attack with four divisions supported by an armoured force of Tiger tanks. The attack drove down the Sele valley towards the beaches and by the early 14th they had driven a salient 2 miles wide between the 10th and 6th Corps, air and artillery attacks on the allied divisions intensified; in places the troops were hanging on literally at the water's edge of the beaches. The American Admiral Hewitt in command of the invasion armada called for heavy sea reinforcements to both support the attempt to push inland against the counter attack, or in the last resort to evacuate the desperately hard pressed invasion force; the call was made to the C-in-C Mediterranean the British Admiral of the Fleet A.B. Cunningham.

Response to the call was immediate and swift, three British cruisers *Euryalus, Scylla* and *Charybdis* sailed from Bizerta to Tripoli, embarked troops and thence sped at high speed for Salerno.

At 1700/14th the main fleet had sailed from Malta bound for Gibralta with jubilant *Petard*, unaware of the crisis at Salerno, and only renewed hopes, that the ship would now find its way back to home waters, as one of the large fleet destroyer escort. Force H had only cleared the Malta approaches when the Commander-in-Chief's order for a recall arrived in the flag ship. *Nelson, Rodney* and the two aircraft carriers had to return to Malta, *Warspite* and *Valiant* with the 14th destroyer flotilla as a screen were to proceed to maximum speed via the Straits of Messina to Salerno. The task

force cleared Malta at 2040, Captain D 14th DF in *Jervis*, leading
the escort comprising of *Penn, Pathfinder, Ilex* and *Petard*, driving hard
through the night, with Mount Etna glowering red and menacing
away to the west, forcing at top speed the battleships into the
Straits of Messina, into the tide torn narrows with little regard for
obstacles or darkened shipping that might have been encountered,
and past the Stromboli island volcano sending up great spouts of
molten fire as if warning the hurrying ships of the death and
destruction that lay ahead. The task force arrived off the Gulf of
Salerno at 1100/15th, and the battleships moved in without delay
to their bombarding stations.

The Gulf was crowded with shipping, transports and supply
ships at anchor, many within gun range of the enemy ashore,
headquarters ships closer inshore with a constant traffic of small
craft of every shape and purpose coming and going in constant
frantic movement; further out moving slowly under way were
several white painted and red crossed hospital ships, focal points
for a steady line of launches and landing craft carrying the many
wounded extracted from the desperate fighting ashore. To seaward,
a line of patrolling American ships and British Hunt class
destroyers steamed constantly north and south, to ward off
submarines that might try to break into the Gulf, firing
intermittently at German aircraft that escaped the Allied fighter
cover, and were attempting to plaster the shipping with glider
bombs.

Inshore, close to the smoke and constant uproar of gunfire and
explosions, Allied cruisers and destroyers stood in firing at the
enemy positions ashore, in many places the gun crews fired over
open sights at targets that were only a few hundred yards from the
ships, and yards from the invading troops who were hanging on a
short distance above the high water mark. The whole area along
the beachhead had been turned into an inferno of constant attack
and counter attack with the warships responding to calls from the
army to break up concentrations of tanks and enemy artillery. The
hills surrounding the Gulf reflected back a pandemonium of
explosions, bomb and gun fire, great palls of smoke erupting
constantly from shipping that suffered hits and destruction of
ammunition and fuel dumps ashore; wrecked landing craft and
vehicles covered the beaches and foreshore.

Warspite and *Valiant* threaded a way through a huge press of
shipping to take up station, *Valiant* to the north off the American

sector, and *Warspite* taking station off the Sele valley and river mouth. No forward observation officers could be supplied by the desperately hard-pressed army to direct and spot the battleship fire, to correct the accuracy of the bombardment; both ships landed their own officers, Naval and Royal Marine.

Petard embarked *Warspite*'s FOOs, landing them quickly from her motor cutter and then remained yards off shore in close support of the army who at that point only seemed to be hanging on by their finger nails, lying in shallow hollows scooped out of the sand above the high water mark. *Petard* and the other destroyers fired at point blank range at counter attacking enemy, men guns and tanks wherever they could be seen through the smoke and dust! The smoke rolled in great dirty distorted billows over the devastation, the air filled with flying steel and a stench of explosions choked the throats and nostrils of men ashore and afloat. *Warspite*'s forward observation officers quickly established communication with the battleship whose great bulk, a mere 2000 yards out from the shore, loomed through breaks of the dense smoke screen laid by the destroyers to protect her from the enemy artillery. Her full broadside of eight 15 inch guns thundered out with a dreadful magnified fulmination that overwhelmed the obscene battle orchestra, for a moment the other sounds of conflict hesitated as the combatants of both sides shrank from the appalling roar from the broadside.

The immensely heavy and accurate fire from the battleship broke up concentrations of armour forming up in the Sele valley, obliterating men and armour; the guns seeking out new areas as soon as the enemy tried to group for a counter attack on the invasion force. *Warspite*'s fall of shot guided the massed smaller gunpower from the cruisers, *Penelope, Aurora, Mauritius* and the USS *Philadelphia*, British and American destroyers, the latter also continuing to lay smoke screens to cover the LSIs and LSTs, scurrying like water beetles across the surface of the Gulf, between transports and the shore, ferrying reinforcements to critical pressure points, men, ammunition, guns and tanks.

Valiant had problems establishing communications with her observation officers, and never really overcame the difficulty, so was delayed from some little time before engaging the targets in the northern sector; when she did finally open fire the effects on the German formations were as decisive as the bombardment further south from *Warspite*.

The devastating accurate fire, supported by the cruisers and destroyers, slowed down and finally halted the German counter-attacks, the enemy having failed to commit all the available reserves before the battleships arrived off the beaches, had lost the certain opportunity of driving the Allies back into the sea; the German C-in-C had hesitated fatally with these reserves, his judgment inhibited by the drive north of Montgomery's Eighth Army towards the southern flank of his army defending Salerno and the approaches to Naples.

The naval bombardment received massive support from Allied fighter bombers that bombed and machine gunned everything that moved; nothing was too small for the attention of the rampaging airmen, single despatch riders, vehicles were attacked with the same ferocity as large and well defended groups of armour, and concentrations of infantry.

As darkness began to close in, *Warspite* and *Valiant* retired to seaward screened by their destroyers, disengaging from the great armada of shipping in the Gulf and its approaches. The battleships steaming westwards into the open sea were subjected to violent and prolonged bombing and torpedo attacks from German aircraft. The destroyer screen as usual were vulnerable to damage and casualties from the anti-torpedo aircraft gun barrage set up by the battleships; 6 inch secondary armament and 4 inch AA batteries fired at low angle, with shells fused to explode at 2500 yards, menaced the destroyers 3500-4000 yards out from the capital ships concentrating their total attention and firing outwards towards the approaching wave hopping torpedo carrying aircraft.

With a grim certainty *Petard*'s turn came to be hit on her blind side from the ships she was defending while her guns and attention of her crew were directed out to starboard, on the succession of Ju 88s roaring out of the closing darkness, over the destroyer screen into the battleships violent barrier of exploding short ranged shells. *Petard* suffered badly, a 6 inch shell incorrectly fused or faulty, from either *Warspite* or *Valiant*, entered the portside of the forward upper seamen's messdeck, exploded and obliterated the ammunition supply party to 'A' and 'B' guns. The seamen's living space reduced to a bloody shambles, did little to impair the fighting effectiveness of the ship which continued to fight off succeeding waves of incoming torpedo aircraft.

While 'A' and 'B' guns crashed out a low angle barrage; below, Doctor and his first aid party from the sickbay flat immediately aft from the now dark and wrecked messdeck struggled in to salvage and save the wounded survivors of the supply party. Able Seaman Huggins and one messmate had been killed instantly, killed working at the ammunition winches, and there were six wounded, the entire remainder of the supply party, three badly; Able Seaman Lofthouse, the Captain's servant, Able Seaman Jack 'Nobby' Hall, one of the asdic team and Brooky's servant, and Able Seaman Curd.

Jack Hall later in a field hospital at Syracuse, wrote down his recollections of the action that terminated his service in *Petard*:

> I was in the forward messdeck passing shells from the top of the magazine hoist, up the shute to 'A' gun on the fo'c'sle deck, when there was an explosion, a terrific flash, a shower of sparks, and then complete darkness. I knew that we were hit of course, but by what, and the extent of the damage I didn't stop to think. I heard moaning and wondered if we were to sink and be caught like rats in a trap before we had a chance to get out. I darted into the port passage, which still had an emergency light burning at the far end, blowing more air into my life belt as I did so. Imagine my horror when I saw blood bubbling from a hole in my chest as I blew into my life belt tube; I made my way into the sickbay where the MO treated my wounds, shrapnel had torn a groove across my back, another piece had entered my chest at the side and had come out at the front. Some more lads arrived with shrapnel wounds and one had to be transferred to a hospital ship in the area for immediate emergency operation, I met him later at the base hospital, from where he was medically discharged. I felt no pain at the time, until later when the effects of the morphia I had been given, began to wear off. Later I learned that two of my shipmates had been blown to pieces, and volunteers were asked for to collect their remains to be placed into their hammocks for burial. No one would volunteer for the awful task, two were detailed and given a double tot of rum. ...

With the complete close down of the night the attempts by the enemy planes to sink the battleships ceased, and at Rupert Egan's request, *Petard* left the screen to close one of the British hospital ships to transfer the Captain's critically wounded servant, Able Seaman Lofthouse.

At dawn next morning, 16th, *Warspite* and *Valiant* returned to their original bombarding positions and resumed the pounding of the enemy forward and support areas. Observations ashore and from the air confirmed that *Warspite* was repeating the heavy toll on enemy personnel and materials, German reports and records later stated that the effect of the naval bombardment at Salerno was conclusive, it had completely halted a major counter attack and caused the withdrawal in the face of the Allied landing forces. *Warspite's* performance is more remarkable, because during the entire period of the bombardment on the 16th, the communication link to the forward observation officers was interrupted by German jamming.

By mid-morning all the bombarding ships were under heavy attack and harassed by guided bombs; the two battleships receiving special attention. The ability to take avoiding action was restricted by the heavy concentration of shipping inside the Gulf. *Warspite* suffered three very near misses, before a fourth bomb hit her amidships, exploding in number four boiler-room causing heavy casualties. The explosion introduced flooding into the adjoining boiler-rooms, reducing the ability to move at speed, immediately. *Warspite* managed to struggle seaward out of the mass of supply and bombarding shipping at 10 knots, before the continuing spread of flooding into the last boiler-room brought the battleship to a halt. One of the attendant destroyers ordered by Captain D14 in *Jervis*, took the crippled giant in tow, and a slow haul south towards the Straits of Messina commenced, *Petard* playing a part in the anti-submarine patrol and anti-aircraft defence. Soon after the start of the 2 knot tow, the ship hauled out to port and paused for a short while still on full action stations alert, and committed the two members of her crew, killed the night before, to the deep after a brief quarter-deck service. Later in the afternoon two American tugs, *Hopi* and *Moreno* replaced the destroyer towing the *Warspite* towards the Straits, passing through during the night. At times the current flowing eastward through the narrows took charge so the battleship and her diminutive towing Americans moved sideways crabwise and out of control on the current.

Soon after midnight early on the 18th *Petard* left the escort and arrived at Augusta at 0300 to land her wounded who then were transported to a British Army field hospital at Syracuse, later to be flown to hospitals in North Africa.

The ship departed shortly afterwards to Malta, arriving early on the 19th, leaving after refuelling had been completed as part of the escort to UK bound aircraft carriers, but this time the ship's company had no opportunity for optimistic and speculative buzzes of a return to 'Pompey' and home leave. Rupert was able to forewarn his men that they were to go only as far as Gibraltar.

By the 24th *Petard* again found herself back in Malta, with a promise of a four day break, leave to each watch for 48 hours at the now improved and more popular St Paul's rest camp came as a welcome bonus, and went a little way to compensate for the First Lieutenant's plan to repaint the ship. During the 26th, while *Petard* rested in Sliema Creek and the ship's company painted over the many rusting patches, under the hot sunshine, away in the Dodacanese their flotilla half section *Queen Olga* with very many of her gallant extrovert crew of Greeks, died in Alinda bay of Leros island. It was some time before the grim news reached the *Petard* and more than a week before the ship learnt that it had been transferred to the control of the Commander-in-Chief Levant and to a hopeless operation, conceived at a time when the Allies had achieved overwhelming superiority in the Mediterranean theatre; an operation that resulted in a grievous defeat to the British land and sea forces denied inexplicably air protection or support from Allied sea and land power by the American Supreme Commander, General Eisenhower.

For a few more days *Petard* revelled in the Ionian sea free from enemy air attacks and only the remote possibility of submarine interference, moving up into the Adriatic with *Jervis* on extended patrols, returning on the 30th to Brindisi. Rupert constantly pressed the doctor for news of progress regarding the men discharged wounded and used all his contacts and influence to see that they received maximum care and an early return to the United Kingdom and their families. He wrote personally to them all and to their relatives; his efforts gradually became known to the men remaining in the ship, through letters that came back to the ship from messmates who found their way home.

For two or three days *Petard* unaware of her future, stayed at Brindisi, her ship's company enjoying the novelty of being at a recently captured mainland of Italy city. The Italians, particularly the members of the armed forces were dazed and wary; they had escaped massacre by the Germans following the surrender of their country to the allies, the city had then been quickly captured by the Eighth Army who had passed on to the north in pursuit of the Germans, leaving a Control Commission to run the city Leaving Brindisi, the ship carried out a patrol and sweep between Iasun island and Dubrovnik, searching coves and inlets of the Adriatic for German controlled shipping. After 48 hours *Petard* received orders to proceed to Malta, fuel then sail to join the Levant Command. The ship entered Malta late on 3rd October, sailing again next morning for Alexandria in company with *Panther* arriving on the 7th to berth straight away on the oiler. Here Rupert Egan received from the depot ship current despatches and signals from C-in-C Levant, a suddenly saddened ship's company learned of the loss of the *Queen Olga*, their Greek friends with the *Intrepid* at Leros.

CHAPTER 8

The Dodecanese Islands
The Destroyers' Graveyard

Immediately oiling finished, *Petard* sailed with *Panther* and the AA cruiser *Carlisle*. The two P's sailed in company for the third and last time, for *Petard* it was to be the start of her role in the doomed Dodecanese operation, beginning with the current Operation Credential; for *Panther*, her part was to be short and end violently.

The main operation started on 7th September, and already had taken its first instalment of men and ships with the sinking of *Queen Olga* and *Intrepid*; the islands of Rhodes and Cos had been captured from the Italian garrisons and their British supporters, with heavy losses in lives and men taken prisoner. The destroyers were caught, and hit and badly damaged in Alinda Bay by dive bombers in the early part of the morning of 26th September. A week after sinking in a broad daylight sweep, north of Stampalia, two German manned merchant ships of 3000 and 1200 tons, *Queen Olga* received mortal damage and sank soon afterwards. The *Intrepid* after frantic efforts by her crew to repair fractured steam pipes was ready to escape at 20 knots when the Stukas returned and before noon she also had been sunk and 16 men killed. *Queen Olga* suffered 70 killed; six officers including the Captain, Commander George Blessas and 64 of his men.

The situation was desperate, the Germans in the Dodecanese islands had gained the initiative and had in fact won; what was to follow after the arrival of *Petard, Panther* and *Penn* to reinforce C-in-C Levant's depleted force of six fleets, now down to four with the loss of *Queen Olga* and *Intrepid*, could only be a bloody and senseless prolonged torture, with no hope of success. It turned out to be a nightmare repetition of the campaign in 1941 when British land and sea forces were blasted out of Greece and then Crete by overwhelming Ju 87 and 88 air power, and superbly led and equipped German airborne troops. A host of proud cruisers and destroyers encasing the bodies of hundreds of irreplaceable men rotted at the bottom of these same beautiful Aegean and Mediterranean seas.

Yeoman Bishop

On the way to Leros loaded with jeeps and trailers

10th November, SS *Trapani* in Kalymnos Harbour

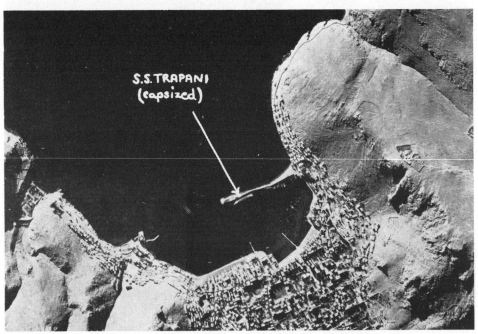

SS *Trapani* after being sunk by *Petard*, *Rockwood* and ORP *Krakowiak*

The origins of this new catastrophe lay with the refusal of the Americans to accept the strategic appreciation of the British Prime Minister; his instinctive opportunist and perhaps romantic concepts of grand strategy were influenced by an overwhelming desire to liberate the Greek nation. He nevertheless received strong support from the British Chiefs of Staff whose assessments were based on cold professional reasoning and logic. Long before the defeat of the Axis armies in North Africa, the possibility of an Italian surrender and the opportunity it would give to open up the Dodecanese for a drive into the Balkans had been foreseen by the British.

The latecomers to the war, the Americans, who because they held the purse strings now dominated the Allied war effort, controlling the pooled resources of men and materials, viewed the British plans with suspicion, describing the British Prime Minister's ideas of grand strategy as coming from politics of the heart, a continuing British preoccupation with colonial ambitions, a desire to meddle in Balkan politics, a recoil from the shadows of Passchendaele in 1917 and the more recent Dunkirk; above all else the Americans would not tolerate any weakening of determination and slowing of preparations for the cross-Channel assault into Europe, Operation Overlord. The Americans later, after their troops suffered hideous slaughter at Kesserine, Anzio and in the Ardennes, understood some of the experience that motivated British strategic thinking.

Under heavy pressure from Winston Churchill, supported by the British representatives on the Allied Joint Chiefs of Staff Committee, the Americans reluctantly agreed to allocate some land forces and ships to the C-in-C Eastern Mediterranean to enable him to prepare to take Rhodes, the essential jumping off base that had to be secured before a drive into the islands could be undertaken. So in fact preparations for a limited operation were well advanced before the Italian surrender; a brigade of the 8th Indian Army Division underwent intensive training, an English Yeomanry regiment was re-equipped with Sherman tanks, and a target date for the taking of Rhodes was agreed.

A three day invasion exercise in the Suez canal area, at the end of August, had just been concluded successfully, when without warning the infantry and tank landing craft, the headquarters ship and three of the four cargo ships allocated to the operation, were ordered to India, to be held ready for an attack on Arakan. The

Americans were insisting, as masters of the alliance, that the long term planned timetable of the Allied master plan had to be carried out; in the event the Arakan operation was cancelled. Shortly afterwards, following the departure of the shipping, the Indian Division received orders to leave the Levant and move into the Central Mediterranean theatre.

General Maitland Wilson, Commander-in-Chief, Eastern Mediterranean, found himself left with a few battalions of infantry, in the main undergoing retraining after a long period of garrison duties within a besieged fortress of Malta, a few Hunt class, six fleet destroyers and a mixed bag of caiques, lighters and small merchant ships. The Italians in the islands failed to live up to rather optimistic hopes that they would attack their late allies, the Germans, and secure Rhodes and Cos for the British. The Germans in Crete after brutally punishing the Italians as a reprisal for General Badoglio's surrender to the Allies, dealt with the 40,000 Italian garrison in Rhodes. 7,000 Germans shared the task of manning the island defences, within three days they overcame a weak and badly organised resistance by the Italians, although a few units fought hard and well, notably the artillery.

The General was forced to cobble together a force to support Italian garrisons on other islands, to hold them until a new invasion task force could be found to carry out Operation Accolade, the capture of Rhodes. The C-in-C had an impossible task, the effective emasculation of the forces under his control by American action, resulted that at Cos where a British force had landed, it did not possess equipment necessary to resist effectively a counter invasion by the Germans. On the day that *Carlisle* sailed escorted by *Panther* and *Petard*, Cos fell, losing at the same time vital airfields without which any further sea operations north of Rhodes could only be a repetition of the 1941 Crete campaign debacle.

At noon, 7th, as *Carlisle* and her escorts sailed north, the cruiser *Penelope* and her destroyers who had been under continuous air attack moving south through the Scarpento Straits, fought off the last of a succession of Stuka strikes, a group of 18. *Penelope* in this last attack received a hit and several near misses, wrecking 'Y' turret and putting her 4 inch anti-aircraft battery out of action through a power cut. *Petard*'s old companion of bombarding raids on Pantellaria was fortunate to escape being sunk, her escorting destroyers succeeded in holding off the dive bombers, and the cruiser managed to clear the Straits arriving back at Alexandria on

the 8th, where repairs took several weeks to complete.

Two 'Hunts' made a rendezvous with *Carlisle* and the two 'Ps' south of the Scarpento Straits, *Aldenham* and the Greek-manned *Themistocles*; during the night of the 7th the combined force Credential received orders to sweep further north through the Straits looking for invasion forces threatening Leros and supply craft to the German island garrisons. The group sailed as far as Stampalia and then on to Levitha without sightings, retiring back through the straits by the dawn of the 8th, releasing the two 'Hunts' to return to Alexandria. They were relieved by other 'Hunts', *Rockwood* and the Greek *Miaoulis* from Limassol; the force would receive air cover from American Lightnings operating in the area out of Gambut for the last time. The air squadrons already under orders from the Supreme Allied Commander, General Eisenhower to be withdrawn; in their last operation over the Aegean, the American pilots were to have a field day. *Carlisle* leading her four destroyers returned north again at 25 knots, north east back through the Straits in broad daylight, seeking the invasion forces reported as assembling at Kalymnos; intelligence reports flooding in from C-in-C Levant's headquarters at Ras el Tin-Alexandria, filled the area with enemy shipping, the command appreciation made an invasion of Leros a certainty for the night of 8th/9th. It was a brilliant day, a smooth unruffled sea beneath a cloudless azure sky and blazing sun, to the sailors' nostrils came a faint, almost elusive, fragrant scent of dried herbage from the sun baked archipelago; but despite faultless visibility conditions, the force failed to sight enemy shipping amongst the islands.

Squadrons of Lightnings patrolled over and close to Leros, made sighting reports of enemy shipping, but failed to contact and home the cruiser and her attendant destroyers onto the sightings. Captain Nalder in *Carlisle*, having reached the limits of his search area, turned the force south and steered 174 degrees for the northern entrance to the Scarpento Straits, while the Germans waited for their opportunity to catch the ships without the protecting cover of Lightnings.

All went well for the ships of Operation Credential until approaching midday when the sky began to cloud a little, and the fifth squadron of Lightnings having completed the half hour patrol over the ships had to depart before the relieving sixth squadron made contact. The Ju 88 shadower keeping its constant and wary vigil, with other enemy watchers ashore on the islands, spotted and reported the break in air cover, and 16 Ju 87s struck. The ships had picked up the approaching dive bombers in good time but were uncertain of their identity, with only a radar contact and no visual sighting, they were unsure that the planes could be the expected Lightnings coming again out of the sun, without the IFF switched on. The Stukas succeeded in getting right over the ships, and commenced near vertical screaming dives concentrating on the *Carlisle*, before the cruiser or the destroyers opened fire in self-defence.

The task force, *Carlisle* and the four destroyers, steered at high speed, a course of 190 degrees into the Straits; the battle between the speeding jinking ships left long winding white course trials in the mirror like vivid blue sea. The diving screaming Stukas must have provided a savage, brilliant spectacle for isolated inhabitants, whose white, widely spaced lonely houses speckled bare but beautiful mountainous islands lining the Straits, Khalkia, Saria, Scarpento, and enemy garrison lookouts on the headlands of Rhodes, Capes Monlithos and Koravola. Each ship shrouded in smoke and spurting flame from its guns, filled the sky with bursting smoke balls and flash points where the barrage set shells exploded.

Two bombs hit *Carlisle*, followed almost immediately by two more as the plunging dive bombers shrieked out of vertical dives. The cruiser had been hit by number four gun, exploding inside tearing her vitals apart, then near misses blew off her starboard propeller and shaft. Only two guns remained in action, her control equipment and director knocked out of action, with heavy casualties the ship was in serious trouble, slewing to starboard out of control, then to a stop shrouded in smoke and steam.

Just as the missing sixth relief squadron of Lightnings arrived nearly out of 'on task' time through expending fuel searching for the rendezvous, finding it only by sighting the air explosions and smoke from the air/sea battle, *Panther* (Lieutenant Commander Viscount Jocelyn) received two direct hits and two very close near misses, all amidships; the speeding destroyer in a spectacular and terrible convulsion broke her back and drove straight out of sight below the lovely calm sea. Most of the gun crews, upper deck and bridge personnel were picked up by the *Miaoulis* following astern; the casualties below decks, in the engine and boiler rooms and magazines were heavy and near total.

The Lightnings tore into the Ju 87s and a solitary Ju 88, massacring the attacking aircraft; eleven, including the Ju 88, were unable to get away and fell into the sea, complete, in parts, some streaming smoke, others flaming torches, around the ships and over a wide area. Four had already been shot down by the ship's massed gunfire.

Rupert Egan drove his ship at near top speed, weaving under extreme helm at times, in and around the location of the stopped and stricken cruiser, all 4 inch guns in local sector and gunlayers' control, in short range barrage, taking on individual targets, each gun pouring out a rate of 22 rounds per minute, backed up by the pom-pom and oerlikons, firing as fast as the supply members of the gun crews could feed the guns. It was a desperate but exhilarating action, the ship surging under the thrust of her twin screws operating with full power heeling violently, taking avoiding action under the direction of the Captain's helm orders.

In the director, the GCO and his team had a bird's eye view of the action, the main armament in the local sector officer of the quarter's control, the director's crew task was only to act as lookout for targets, talking down over the gun phone net to encourage and steady the individual guns in their efforts to fight off the plunging dive bombers. In this incredible setting, out in the Scarpento Strait, aloft in the director, it seemed almost possible to be detached from the reality of the death struggle taking place, the warships covered in smoke and flame from gunfire, bomb hits and near misses, the sea erupting from bomb explosions and crashing aircraft, while overhead against a matchless sky, spotted with great groups of black/brown shell bursts, nearly thirty aircraft were locked in a swirling air battle.

For the *Carlisle* this was the end of the line for the old lady; the ship had survived the 1941 desperate Greece and Crete battles in these very same waters against these same savage Ju 87 and 88s, and now two years later the nightmare had repeated itself, the old tough hull now received critical damage. Rupert closed the cruiser, in the sudden stop to the bombing following the Lightnings arrival and the destruction of the Stukas, to assess the damage and to arrange a tow for the stopped ship. With very considerable skill and speed, the Hunt *Rockwood*, passed a tow to *Carlisle*, and with *Miaoulis* and *Petard* in close attendance, the cruiser started a stern first tow at twelve knots for Alexandria, clearing the southern end of Scarpento Straits without further attacks. *Carlisle*'s casualties were one officer and nineteen men killed, seventeen wounded, the ship built in 1918 was beyond repair, at Alexandria she remained until the end of the war as an immobile base ship. The Lightnings escaped losses; all returned to the North African bases.

The decision to withdraw them from further support over the Dodecanese, spelled complete disaster to the attempt to hold the islands, Leros and Samos deep in the Dodecanese, north of Rhodes and Cos, with airfields that swarmed with German planes who now found it possible to attack shipping inside visual distance from these base airfields. The British fleet operating in the central Mediterranean theatre had two fleet and six escort aircraft carriers, and it still seems a bizarre, almost criminal neglect that not one was diverted to support the continuation of the struggle to hold the isolated islands.

Rupert Egan in his role as senior officer of the escort, successfully shepherded *Rockwood* and her tow *Carlisle* into the Grand Pass Alexandria where tugs took over the last short lap into the harbour. *Petard* after refuelling moved longside the depot ship *Woolwich* to get the worn linings of the 4 inch guns changed. The following evening, Rupert with perhaps a premonition of what lay ahead for his ship, obtained permission first from the Commodore Levant destroyers, Percy Todd, and then the Captain of the depot ship *Woolwich* for some of the base ship's officers to take over for one night, duty officer responsibility for *Petard*, to enable Rupert to dine all his officers ashore.

Embarked in twin two horse gharries, white clad officers primed with generous apertifs, hilarious to the point of mild hysteria, moved out of the dock area up Mohammed Ali Square, Rua Sherif Pasha to a restaurant owned and run by one of Rupert's acquaintances. The evening shewed up his talent and skill as a *bon viveur* and *gourmet*; the company came from his wide circle of friends in Alexandria, British and resident, service and civilian. For some of his officers strained mentally and physically by the months and long hours of continuous watchkeeping and action stations at sea, added to by the recent sample of renewed enemy air threat which served as a sombre setting for their privileged knowledge that adequate counter air protection would be denied for the future, spoiled the chance that the party offered for relaxing.

Once the initial excitement and stimulus of drink wore off, some of the female guests found one or two of the *Petard*'s officers lacking in animation, preoccupied and even showing signs of exhaustion. It was nevertheless a brave effort by their Captain, who showed no sign of his long hours of continuous and unremitting responsibility without the reinforcement of sleep or rest; concealed in his short, rather overweight frame he had an enormous store of energy, a huge capacity for enjoying other people's company, that he rewarded by being an entertaining and generous host. He was quite inexhaustible, not until close after the arrival of dawn, shortly before both watches of the hands were due to muster in his ship, he led his party back in gharries through an Alexandria bracing itself to face another day, to the ship and the hopeless Dodecanese battle.

The attempt to sustain and reinforce the beleaguered British island garrisons and the Italian allies now developed into a pattern of nightly infiltrations by Fleet destroyers, either singly or in pairs, accompanied by one or more Hunts. The army units in the islands had none of their own artillery, tanks or heavy weapons, no transport other than jeeps or what the Italians had to offer from very rudimentary vehicle stores. The troops carried almost everything they had on them; there were no suitable craft that could survive a run by day into the enemy air dominated Dodecanese to supply the heavy weapons so urgently required. The Fleet destroyers handed over boats, whalers and cutters, to the care of the *Woolwich* at Alexandria, and hoisted fully loaded jeep trailers at each vacant davit head with others finding space on the upper deck. Torpedo tubes trained out to port and starboard allowed six to eight jeeps loaded with petrol filled jerrycans, to be carried on the iron deck, other additional cargo of ammunition boxes and small arms piled wherever space could be found. Below decks fully accoutremented soldiers, up to sixty were crammed into the messdecks where they stoically bore the miseries of sea sickness and frequent action in unfamiliar conditions, unable to help to defend the ship or themselves. Stores and men were embarked for each of the double night runs to Leros and Samos. So that every destroyer returning from a supply run could be replenished without delay, dumps of jeeps with trailers, ammunition, stores and troop reinforcements had been established at immediate readiness in Haifa, Limassol, Casteloriso and Alexandria. The Hunts also carried stores and troops on every run.

The air support available now that the Lightnings had been withdrawn and departed to the Central Mediterranean war theatre, was inferior to the German strength; it consisted mainly of Beaufighters operating from bases far from the operational area, the nearest squadrons being based in Cyprus, 250 miles from Rhodes. The Middle East air commander, Air Marshal Sholto Douglas informed the C-in-C Levant that he was unable to supply sufficient air cover for ships operating in daylight near Rhodes. This meant that the German land and sea forces were able to build up their strength north of the island with minimum interference. C-in-C Levant, Admiral Willis, reported to C-in-C Mediterranean, and Admiralty London, that he could not operate sea patrols of surface ships by day inside the Dodecanese without accepting prohibitive losses; nevertheless the doomed operation proceeded.

Small groups of destroyers heavily loaded with military equipment, loaded to a point of near instability, sailed every day with one cruiser as escort from Haifa, Limassol or Alexandria, bound for the passage between Rhodes and the Turkish mainland, timing their arrival a little before dusk, slipping through to lie up during daylight hours the following day inside the Turkish territorial waters in one of the innumerable bays that lined the Gulfs of Doris, Kos and Mandeliyah. During the second night the cruiser and destroyers entered Alinda Bay, Leros, to discharge cargo and passengers within a short span of one or two hours, into barges manned by nervous, at times panic stricken Italian crews. Unloading had to be completed to allow the ships to depart and escape at high speed back the way they had come, before they were caught in daylight north of Rhodes or outside neutral Turkish waters by free ranging Stuka squadrons.

On 19th October a third cruiser, *Sirius* received serious bomb damage moving up the Scarpento strait with the *Aurora* and destroyers under constant air bombardment, to shell the harbour of Cos. There were Beaufighters in the vicinity but they were unable to prevent the cruiser being hit and near missed; the ship's two after 5.25 turrets knocked out and the radar and aerials out of action made it imperative to withdraw the ship before she was sunk. The destroyers without the cruiser, *Eclipse, Pathfinder* and *Belvoir* loaded heavily with troops and stores went on to lay up in Turkish waters while *Sirius* escaped south to Alexandria. From that moment, no further cruiser ventured north of Rhodes, they would in future only accompany the destroyers as far as a line south of the island to give extra anti-aircraft gunpower, then return to leave the laden destroyers to slip north under cover of darkness to a favoured lying up bay inside neutral water.

Petard had made two runs into Alinda bay, each run taking two nights carrying troops and jeeps. The passage north had on each occasion been from Alexandria through Scarpento Strait passing west of Niseo island rounding Cape Krio keeping inside Turkish waters into a bay near Budrum, there to remain during daylight hours, under way moving slowly round the small bay while Ju 88s and 87 aircraft made threatening runs out of the sun in an attempt to unnerve the British destroyer gun crews, tempting them to open fire so that they could retaliate on the excuse that the British had broken the Geneva rules.

It became a severe trial and test of discipline as the planes dived low over the isolated bays, so low that the plane squadron markings could be read clearly. It turned into an unreal but deadly game, both sides under strict orders not to infringe the Geneva rules and offend the Turks unless attacked by their opponents. The Turkish army and coast guards kept *Petard* and the destroyers with her under close observation, taking the occasional pot shot with a rifle to while away the time, otherwise making no effort to stop the ships using territorial waters for sanctuary. On the first two runs *Petard* with her two Hunts were able to get through into Alinda bay on the second night of the trip without serious air opposition, disembarking men and stores into barges as they lay to anchor. The barge crews were extremely nervous and almost rendered useless as soon as the sound of aircraft engines could be heard out of the dark, but somehow the soldiers, stores and jeeps in the complete dark were passed out of the ship without loss or serious injury in time for the ships to sail at high speed with sufficient time to be clear south of Rhodes by daybreak.

Other destroyers using the east about Rhodes channel were having a rougher time, fighting desperately under a huge umbrella of flares dropped from planes detailed for this task while Stukas plunged unseen from above the blinding light to drop bombs on the overloaded desperately jinking ships steaming dangerously close to islands and mainland in an effort to put off the bombers. For a couple of nights despite the vicious attacks, no destroyer received hits, and reinforcements got through. It was a source of wonder to the sailors how calmly and courageously the soldier passengers without exception accepted the alarms and action on passage to the island garrisons, loaded down with huge packs, arms and ammunition, they would have no chance of survival if the ship foundered. When being disembarked in total darkness at Leros or Samos they went quietly without complaint to the hopeless task that could only finish with death or at best as prisoners of war.

For the ships' third run out of Alexandria, *Petard* sailed in company with the *Faulknor* and *Dulverton* with *Aurora* giving cruiser protection up to the so called safety line south of Rhodes, the destroyers slipping into the Aegean under cover of darkness of the night 19th/20th. While at Leros *Fury* and *Beaufort* unloaded under heavy air attack, escaping without damage to bombard Cos harbour on their return to Alexandria. They were successful, perhaps unwittingly, in keeping the German aircraft away from the *Faulknor* and the other two destroyers with the flotilla leader who successfully made Guvercinlik Bay, there to lie up throughout the daylight hours of the 20th.

That night leaving *Dulverton* in the bay, *Faulknor* and *Petard* slipped out and sped quickly between islands and mainland for

Partheni Bay at the north of Leros island to offload the troops and stores, but this time they were quickly located and subjected to intense flare dropping attention. Under the brilliant white light, every gun firing upwards into the black night above in blind barrage fire, the uproar and crash of gunfire could not overlay the scream of descending planes and the explosion of bombs.

In this inferno, Rupert's calm control on his exposed bridge blinded and showered by cascading lumps of burning magnesium from flares that threatened to entangle in the foremast and shrouds, was matched by Brooksbank going about his navigational duties plotting, fixing and advising his Captain of the ship's position with complete disregard to the pandemonium of the ship to air night battle. *Faulknor* began to lay smoke as a ruse to confuse the low flying bombers, *Petard* found herself plunging out of stark exposure into a dense black wall of smoke, adding to Brooky's problems of navigation; Captain D's short emission of smoke confused the bombers for a moment and the flare dropping aircraft lost contact with the destroyers. Using a pre-arranged signal both destroyers then dropped several large white smoke canisters, these left a long trail blowing down wind.

The aircraft diverted their attention to this *ruse de guerre* taking some time to discover that it was only smoke, allowing the two ships to slip away and into Partheni Bay hoping to find the lighters waiting for them. It was only after precious minutes had slid away bringing the time for moon rise nearer that the naval shore party finally forced terrified Italian crew members to move barges longside the two shadowy shapes in the bay, and the frantic off-loading began. Some jeep trailers, those on the port and starboard whaler davit heads had been lowered into lighters, cases of ammunition followed with other stores manhandled by torpedo crews and ammunition supply parties helped by some of the soldiers.

Moon rise coincided with a return of the bombers who came in to press home hard, an attack of first flares followed by bombs making it impossible for unloading to continue; with every gun in action joining the great eruption of tracer fire rising from the dark shore line of the bay, the two destroyers dropping white smoke canisters left the bay at speed and without damage escaped back to rejoin *Dulverton* in Guvercinlik Bay the ancient port of Karyenda, to spend another day being buzzed by provocative German aircraft and under suspicious surveillance from the Turks.

At 1910 with *Dulverton* to give extra fire power to the joint AA defence, *Faulknor* and *Petard* left again for a second attempt to land the troops and remaining stores at Leros. The ships were baulked in the effort to approach Partheni via the Pharios channel despite the use of smoke floats. Bombers were waiting in force and pressed home with determined and heavy bomb attacks with the alarming addition that the ships suspected one aircraft was trying to use a guided missile, only the fact that the ships had not been caught effectively silhouetted against the flares by the controlling aircraft allowed the targets to escape. It seemed clear that to wait for the moon to rise would court disaster if the stand off bomber returned with a new bomb load. The destroyers proceeded north round Pharmako and Arki islands crossing west and south to Levitha, where *Dulverton* approached and bombarded the north side of the island and demolished Sparo lighthouse while *Petard* and *Faulknor* swept round the south looking for enemy shipping.

Here the flare dropping aircraft found them again. With skilful use of white smoke floats the destroyers confused the flare planes and slipped away south to wait and allow *Dulverton* to catch up with them; the three ships then retired and sped south through the Straits of Scarpento and were clear by dawn to join *Aurora* waiting anxiously for the destroyers. They arrived back safely with the troops still embarked, in the late afternoon at Alexandria. Refuelling and ammunitioning started immediately, at the same time the few stores that had been landed at Leros were replaced.

During the short turn-round hours in harbour, fitted in between visits to the Commodore Destroyers and probably the office of C-in-C Levant for briefing conferences and orders, the commanding officers of the ships of the Royal Navy without fail had to draft and submit typed reports of proceedings.

This chore ate into the short and rare opportunities for the commanding officers to rest and sleep, and was a special agony in small ships where there were no staff officers to prepare preliminary drafts for the ship's Captain. Rupert somehow found in his great reservoir of strength a capacity to produce reports that were frequently longer and more detailed than those submitted by the Captain D ships who all had staff officers in relatively generous numbers to write the first drafts. Rupert Egan's reports always had humour, a light touch and never failed to contain generous comments, conclusions and ideas.

While *Petard* snatched a brief chance to rest her crew, the *Eclipse*,

Commander E. Mack, DSO DSC RN, fully loaded with her quota of jeeps, the trailers at davit heads and deck stores, embarked the Headquarters unit and 'A' company of the territorial 4th Battalion of the Buffs, some 120 fully accoutremented soldiers. In *Petard* 'B' company of 188 men had now been confined in crowded messdecks for four days, a dismal and unfamiliar situation for men ill-prepared after serving three long years in Malta. The battalion had only recently landed in Egypt for rest and retraining, now found themselves bound for the perils of the Dodecanese islands without having started their training.

The two Fleets heavily laden, upper decks and between spaces crowded with men and stores to a point where efficient manning and fighting of the armament was at risk, sailed at 0630/23rd escorted by four Hunts, *Aldenham, Exmoor, Hursley* and *Rockwood*, the attendant cruiser *Phoebe* to go as far as the 'safety line', south of Rhodes. Shortly before sailing, David Nasmith managed to get the *Petard*'s two whalers back and with some difficulty because of cargo cluttering the iron deck rehoisted at the davits from which jeep trailers had been lowered at Leros; it turned out to be a fortunate decision by the First Lieutenant, one that within a few hours saved some lives.

On the night of the 22nd/23rd while the Fleets, *Jervis* and *Pathfinder*, successfully offloaded men and stores in Alinda Bay, two Hunts, *Adrias* and *Hurworth* ran into a mine ambush. With terrible losses in lives, *Hurworth* sank surrounded by ignited fuel oil, and *Adrias* with the forrard third of the ship blown off managed to get clear and beach inside the sanctuary of Gurvergenik Bay. The Greek ship's commanding officer, the wounded Commander J.H. Toumbas, RHN, was able to pass details of the disaster and estimate the position of the minefield by the Aldis light of a patrolling Beaufighter. The warning, in retransmission to *Eclipse* and *Petard* became mutilated in its urgent relay and gave the location of the mine trap off the west instead of the east route round the north tip of Kalymnos.

Commodore Levant destroyers, Commodore P. Todd, DSO OBE RN, disturbed by an increasing volume of complaints from the commanding officers of Levant destroyers, on the futility of the operation, embarked in *Eclipse* just before Commander Mack led the mixed group of four Hunts and two fleets out of Alexandria. He received the grim news of *Hurworth*'s sinking and the damage to the *Adrias* as the ships sailed north. Percy Todd hoped that he would be able to see and assess for himself the situation which seemed to be going from bad to worse; in addition to the cruisers damaged, the British and Greek destroyers sunk and damaged, about eight Italian ships, destroyers and a minelayer and transports working for the Allies had been sunk at Leros.

Shortly after the attendent cruiser *Phoebe* turned away south, and as the destroyers moved on into the gathering dusk, still south of Rhodes, *Rockwood* found herself in trouble and unable to maintain speed, oil fuel had become contaminated with sea-water; *Eclipse* ordered the Hunt to return to Alexandria escorted by *Exmoor*, the remainder carrying on, passing between Rhodes and Scarpento on a course to round the western end of Kos. Instead of continuing north leaving Kalymnos to starboard, then north about Leros to approach Alinda bay from the north and east, the received mine warning retransmitted from the damaged and beached *Adrias*, influenced a change of plan. Ordering the two Hunts *Aldenham* and *Hursley* to keep clear of the suspected minefield west of Kalymnos, then to close Levitha and create a diversion by bombarding the harbour, *Eclipse* with *Petard* astern at one cable distance, turned to pass to the east of Kalymnos towards Sandamar bay where the destroyers were to anchor and transfer the Buffs into MLs and MTBs for onward passage across a short stretch of water to Leros.

Proceeding in the intense darkness that came before moonrise, into the Karabalka channel, *Petard* clung to the dim blue glow of *Eclipse*'s stern light, every man in the ship at extreme tension because patrolling aircraft could be heard overhead, about three had been identified on the radar screens. Loading numbers with ready fused ammunition cradled in their arms, stood-to at guns trained and elevated in four sectors ready to pour out a barrage blind into the night above an anticipated umbrella of falling magnesium flares. None came; instead the ship reeled under a huge impact, men cowered with shocked nerve systems, as a giant explosion and flame erupted dead ahead where the *Eclipse* led unseen into a night made darker by the proximity of high land masses; at 0050 less than 200 yards ahead of *Petard*, the *Eclipse* blew up on a mine moored in 48 fathoms, sinking in speeding seconds.

Reacting instantly, Rupert Egan turned his ship hard a port with engines thrown into full emergency astern, bringing *Petard* to a stop, lying across the path of a stiff breeze blowing from the north. The crowded ship listened to the awful silence that followed the nightmare destruction of the leading ship loaded beyond normal safety limits with men and stores; every man, soldier and sailor cramped with his own private fear of the same thing happening to the ship drifting on the wind in mined water. Smoke and the smell of oil fuel blew down onto the *Petard* as David Nasmith organised to clear away the two whalers on dark and crowded decks. The task of turning out the davits and lowering the boats manned by scratch crews was one of great difficulty but done with little delay and no lack of volunteers.

The boats lowered and under the command of Canadian Midshipman Rothwell, disappeared into the dark under oars to search for survivors. For four hours, in extremely hazardous conditions, in a sea thick with oil, with enemy aircraft overhead trying to locate his ship, the young midshipman, little more than a boy, with his two whalers looked for men in the roughening sea. The casualties were terrible, out of a total of over 420 men, 220 ship's company, the remainder soldiers of the headquarter unit and 'A' company of the Buffs, only 44 were found. The tall red-headed midshipman and his boats carried on bringing back to the ship the few pitiful oil covered survivors until Rupert was forced to stop the search as daylight came nearer, putting his own ship and its vital passengers at unacceptable risk. The whalers smothered in fuel oil were hooked on and hoisted awkwardly, the inexpert fully armed and accoutremented soldiers crowding the darkened ship could not assist, and for no fault of theirs, hindered the seamen stumbling on the encumbered jeep and ammunition box crowded blackened out iron deck. Among the survivors, Commander Mack was saved and also the colonel commanding the Buffs, Colonel Iggulden and one of his majors. Apart from the few found by the whaler crews, a handful of immensely strong and lucky swimmers managed to cover the distance and crawl ashore on the Turkish mainland. Among those who perished was Commodore Percy Todd, who died in the attempt to see what his destroyers were asked to endure.

After recovering the whalers, Rupert withdrew his ship and felt a way into Turkish territorial waters to lie up for the day at Budram, where *Petard*'s men did what little they could to lift the gloom and near despair, that not surprisingly afflicted a few of the soldier passengers who had now shared the destroyer's crowded accommodation for five days. In this the latest episode of a doom threatened struggle by 'B' company to reach and reinforce the Leros garrison, they had seen friends and companions of 'A' company destroyed while they remained as helpless spectators.

That night 24th/25th still lying up at Budram, ML359 moved in longside *Petard* and embarked a naval base party for Leros, landing them at Alinda without difficulty. Soon after the transfer of the naval passengers, Rupert Egan moved his ship south across the Gulf of Kos into another Turkish bay, remaining there for a further long day under continuous joint surveillence by the local Turkish coastal defence unit and the German aircraft repeating the now familiar tactics to provoke the tired and edgy ship into retaliatory action. The ship did not anchor because it seemed very obvious that the Turks wished to board the crowded British destroyer, and the only way to avoid them and keep clear of a small motor launch, short of using force, was to remain under way.

After dark the two Hunts who had also remained inside the Aegean to help *Petard* after the *Eclipse* had been mined, nosed cautiously into the bay and placed themselves longside the fleet. Ammunition cases and other arms were transferred quickly, followed by the men of 'B' company, 50 into each ship, but the main deck cargo had to remain, there was no room for the six jeeps that had crowded the decks for so long. The *Aldenham* followed by *Hursley* slipped away, within two hours entered Alinda Bay and were able before the moon rose to land the soldiers without loss or injury. Soon after the Hunts had left, *Petard* retired at speed south round the eastern end of Rhodes, entering Alexandria in the early afternoon of the 25th and landed the few survivors from the *Eclipse* while she refuelled and prepared to return to the islands.

The ship began to see changes in the ship's company, men going sick under the strain of long months of active service conditions, others mainly the regular engagement members of the ship's company leaving either on promotion or for professional courses prior to promotion. One of the first to go was the Yeoman of Signals Chapman who left on 16th October discharged to the *Woolwich* following *Petard*'s arrival back at Alexandria escorting the crippled *Carlisle*. The Yeoman, a large ebullient extrovert rather untidy petty officer, had exhausted himself serving two commanding officers. Long endless hours at sea at the captain's elbow, constantly ensuring that no signal from the senior or other ships in company, by light, semaphore or flag hoist was missed by his signal staff, always available or on call to interpret the meaning of signal groups and in his role as custodian of the fleet signal book. With a small signal department he had to provide the only back up to the man on watch while the junior men off watch rested. While operating with the fleet the yeoman often had to read and interpret correctly and log 200 plus signals in a day, and it became gradually obvious that this rugged character, was exhausted and physically ill. Doc Prendergast knew that he had to be rested and the arrangements to get Chapman relieved were put in train before the ship arrived back on the Levant station.

Petty Officer Yeoman Bishop who arrived to take over from Yeoman R. Chapman DSM, was another professional, but a smaller and slighter physical build, always immaculate straight correct and carried himself like a product of the gunnery school, a strong disciplinarian and a first class signalman. His almost continuous presence on the bridge or the flag deck spruce, alert, miraculously always shaved; the meticulous attention to signal drill and technique had a strengthening effect on the morale of tired men, not only those within his signal department but others in the bridge team, including the officers.

Others left the ship at Alexandria including Telegraphist Neil Allen en route to HMS Mercury in England for his Leading Telegraphist course.

During daylight hours the islands that were being so laboriously supplied and reinforced by the destroyers shuttling up under the cover of darkness, endured constant and merciless bombing by the German air force now reinforced by squadrons withdrawn from the Balkans and the Russian front. At the same time the German preparations were advanced for the sea and air invasion of Leros. Without the threat of surface ship attack by day, invasion shipping from Greece was able to be deployed subject only to Allied submarine gun and torpedo threat; several transports and landing craft were sunk with heavy loss of lives by the British, Greek and Polish submarines that operated in the archipelago. The British air squadrons operating from distant bases also took their toll and carried out constant reconnaissance patrols; but they were unable to provide cover against the German bomber units so that cruisers and destroyers could take advantage of the reconnaissance aircraft sightings or finish off convoys attacked by the submarines and British bombers. After dark, enemy shipping was able to move from the reported locations before the fleet and Hunt class destroyers lying up in neutral waters caught up with them. The invasion forces for Leros inexorably moved closer through the islands building up strength, while the Ju 87 and Ju 88 squadrons destroyed the Leros defence positions, coastal batteries, roads and stores.

In a desperate effort to break up and destroy the enemy sea forces the Levant destroyers were being turned back on the return run from the store and troop reinforcement shuttle service to spend an extra night on offensive sweeps round the islands, probing into harbours and bays seeking out German E-boats and transports. It called for tremendous endurance and navigation skills of the highest quality, operating under almost continuous air attack below flares and bright moonlight, in waters full of natural hazards with only few navigational beacons in operation, and these only on the Turkish mainland and offshore islands.

While a strong force of Fleets and Hunts including the *Pathfinder* supported by *Phoebe* roamed north and south of Rhodes and round Kos without success, *Petard* with the Hunts *Beaufort* and *Belvoir* left Alexandria in the afternoon of 29th to rendezvous with the cruiser *Aurora* off Kastelorizo Island before entering the Dodecanese, rounding the north east cape of Rhodes to pass Symi before lying up in the Gulf of Kos. *Petard* loaded with eight jeeps and the trailers fully loaded with military stores also had embarked sixty soldiers and nine naval personnel. The Hunts also carried a full load of men and materials; *Belvoir* had five jeeps and sixty soldiers, and the *Beaufort* the same number of soldiers, but only one jeep and mail for the Leros garrison.

Rupert Egan commanded the force of three destroyers that made a rendezvous on the afternoon of the 30th with the cruiser waiting to give extra AA gun power until for force moved north of Rhodes under cover of darkness. A fighter escort of Beaufighters closed the ships as the cruiser and destroyers proceeded along the Turkish coast inside neutral waters in the area of the Seven Capes, while the *Aurora*'s radar plot warned of the approach of a large formation of aircraft from the west, from the direction of the setting sun. The fighter escort quickly sighted three formations of Ju 88s escorted by six Me 109s. The enemy flew at high level and were at once engaged by concentrated gunfire from· all four ships before the fighters attacked the enemy squadron. One Ju 88 fell to the anti-aircraft fire as the formation released bombs from 12000 ft; there was little room to take avoiding action, *Aurora* turned to port at high speed with one bomb falling close astern and immediately ahead of the following *Beaufort*. *Belvoir* completely surrounded by huge spouts of white/brown water survived in the main concentration of the bomb fall, while *Petard* turning at full speed to starboard found herself driving straight at the high steep cliffs on the Turkish mainland only a few cable lengths to starboard of the ship's course through the territorial waters. The ship's company's alarm at the closeness of the rocks and cliff face, turned to admiration of the Captain's seamanship as he manoeuvred the top-heavy ship, pursued by bombs with every gun in action, out of the close and dangerous proximity to the shore.

The first concentrated high level attack failed to damage any ship, but as the group continued to steam north, further waves of mixed Ju 87 and 88 bombers drove down onto the ships. The disciplined and concentrated gunfire succeeded in deflecting the bombers' aim, who also found the need to defend themselves against determined attacks from the Beaufighters a severe handicap. Then came fourteen Stukas, escorted by Mc 202s who ignored the Beaufighters and with a grim relentless dedication that identified the squadron as veterens from the Russian front and probably also the earlier Crete campaign, the planes plummeted down through the barrage of fire onto the ships.

One bomb hit *Aurora* amidships dead centre in the middle of the four twin four inch anti-aircraft mountings. All four mountings were trained outboard, elevated to maximum elevation exposing every member of the gun crews to the bomb explosion behind them. Forty-six men were killed and twenty wounded, the after control tower was destroyed and the 'X' and 'Y' six inch gun turrets put out of action. The cruiser's speed had to be reduced to prevent the after funnel, damaged and distorted, from collapsing onto the rescue and fire parties working in the area of the bomb explosion.

Aurora with her gallant crew had to retire escorted by *Beaufort*, leaving *Petard*, and *Belvoir* to try to make the entry into the strait between Rhodes and the Turkish mainland with only the Beaufighters to help them fight off German aircraft determined not to let the destroyers through. The ships felt lonely and exposed without the famous cruiser to aid and encourage the smaller ships, crowded with troops and stores fighting desperately to hold off the succeeding air attacks until reaching the shelter of neutral waters and darkness.

The Beaufighters did what they could, but the sheer weight of the attacks and numbers of bombers were too much; shortly after *Aurora* and her escort disappeared to the south, sixteen Ju 88s struck at 1700. The two ships using every trick known to the commanding officers jinked at high then reduced speed with guns, 4 inch and close range pouring out a massive fire rate, first at long range controlled fire then at close sector gunlayers control barrage. The attack went on for almost three quarters of an hour before the Junkers retired harried by the three Beaufighters who continued to mix it with the larger number of enemy, always at additional risk from the gunfire of the attacked ships. Barely five minutes after the scattered Ju 88 formation had retired towards Rhodes a second 'V' formation of eight Ju 88s appeared flying high, intent on a formation attack. This they delivered at 1755, the two destroyers twisted and dodged away from the falling bombs, then steamed together to give mutual support against the planes coming in singly after breaking formation.

This time one Junker instead of flying over the ship, banked before reaching *Belvoir* and released a bomb that hit squarely at the front and at the base of the bridge behind the crew of the fo'c'sle gun who failed to notice the bomb entry hole until fire was checked. From *Petard* ahead, the bridge crew on the Hunt could be seen cranning over the front of the bridge trying to spot where the bomb had gone. It did not need the grim comic obscenities about exposed orifices, signalled from the fleet destroyer to disguise a concern for the smaller consort, to help Lieutenant J.F.D. Bush RN and his crew to quickly find the unexploded bomb deep inside the ship resting on one of the stabiliser fins. The First Lieutenant and engineer officer assisted by a couple of volunteers manhandled the bomb up on deck; then carried by the largest man in the ship, cradled in his arms, the bomb was carried aft and dropped over the stern.

The pressure from the German bombers showed no sign of slackening, there seemed to be every chance that the squadrons would again launch an attack with greater numbers before dark, so Rupert turned the small force back on a reverse course away from Rhodes and retreated at speed to the island of Kastelorizo still pursued by harassing Ju 88s. The destroyers arrived off the small port where the AA batteries ashore helped the hard pressed ships to keep the Germans at a respectable distance. It was a bad day for Allied shipping losses; two large landing craft that had left Haifa the previous afternoon escorted by three MTBs and heavily loaded with soldiers, were caught by Stukas and sunk shortly after *Aurora* had been hit, the casualties again were heavy, with only about thirty men surviving the sinkings.

By 1900 it was quite dark, and Rupert Egan turned with *Belvoir* back north west past Rhodes and Symi without being caught by flare dropping aircraft. With considerable relief and not a little surprise the two destroyers were allowed to move into the Gulf of Mandelyah, there to move into a deep bay surrounded by steep cliffs that permitted the ships to lie only yards off shore and reduced the chance of being sighted by German reconnaissance aircraft patrolling the Gulf of Kos. The bay found and recommended by Brooksbank to Rupert, proved a safe haven; the ships lay at anchor undisturbed by aircraft, sighted several times by the watchful ships, or the Turkish patrols ashore. That night 31st October/1st November, *Petard* led the way successfully into Parthani Bay by the SW entrance, and there disembarked troops and stores quickly; before moonrise the destroyers had given the bombers the slip, and were back in Iasus bay.

The usual restless day followed, with the occasional Ju 88 buzzing the two ships provocatively, and enlivened by the visit of Turkish officials who had to be persuaded by a pantomime played out by Bertie's ERAs stripping down a working but non-essential auxiliary engine, that *Petard* had anchored to carry out vital repairs, and that *Belvoir* had anchored also in case a tow had to be organised. A long day, 1st November, passed with few men in either destroyer able to have more than a short catnap at their action stations, everyone keeping a wary eye on the Ju 88s who swept low over the discovered hideout. The German aircraft also made the Turkish examination officers nervous, it was very obvious that they half expected the ships and aircraft to attack each other and became very anxious to leave.

For the British destroyers the patrol craft lying alongside, flying large Turkish ensigns became a guarantee of immunity against bombs from the Ju 88s, so a battle of wits ensued to keep the reluctant Turks on board each ship for as long as possible. In *Petard*, one Turk invited down to the engine room to examine progress on the bogus repair, found that the engine room staff had to remove the ladder up to the entrance hatch for an apparent urgent job that could only be tackled with the ladder unshipped. The replacement of the ladder took a long time to effect as the securing bolts had somehow been mislaid. Other members of the boarding party including the Mayor of Gulak, the Chief of Police and Harbour Master were taken down to the wardroom for refreshment and plied with drink by a persuasive Doctor. Under the care of the Irish medic the Turks, without any knowledge of

English or a third party language to defend themselves, were overwhelmed by the variety and quantity of drink. From time to time reports reached the bridge that made the jaded watchkeepers envy the doctor's task, the more so as the afternoon passed and the sounds of song in the still air of the bay confirmed that Prendergast was applying himself with dedication and enthusiasm to his duties. The Turk in the engine room finally had to be released to join his companions dancing away the last of the twilight in the arms of a wild red headed and bearded officer in the wardroom.

The four guests with their presence and craft having helped to deter any Ju 88 pilot who may have been tempted to ignore his orders to observe the sanctuary of neutral waters by attacking the anchored destroyers, were led to the Mediterranean ladder, and there, two clutching photographs of the ship, had to be urged rather forcibly to leave the ship and its generous doctor host. Rupert ordered both ships to weight anchor as the Turks left, the destroyers slipping away out of the bay in darkness to pass to the north of Kos, hopeful that the flare dropping airmen would not catch them as they passed through the narrow straits between the island and the mainland of Turkey out into rather more open water south of Kalymnos. In the approaches to the small harbour serving the island, both ships dropped delayed action devices timed to explode at intervals over the next 24 hours, to alarm and puzzle the enemy who were using the harbour as a staging point for the invasion preparations. The lay completed, the two ships turned south and left the Aegean using the Kaso Strait, arriving back at 1500/2 November Alexandria without being located by the German air fleet.

Petard had a night in, only a handful of the hardier spirits appeared when liberty men were piped, most turned in to hammocks as soon as the stores and ammunition had been struck below, the ship empty of soldiers, silent except for the watchkeepers keeping a quiet vigil, seemed to sleep like her exhausted crew.

By first light men and stores began to arrive longside in barges and landing craft, and soon after mid-day the ship was on the way again with two Hunts, similarly loaded, to rendezvous with the only surviving undamaged cruiser *Phoebe*, still on station to the south of Rhodes to give moral support and gun power to the destroyers moving north every night into the hostile Dodecanese waters. This run that kept *Petard* three nights out amongst the islands followed by two days in the bays lining the many Gulfs of the mainland of Turkey was relatively quiet, the main weight of the air attacks seemed to be concentrated.on the destroyers and MTBs hunting round the islands looking for craft bringing together the German invasion forces to the jumping off islands, Kalymnos and Kos. The men and stores were off loaded into MTBs and landing craft in a bay near Burdram disturbed only by a brief attack, before *Petard* slid away to reinforce the destroyers patrolling round Leros. After an hour or two of false alarms, *Petard* returned to Alexandria south through the Kaso strait without sighting enemy shipping.

While aircraft, Beaufighters and Wellington bombers continued the daylight search, and destroyers at night with limited success sank a few caiques and lighters; *Petard* had two nights in Alexandria with the ship's company out on the town in a big way keeping the provost marshal's staff busy returning men from brothels and the bars of 'Sister' street and further afield, where they had tried to drink themselves into a short break of alcoholic forgetfulness. The few who had been removed from a bar fracas or for breaking up an establishment, found the First Lieutenant tolerant and merciful when they appeared at the defaulters' table. Their biggest problem was the agony of a hangover to be coped with as the ship sailed north again.

Petard sailed at 1530/7th, Rupert Egan in command of a force of three destroyers, the others were two Hunts, *Rockwood*, Lieutenant S.R. Le H. Lombard-Hobson, and the Polish manned ship ORP *Krakowiak*, Commander Naracewisz. The ships arrived in the early hours of the morning at Limassol, Cyprus. A few hours later after the commanding officers had been briefed with the latest intelligence, in the early afternoon from Limassol, *Petard* led the Hunts towards the Aegean entering via the Scarpento Strait after dark, with orders of critical urgency to seek and destroy enemy shipping about to assault Leros.

German air attacks on Leros had increased in number and severity, over half the heavy anti-aircraft artillery manned by the Italians had been knocked out with heavy casualties to the gunners. The British garrison brought to the island a few at a time, in hazardous conditions and at a heavy cost in men and ships, without armour, field artillery or heavy equipment, suffered badly from the incessant daylight bomb attacks. Some two dozen enemy landing craft had been sighted and were known to be hidden in and around Cos and Kalymnos ready to transport highly trained and seasoned German assault troops.

Harried by flare dropping aircraft and their accompanying

bombers, Rupert Egan drove his ships round the islands in almost desperation, probing into bays and inlets looking for the elusive invasion craft. To the alarm of his ship's company several times *Petard*'s commanding officer ordered the searchlight to be switched on, the stabbing beam briefly flickered across the rocky shore line, revealed nothing and twice the ships were punished in return by more attacks from the air and darkness of the pre-moonrise sky; fortunately all escaped without damage or casualties. They were probably saved from an overwhelming mass attack by the fact that two other destroyer groups were out amongst the islands and received the main weight of the bombers attention.

Frustrated and with moral at a low ebb, the ship with the Hunts, *Rockwood* and *Krakowiak*, moved into the Gulf of Mandelyah to lie up during the daylight hours of the 9th. While sweating out the long day Rupert received a succession of signals reporting the sightings made by Beaufighter reconnaissance patrols. The landing craft and supply ships on the move round the islands clearly closing in on Leros included one 3000 ton ship with several smaller craft, inside and berthed on the breakwater of Kalymnos harbour.

Before darkness had fully returned *Petard* led the way out of Gurvergenik Bay into the Gulf while in the far distance, to the west, squadrons of Junkers could be seen either closing or returning from raids on Leros where the pressure and destruction had continued without slackening. At speed Rupert took his unit past the southern tip of Leros and across to Levitha without finding anything. The orders for the three destroyers, gave an area of search round Levitha and South to Stampalia, then down the west coast of Kalymnos before withdrawing out of the Aegean to Limassol. Nothing could be found in the bays and inlets of Levitha, then withdrawing south towards Stampalia the destroyers found at last.

The first sighting about 10 miles from Levitha was a large float that turned out to be empty; as Rupert slowed the unit steaming in line ahead, with the Polish Hunt bringing up the rear, the bridge buzzer and voice pipe from *Petard*'s radar 286 office alerted Rupert that several surface echoes existed out on the port bow less than 3000 yards away. Turning to starboard 20 degrees to take up the down moon position and to bring all three destroyers round so that their full main armament could bear on the target, Rupert ordered the searchlight to expose the target followed seconds later by *Rockwood*'s beam. At the intersection of the beams there were two caiques and a landing craft closely bunched together with the caiques nearest to the Allied ships, all three packed with troops so tightly that there seemed to be no room for men to move from the position they had occupied when the craft were loaded.

The destroyers opened fire simultaneously; 4 inch shells churned the sea round the invasion craft into a boiling cauldron of explosions and spray. The wooden caiques were hit many times by the first broadside salvoes, bursting into flames almost immediately, turning into violently burning funeral pyres for the men crowding the decks and holds. The sudden leaping flames lit the sea and replaced the now doused searchlights, *Petard* and *Rockwood* checked the 4 inch fire, the lighter had disappeared masked by the flames and smoke from the burning caiques. Hauling clear of the heavy smoke blowing down onto the three destroyers Rupert ordered *Krakowiak* to open fire with star shell to the east of the burning craft; two flares falling on their small parachutes lit up the low silhouette of the lighter and before the flares fell to expire in the sea, the joint broadside of the unit, steaming still in close line ahead formation, had torn the hull apart and finished it as a floating transport, killing all but a few of the crew and soldiers who had filled the large open hold. At that moment one of the caiques blew up leaving only the flames of the second flickering on the water line before it also disappeared to leave the sea again in starlit dimness. *Petard*'s searchlight flicked quickly over the sea to confirm that nothing remained of the invasion transport group, the hard brilliant beam shewed up only debris of shattered wooden hulls, lighting up here and there amongst the scarce evidence of the short merciless action, the white faces and arms of the few swimmers that remained.

The patrol south to Stampalia was abandoned, Rupert on the assumption that the caiques and lighter might be part of a general move to the east and Kalymnos from islands to west, turned towards the dark bulk of Kalymnos seen against the eastern sky, hoping to overtake other troop transports. The three destroyers closed the land without making further contact then turned south keeping close to the sheer cliffs of the island searching anxiously for E-boat escorted landing craft convoys or stores carrying vessels. The west coast produced no targets, so *Petard* rounded the western tip of the island and closed the harbour with only a partial hope that the merchant ship reported and photographed by the reconnaissance Beaufighter would still be in port. Surprised to have arrived off the harbour without being detected by patrolling aircraft, especially after the searchlights, gunfire and star shell used only 1½ hours earlier to the west, Egan again ordered the Polish ship to fire star shell over the harbour area while *Petard* led the line on a course parallel to the breakwater, keeping a distance of 6000 yards to clear the area of a suspected minefield. In the bay overshadowed by the mountains that lined the two sides and extended back into the interior, the darkness before the moon rose over the eastern mountain summit was total, no glimmer or pinpoints of light escaped from the harbour or the little town jammed in the narrow ravine that rose steeply from the harbour. *Krakowiak*'s star shells exploded harsh brilliant light with a suddenness that startled even those in the ships out in the bay expecting the illumination; four magnesium flares slowly descended on the town and harbour, exposed the cluster of white houses at the base of the crack between the two mountain ranges, and the breakwater that grew out of the western side of the bay. Standing up above the breakwater wall, exposed by the flares, the masts and superstructure of a medium sized merchant ship could be seen by the raiding destroyers with almost disbelief at the evidence of their eyes, a ship reported by the reconnaissance planes still at its berth after nightfall.

Krakowiak continued to lob in star shells as the three ships opened fire on the ship berthed inside the breakwater, it was a difficult target, the lower hull concealed and protected by the masonry of the sea wall. For nearly an hour *Petard* preceded the column of destroyers back and forth across the bay pounding the ship and harbour, many of the 1500 shells fired, ricochetted off the top of the wall and bounded up the hill and mountain sides to explode on the barren terrain. Others to the sickening despair of the control teams and the directing GCO, crashed into the houses of the innocent islanders caught up in the terrible inhumanity of war. Greeks first overrun by the Italians in 1941, now in the power of the Germans who were forcing their late allies and the Greek islanders with great brutality to service their continuing fight in the Aegean, were in their small Kalymnos homes being bombarded by ships of their allies, British and Polish.

Before the awful messy action finished, the moon rose clear of the mountain curtain and shone down onto the ships and the bay. The time was 2300 and the merchant ship's superstructure blazed with large fires as the hull began to heel away from the breakwater; Rupert ordered the destroyers to cease fire; no return gunfire had been reported but the cannonade unleashed a hornet's nest of aircraft that unseen in the clear night sky could be heard positioning themselves to attack the ships.

Rupert took *Petard* in to the entrance of the harbour at the same time ordering the Hunts to withdraw clear of the bay and await his return; turning his ship in the entrance it was possible to see that the merchant ship, SS *Trapani* had been effectively put out of service, but it was disappointing to see that there were no concentrations of landing craft. At the head of the harbour, difficult to see clearly because of the smoke and dust from the long bombardment, it seemed possible that some lighters and other craft had taken shelter, so Rupert Egan fired a torpedo while turning *Petard* 180 degrees to retire seawards; the torpedo exploded violently against the jetty of the unhappy little township, the great orange glare of the explosion exposing the cluster of buildings momentarily astern of the ship. *Petard* hurried out of the bay with more and more aircraft buzzing the ship firing frantically blind in retaliation into the clear moon drenched sky. Rejoining the anxious Hunts, *Petard* resumed position at the head of the three ship column, the time was 2320, the destroyers stood out clear and marked by their wakes in the sea sparkling with moonlight.

The planes were acting in a new and curious way, several made shallow dive passes at the column, down moon along the line and from port and starboard, coming in low in the face of the 4 inch and close range barrage thrown up by *Petard* and the two Hunts, but no bombs were released for a time. The island of Cos stood out on the port hand less than three miles away, and from the airfield at Marmari planes could be seen with navigation lights switched on, taking off to attack the ships. *Petard* turned her guns from the defensive AA barrage and for a short time lobbed several salvoes of shells onto the runways less than 9000 yards away, while the short range pom-pom and oerlikons continued to engage the aircraft overhead.

It soon became clear that the Germans were trying to use glider bombs from planes standing off down moon; several single bomb explosions occurred in the sea close to the ships' line of advance, Rupert altered the formation into a V, with *Petard* at the head of the triangle, *Rockwood* and *Krakowiak* station respectively to port and starboard 45 degrees out on the landing ship's two quarters. This increased the bombers' difficulties simply by dispersing the targets and presenting three wakes in the sea, at the same time the ships were able to give more effective mutual protective gun cover. For the next hour the ships steamed south at 20 knots under continuous harassment from aircraft running a shuttle service from the three airfields on Cos, all less than 10 miles from the targets. At 0020 *Rockwood* was hit by a glider bomb as the formation passed through a position 5 miles due west of Krokelo Point on Cos. The ship heeled round under full rudder through damage in the gearing room that also affected the steering. The bomb did not explode; it passed out of the ship below the water line in a fuel tank, a fire started in the switchroom which the electrical party got quickly under control. For a short time the commanding officer, Lieutenant Lombard-Hobson, tried to steer his ship using the main engines and to keep up to the speed of the formation, but his ship began to settle aft and took up a list to starboard, indicating rather serious damage.

Still keeping his ship going at twelve knots, Lombard-Hobson signalled to Rupert Egan with one word 'Turkey', the three ships altered course to leave the island of Nisero close on the port hand, all the time the Ju 88s came out of the clear night sky like angry hornets, releasing their bombs at the ships firing back at vague radar echoes and the sound of screaming engines. By 0130 *Rockwood*'s gearing room was totally flooded and *Petard* received a request for a tow. Aircraft still came at the ships in single plane attacks requiring the guns of all the destroyers to remain in action, this hampered the men in both ships arranging the tow; in *Rockwood* the twin 4 inch forward gun mounting fired barrage salvoes over the heads of the mixed bag of cooks, stewards and stokers who struggled under the muzzle blast of the guns to pass out unfamiliar wire and cable to the *Petard* on whose after-structure and quarterdeck, 'X' and 'Y' guns continued to fire at the unseen enemy bombers, while men hauled in the heavy towing gear from the damaged hunt. With *Krakowiak* stationed down moon putting up a furious barrage over her two consorts and allies overcoming daunting difficulties, the tow preparations took less than half an hour, and the ships were under way making 15 knots, steering a course to pass close under the towering cliffs of Nisero. Rupert Egan followed a course plotted by Ken Brooksbank, taking the ships within yards of the steep and precipitous coastline, giving some protection to the ships from planes on the port hand. The cliffs multiplied the crash of gunfire, and lit up with a terrifying nearness in the light of *Rockwood*'s full flash propellent; all her flashless ammunition had been expended.

Before the ships cleared Nisero, the attacks stopped, and all were hopeful that they would get across the 10 miles of open water to Cape Krio on the Turkish mainland making the entrance to the Gulf of Doris without further harassment, now that also the moon was setting, but this was not to be. Another task group, *Faulknor, Beaufort* and *Pindos* were out searching round Kalymnos and attracted the aircraft out from Rhodes as well as Cos. Those flying in from Rhodes located the *Petard* with her tow, and the attentive *Krakowiak*; before the ships reached sanctuary, two flare and bomb attacks were launched. The ships were again fortunate to avoid further damage, although *Petard* began to have trouble with 4 inch fused ammunition that burst prematurely a short distance from the gun muzzles, spraying the hull, open gun decks and bridge with shrapnel, a clear indication that the gun linings were again worn out. Fortunately no one was hit but this added hazard did little to bolster optimism that the tow would escape the enemy. The second attack passed and again somehow the ships avoided damage. Out of the blinding shambles of falling flares, crash of gunfire and explodind bombs, Brooky and Rupert Egan navigated the formation through the natural unmarked hazards of islets and rocks which littered the coastline waters, into the neutral waters inside the Gulf of Doris. Brooky found a landlocked bay called Losta, where the three ships anchored at 0750/11th.

During the day, *Petard* moved alongside *Rockwood* and transferred oil out of the Hunt so that the bomb hole could be brought above the water line. The Hunt had only suffered one casualty, although the first impressions in the dark caused short term alarm. The unexploded bomb had bounced twice along the iron deck before ploughing down into the ship, and on its way tore through the beef screen full of meat thawing out after removal from the refrigerator by the ship's Tanky. The gory mess of meat carcasses scattered over the deck presented a nightmarish situation when the damage control party and rescue parties arrived on the scene, it took a few shocked minutes before a relieved commanding officer learnt that a number of his crew had not been massacred.

After dark on the 11th, *Petard* led *Krakowiak* away south past Cape Alupo marking the southern entrance to the Gulf of Doris, rounding the north east tip of Rhodes clearing the Aegean long before daylight. *Rockwood* now joined the *Adrias* beached inside the Gulf of Cos to the north as the second damaged destroyer left to the constant scrutiny of patrolling Ju 88s, the interested observations and occasional visits by the Turkish coast defence officials; equipment and welders were ferried up to her under cover of successive nights and the hole made by the bomb closed. On the 19th the Hunt made her escape towed by the *Blencathra*.

Petard immediately on arrival at Alexandria during the afternoon of the 12th, following routine refuelling and reammunitioning, moved longside *Woolwich* to have worn gun linings renewed, the second time in four weeks, during which period the ship had fired her entire outfit of 800 fuzed 4 inch ammunition three times and in addition many hundreds of semi-armour piercing and direct impact ammunition.

That same day the long threatened invasion of Leros started, hard bitten action tested troops swarming ashore under overwhelming air cover, Stuka dive bombers used in their classic role as aerial artillery, followed by waves of paratroops. The battle continued from the 12th to the 17th, with the British troops so laboriously ferried to the island being cut to pieces without adequate arms or air support to assist them, receiving little support from the poorly disciplined and trained Italian allies. By the early hours of the 17th, resistance had ceased, very few of the troops were able to escape, only about 250 British soldiers, airmen and naval personnel managed to clamber aboard MTBs, MLs and caiques under immense air attack, and through the great bravery of their crews, were slipped into Turkey, many going into temporary internment. With the exception of this handful who escaped into Turkey or to the north and the island of Samos, four complete battalions of British troops became casualties or were taken prisoner. Some 200 officers and 3,000 men of the British army became captives, 350 officers and 5,000 men of the Italian forces were also captured. The Germans repeated the brutal retaliation meted out to their former allies on the other captured islands; most of the officers were shot.

In Alexandria *Petard* had been held up with problems caused by the worn gun linings. On two guns, these refused to be removed and the guns had to be taken out of the ship and into the workshops of the *Woolwich*. So while the five days of the final agony of Leros passed, *Petard* remained in harbour sailing only late on the 18th bound via Kasteloriso island to the Gulf of Cos to help in the organisation of an evacuation.

Rupert Egan had under his command, the two Hunts *Croome* and

HHMS *Themistocles*, and proceeded to Cyprus, the Port of Limassol for orders, arriving there next morning. The orders arrived at 1300/19th, *Petard* was to sail via the eastern entrance to the Aegean, north about Rhodes and take the destroyer group into Alakishi Bay located on the northern fringe of the Gulf of Cos, there to act as a focal point for small craft, the surviving MTBs, MLs and caiques, still ferrying out escapees from Leros and the garrison from the abandoned Samos.

The decision to abandon the island of Samos instead of trying to repeat the torment of Leros, was the only sane decision to emerge out of the ill-conceived campaign. The relatively small British army units, the Greek Sacred Heart Regiment, naval and RAF support groups and several hundred Italian troops had started to pull out on the night of the 18th/19th; many were already being collected into temporary holding camps by the Turks prior to being transported by freight trains to the Lebanon and Israel. These arrangements were the culmination of frantic diplomatic activity.

The evacuation of the highly disciplined, patient British army units, survivors from the latest of the many forlorn and hopeless expeditions or adventures to which it had been transported by the navy, always in the face of overwhelming air attacks, was the concern and priority of the Levant Command.

Arriving in Alakishi Bay after a passage that had been enlivened by powerful searchlights sweeping the narrows north of Rhodes and the entrance to the Gulf of Cos, the lights above Villa Nuova on Rhodes being particularly powerful and menacing, the two ships anchored in very deep water that made the location less suited for small vessels than other bays in the Gulf. On passage *Croome* had developed problems with an overheated stern gland on the starboard propeller shaft and had to turn back to Alexandria, leaving only *Themistocles* to accompany *Petard*.

Waiting through the day without any craft appearing, Egan ordered the destroyer motor cutters to be lowered and sent to patrol round the edges of the Gulf after dark, to collect and shepherd any shipping found, to the waiting destroyers. The cutters completed the night reconnaissance without sightings, so a party was landed with orders to climb the large hill that dominated the bay and gave a view from the summit of a large part of the Gulf and into the next bay, Kishle Batu. The reconnaissance party again drew a blank; *Petard* reported by signal that no shipping could be found.

Air surveillance by the enemy was surprisingly restrained, only a single Ju 88 toured the Gulf at about 0900 on both mornings the destroyers remained in the bay, and one appeared for a short time at 1700 on the first evening.

At 1900/22, *Petard* lead away south from the Gulf of Cos for the last time, crossing the Gulf keeping close to the Dorian promontory from Cape Shuyn to Cape Krio, then passing between Niseros and Piskopi group of islands. Again a number of searchlights shone across the entrance to the Gulf and others could be seen at a distance from the direction of Kandelusia, but nothing menaced the destroyers slipping away towards the Scarpento Straits. A few planes were seen with navigation lights switched on, landing at Cos, but to use Rupert Egan's own words, 'nothing disturbed the ship's decorous progress'.

The destroyers arrived back at Alexandria, passing through the boom at 1400/22nd, refuelled then berthed together at Kamaria docks.

So ended the campaign that should not have occurred once the Americans decision to withdraw support had emasculated the original plans to take Rhodes. The fact that the Aegean would eventually be bypassed, and that later the islands with the German garrisons would fall into the Allied hands while the German war machine was being smashed in northern and central Europe, should have been foreseen by the professionals who shaped strategy and conducted the operations. The campaign did nothing except to increase the suffering of the hapless Greeks, the Italian occupation forces were surplanted by the Germans, and many innocent islanders became the victims of the conflict in the Dodecanese.

Allied losses, mainly British in terms of men killed and taken prisoner, were heavy, and so was the toll of ships operating under the command of C-in-C Levant.

Destroyers sunk	6
Destroyers damaged	3
Cruisers damaged (one beyond repair)	4
Submarines sunk	2
MTBs, MLs, Minesweepers sunk	8

The losses inflicted on the enemy were also substantial; Allied aircraft, surface ships and submarines sank

(*Right*) Doc and Sub-Lieutenant
A. M. M. Wood

The ship wearing her Eastern Fleet livery

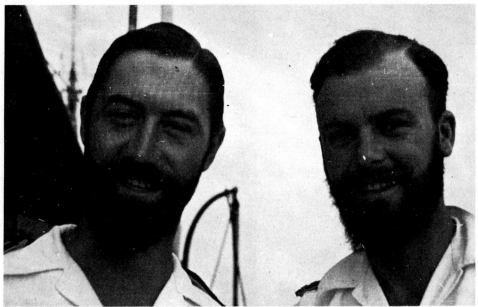

Brooky and the Gunnery Control Officer, two years after joining *Petard*

(*Centre*) The Japanese submarine *I 27* manoeuvering to ram the crippled *Paladin* and (*bottom*) *Petard's* seventh torpedo destroys the *I 27*

Merchant ships	8
F lighters and landing craft	14
Torpedo boats, Escort vessels	13
Floating dock	1
Armed caiques	5

CHAPTER 9

With the Eastern Fleet
The Japanese Submarine

Final remnants of the Leros garrison continued to filter back by island and coastal hopping in the few HMMLs, MTBs and caiques that survived, out of the Aegean to Casteloriso, later to be embarked in destroyers sent to collect the men, returning to Alexandria and the great empty transit camps outside the city. The Samos evacuees, mainly by rail had now reached the Lebanon, and were also being pulled back to the camps to rest and later to be reformed into new units, or sent home.

The Aegean and the Archipelago completely under German control, saw no further Allied shipping for many months, except for a few submarines and caiques slipping into the islands to land raiding and reconnaissance parties, otherwise Crete and Rhodes marked the northern limit for Levant Fleet operations.

The Commodore Levant Destroyers, dispersed destroyers that could be spared from patrol and escort duties, to give leave, rest the crews and for boiler cleaning. *Petard*, one of the fortunates, sailed for Haifa for a boiler clean and to give leave, arriving there on 23rd November. One whole watch by the same afternoon had departed in army transport to rest camps, one close to Jerusalem and another not far from Tel Aviv. There was a need for the break, the lower-deck had been going through a bad patch, the Dodecanese had taken its toll, men were dispirited and morale had suffered badly. But with the arrival at Haifa there seemed to be a decided lift to depressed spirits when the first party left for the break ashore; arrangements were immaculate, everything had been laid on to get the libertyman away, transport stood ready on the jetty as the ship berthed. The ship, the commanding officer and officers were fortunate in the Naval Officer in Charge Haifa who understood the probable mood and condition of the ships returning from the Dodecanese defeat.

In recent weeks several casualties and men leaving for courses, promotion, medical or compassionate reasons, had been replaced by junior very raw conscripted hostility only ratings. They arrived in the ship after long sea journeys in crowded transports, and in some cases after many days, even weeks in a desert transit camp. Some joined while frantic refuelling and reammunitioning was taking place to turn the ship round while men and stores were being crammed into every available space by a ship's company that showed signs of exhaustion and were jumpy. The depression of the tired men can only have increased the apprehension of the new men, who at times joined as one lonely individual without a companion to share a bewildering ordeal. A replacement might join to find the ship sailing inside the hour of getting himself and his kit inboard; there would be no time to settle into a crowded and very frightening ship of war, before the ship sailed into the Aegean and two or three nights of action and terror for the new draftee. Bombed and flared, to be in close proximity to 4 inch guns and close range weapons firing for long periods, was a situation for which the conscripts were totally unprepared by the short basic training in the UK, they came utterly unfamiliar with any aspect of life in an active service destroyer.

It was hardly surprising that on return to Alexandria, one or two, made blind futile attempts to run away to hide from fear in the hot desert city and port, unaware that there were many and perhaps worse perils for them in the teeming alleys surrounding the dock area; they were fortunate to be picked up quickly by one of the many Provost Marshal's patrols.

Changes were taking place in the officer complement which commenced to alter the regular to temporary officer ratio, from the six regular to the three temporary that had existed since the ship commissioned, and at the same time increased the total number. On return to harbour on 12th November after leaving *Rockwood* in Losta Bay, a university graduate, A.M.M. Wood, now commissioned as a temporary sub-lieutenant (E) RNVR, joined the ship and Bertie's engineering division. Tall slim freckled articulate and self possessed, he came just when a new face and personality was needed to stimulate and refresh the wardroom members, and to break the deadlock of depression and war weariness. Bertie took to his extra man, and Ken Brooksbank because perhaps he was also a graduate had much in common with the newcomer.

A week afterwards, the day following the arrival at Haifa, David Dunbar Nasmith suddenly received orders to leave the ship for a new appointment in command of the Type 3 Hunt, *Hayden*. His departure thirteen months after arriving to fill the vacancy left by Tony Fasson's death in *U-559*, resulted in a step up of the three lieutenants who had commissioned the ship together as sub-lieutenants, Robert de Pass now became the First Lieutenant, the GCO and Kenneth Brooksbank, the Second and Third Lieutenants respectively. For Robert the task at first seemed a daunting one, the lower deck in a dispirited mood, his own appearance of extreme youth that belied his age, tended to make the senior ratings in particular, suspect his ability to take over as the second in command and senior executive officer.

These doubts were dispelled, aided by two factors that helped to reinforce Robert's rather surprising determination, toughness, and the use that he made of friends, acquaintances and contacts to the advantage of the ship and the ship's company.

He was fortunate that the ship started a period of leave and recuperation at the commencement of his appointment as First Lieutenant, and the fact that the Naval Officer in Charge Haifa made the arrangements to entertain and rest the crews from ships that survived the Dodecanese campaign his main concern and lent his ear to new and unconventional ideas. Almost before the first complete watch of the crew had disappeared in the transport to start seven days leave, the NOIC had arrived onboard to discuss his proposal for getting the officers away from the ship; up to this moment none of the original members of the wardroom had had a single night ashore to sleep since leaving the United Kingdom. The several visits to dry and floating docks had not enabled the officers to get clear of the ship for a night; quite correctly the priority had been to get the ratings away from the crowded, noisy, machinery filled and comfortless messdecks, there was also the assumption that still persisted, even at this stage of the war, that in the officer corps, all had private means, could make their own arrangements, had sufficient comfort in their cabins, too much to do and could not be spared.

For these reasons and others of equal or less substance or validity, there were in fact no funds or rest camps for officers in the Levant, and it required the ingenuity of the NOIC Haifa to break the deadlock. He reasoned that because officers based in the UK, ashore or afloat were entitled to three free travel warrants per annum plus ration allowances while on leave; most of the *Petard* officers could consider that they had an entitlement of four or probably five travel warrants. Using some obscure method of calculating how this should be converted into a cash allowance, that no doubt gave his Supply and Paymaster officers' nightmares, he decided that transport in the form of taxis hired on the basis of one to every four officers had to be laid on for a period of five days, plus an allowance to assist pay hotel bills, in addition he ordered his staff to locate a good hotel and book rooms for *Petard*.

Immediately after lunch, the first for many weeks to be held in a relaxed mood and free from tension, four delighted still unbelieving officers, Bertie, Robert, Doc and the GCO uniformed but unarmed, embarked into a large Chevrolet taxi driven by a handsome Greek Cypriot who had a working command of English and an unrivalled encyclopaedic knowledge of people and places, entertainment and women to suit every need, mood and occasion.

During the 150 mile run south to Tel Aviv, the road bordered by miles of citrus groves, the four officers listened to their guide chauffeur in silence, savouring their unexpected freedom, while he laid out his verbal display and description of the delights he had on offer for his passengers. The hotel booked, was small but a modern establishment on the seafront and named the Gat Ramon, which some years later became part of the Russian Embassy. For the present it accommodated mainly British Army officers on leave, a few RAF and the four naval 'liberty men' from *Petard*. The leave fulfilled the promise it offered from the start; collectively and singly each of *Petard*'s group was able to find in the five days at Tel Aviv something to refresh the mind and body, in spite of the drinking as if none had a future beyond a few tomorrows, and the parties organised with the envied assistance of the Greek Cypriot procurer and his taxi. The taxi remained always at instant readiness outside the Gat Ramon, the driver living and sleeping in his vehicle.

On the 28th the party returned to Haifa so that the remainder of the wardroom could in their turn get away; the drive back helped to clear heads that still suffered from the previous night's farewell excesses shared with new Tel Aviv acquaintances.

Next day a newcomer joined the ship, Lieutenant (E) E.W.K. Walton, DSC RNVR, to replace Bertie. Walton had previously served in the destroyer *Duncan* where he had won his DSC, and now came to *Petard* to allow Faunthorpe to leave after $2\frac{1}{2}$ years with the ship. Bertie deserved his break from sea service but it was a wrench for those left behind, he was the first to depart from the ship to leave a personal and emotional gap in the wardroom. For Bertie, the ship had given little in return for his civilised and unflappable approach to the many crises he had helped to weather, and for his skill as an engineer. In *Petard* he lost whatever chance that remained to him for promotion, and he left the ship without a recommendation for a decoration to add to his mention in despatches, this was to be the sole tangible recognition for his almost nonstop and successful efforts to keep the ship afloat and steaming during and after the many actions when damage had been sustained.

To his friends, the failure to recognise his professional skill was a bewildering oversight or a deliberate act for reasons that they could not begin to comprehend. The party that preceded his departure was spectacular, it flowed and ebbed into the night and out of the ship into the night spots of Haifa, with Doc treating it almost as a wake because of the departure of his friend.

The ship's company thrived on the leave break, even those who remained on board to paint ship and help carry out the self refit and boiler clean found much entertainment ashore, and for the first time since Durban, opportunities to meet civilians ready and anxious to take them away from the ship to their homes.

Three weeks after arriving at Haifa, *Petard*, boiler clean and self refit completed, repainted and every man, officers and ratings, refreshed after several days away from the ship, sailed for Alexandria on 18th December undertaking sea trials and exercising on the way, arriving to berth in Kamaria docks on the 22nd. Shortly after berthing a further addition to the officer complement joined, P.G. Wright Sub-Lieutenant RNVR, dark featured and bearded, he acquired the immediate nickname, Bringham Singh. He arrived to take from Ken Brooksbank the Ship's office duties that had been previously Robert de Pass's responsibility before he had been elevated to the First Lieutenant appointment.

The ship remained in harbour and longside at the dock into Christmas eve, and unbelievably was still there for Christmas Day. While most of the ship's company had now been away from home for three or four, and some even five Christmases, they were all conscious of being fortunate to have the second spent in *Petard*, in harbour, and this one away from the noisome Gabarri dock at the other end of Alexandria harbour. With the joint influence of the Captain and the First Lieutenant, the first with his appetite for entertaining and the second his flair for fixing and obtaining through contacts anything in short supply, the festivities in the destroyer were as good as anything possible on the station. Mess rations contained extras in the form of pork and poultry, augmented by steam puddings that had been manufactured in the depot ship *Woolwich*. Petty Officer Cook Inkpen and his henchman Tug Wilson worked through the entire night fortified by rum and kye, baking special bread rolls and cakes for every mess in addition to cooking the main and special Christmas dinners put up by the mess cooks and caterers.

By the time that Rupert led his officers forward at noon to do the rounds of the messes, the ship below decks had once again been transformed, the Yeoman's flag lockers as usual had been raided to decorate the mess decks; stanchions, hammock rails and table supports carried green foliage collected by liberty men from gardens and villas after dark, the mess tables laden with food and beer, this year were bright with the colour of Christmas cards that had arrived with the mail on Christmas Eve.

This mail the first to come through to the eastern reaches of the Mediterranean by air, brought with one spectacular leap the families and friends at home close to the ship. The mail left England only three days earlier, and for the first time since leaving home waters, mail was not weeks old. The cards not only brightened the scene but lifted the spirits of everyone, the large bunch of greenery at the upperyard arm indicated the festive scene and the mood of the men. Rupert was in his element, exchanging banter and accepting offers to sample food and drink with enthusiasm, joining in the singing lead by an impromptu stokers messdeck glee club.

Finally the party from the wardroom escaped from the chief and petty officers' mess rather worse for wear to start their own Christmas fare in the mid-afternoon but not before releasing the wardroom staff for the remainder of the day, taking over themselves the normal domestic chores, which included the preparations for a party that later took place with a few invited guests from other ships also in for the day, and some of Rupert's civilian friends.

Next morning, Boxing Day, *Petard* returned to reality, sailing at 0800 to relieve one destroyer from the standing patrol south of Crete. For the next two days with two others, one fleet and one Hunt, patrolled across the southern approaches to the Kaso and Scarpento straits without incident. One group of Ju 87s sighted the ships, closed to identify the destroyers then sheered off without an attack developing. *Petard* returned to Alexandria on the 30th, and following refuelling received on board a new warrant officer, Mr S.

Leuillete Gunner (T) to relieve Malaya MacAllan who had been promoted lieutenant in August and had since that time anxiously with increasing impatience waited to be released from the ship to return to UK for courses. Malaya's promotion was well deserved and long overdue, but everyone was sorry to see the proud conscientious officer go. Lieutenant MacAllan wasted no time in handing over to his relief and departed to await passage to UK before the ship sailed again at 0800 New Year's Eve 1944, with *Pathfinder* for the Kaso strait to intercept a merchantman, the SS *Leopardi* reported by intelligence agents in the Greek mainland to be about to sail from the Port of Piraeus, bound for the Dodecanese garrisons. The destroyers returned two days later after an abortive search.

The next eleven days saw *Petard* at sea most of the time searching seas that now held little threat from U-boat or air attack; it seemed a strange almost routine training exercise carrying out long patrols down sea lanes that bordered the empty silent battlefields of the Egyptian and Cyrenaican deserts. The ship and other destroyers were engaged as part of a shuttle service of escorts to great capital ships moving east singly or in groups to gather at Alexandria. The battleships, *Queen Elizabeth* and *Valiant* came from the central Mediterranean theatre, followed by the aircraft carrier *Illustrious*. Then the battle cruiser *Renown* and the carrier *Unicorn* who had come from the west out from the United Kingdom.

The assembled capital ships sailed out of Alexandria on the 14th, in a majestic line down the Grand Pass and turned east for Port Said, entering the canal early on the 15th. *Queen Elizabeth, Valiant, Renown, Illustrious* and *Unicorn*, led and followed by the fleet destroyers took the entire day to pass south to Port Suez. On the 16th escorted by only four destroyers, *Paladin, Pathfinder, Petard* and *Rocket*, the great ships sailed down the Gulf of Suez into the Red Sea on passage to join the Eastern fleet and to prepare for battle with the Japanese high seas fleets.

Petard and *Paladin* returned to the tortured burnt landscape of Aden on the 19th, entering after *Renown* and *Illustrious* had passed in through the boom defences to fuel before the remainder of the fleet followed to take their turn at the fuelling buoys. At Aden awaiting the arrival of the capital ships, the flotilla leader *Rotherham* of the 11th Destroyer Flotilla lay at the destroyer trot with six other destroyers, fuelled and ready to form a reinforced escort across the Arabian sea to Ceylon and the Eastern fleet base at Trincomalee.

On the 21st the fleets lead the way out of Aden through the boom defences and deployed into the screening formation outside. Eleven destroyers, *Rotherham, Rocket, Racehorse, Roebuck, Rapid, Nizam, Napier, Norman, Pathfinder, Paladin* and *Petard* preceded the two battleships, the battle cruiser and the aircraft carriers, formed soon after into two columns as the fleet steamed east to leave Socotra island to starboard before turning southeast on course to pass between the Laccadive islands and Maldive groups 1400 miles ahead. After two days of almost nonstop exercising it was with relief that *Petard*'s ship's company welcomed the information that they were to form part of the escort for a section consisting of *Renown* and *Unicorn* diverted to Cochin. The break away took place on the 24th and the squadron arrived three days later at the port and naval base, the former capital of Kerala province in the south west corner of the sub-continent of India.

Cochin provided new experiences for *Petard*'s men, the bustle of the harbour with constant movement of arriving and departing ocean lateen rigged dhows, quays crowded with craft and teeming throngs of humanity, markets equally crowded with men and women from every race that populated the huge Imperial possession provided a spectacular source of wonder to the visitors to India, to spice and flavour all the traditional offerings a sailor expected to find and found in this seaport.

After three days at Cochin, with *Paladin*, the ship sailed for Colombo there to enjoy for a further two days the colonial attractions of the capital of Ceylon that still had much to show of its occupation history, first by the Portuguese followed by more than one hundred years of Dutch rule, then the present British.

The main fleet units escorted out from the Mediterranean, arrived in Trincomalee on 28th January, and finally *Paladin* and *Petard* rejoined the escort of the *Renown* and *Unicorn* arriving in their turn off the great naval base facing the Bay of Bengal on 2nd February.

The destroyers, *Norman, Roebuck, Quiberon, Paladin,* and *Petard* turned and swept to seaward to protect the two capital ships from submarine attack while they formed in line ahead to pass through the boom defences into the great natural harbour, anchorage and naval base. The three Eastern fleet destroyers then entered next, leaving the newcomers to the command to enter last. Finally Rupert Egan turned the two 'Ps' towards the entrance ordering *Paladin* to take station astern, led the destroyers like two shabby orphaned waifs from the disbanded 12th and laterly the 14th DF coming to join their new 'foster' flotilla, the 11th Destroyer Flotilla of the Eastern Fleet.

Both ships approached the fleet anchorage with a defiant swagger mixed with a fearful bravado. All were convinced, probably with little foundation, that their puny 4 inch guns, elevated to an impudent 10 degrees, had fired more rounds in anger against the enemy than the collective artillery might of the fleet. The ships' companies of the two destroyers ranged in ranks facing outboard at their stations for entering harbour, on the fo'c'sle, iron deck, quarterdeck, bridge and flag deck, wore only white caps and shorts; torsoes and legs burnt brown and near black by long months of Mediterranean and Red Sea sun, were bare and uncovered. Only the officers fallen in with their part of ship divisions wore shirts, shorts and white stockings. Alone the two sea-strained ships moved down the great lines of battleships, cruisers, aircraft carriers and destroyers berthed in pairs at the trots, wearing proudly their scars, shell and bomb splinter patches that weeped red rust stains. The men looked from their ranks with an awed astonishment at the immaculate fleet as their ships passed.

Fresh paint gleamed, brass brightwork and polished steel shone from fittings and gun tampions, white awnings were spread over holystoned quarterdecks and fo'c'sles, even the destroyers had wing awnings spread; brilliant boats lay to scrubbed booms with canvas covered and painted fittings, completed the magnificence of the fleet in the great harbour fringed by the greens of jungle foliage. As progress continued down the lines of moored ships a feeling of unease infected officers and men of both destroyers, it was becoming clear to the newcomers that the fleet was too 'pusser' for the 'Ps' to be acceptable, the rig of the day in every ship was tropical rig, no one went about the upper decks minus shirts or seamans singlet, the bronzed chests in *Paladin* and *Petard* were clearly not *de rigueur* for the Eastern fleet in its traditional splendour. There were too many flag and senior officers looking long and critically through disapproving telescopes at the action scarred ships to be healthy; there was no friendly wave, rude gesture or shouts traded with chummy ships following the formalities of piping salutes to senior ships, something that was common place in the Mediterranean bases.

Paladin and *Petard* berthed and secured, one on each side of a fleet tanker, quickly and expertly, with ship companies subdued and apprehensive. Before refuelling had been completed, the two ships received orders to moor on completion in a creek away from the destroyer trots and to paint ship to conform to the fleet colours, light blue hull except for the bow sections, and light grey upper works including masts and funnel. When Rupert led away to the isolated moorings men in both ships were in the fleet dress of the day, everyone a little shaken by the lack of welcome, perhaps they expected too much and had overated the knowledge that the men of the Fleet had of the Mediterranean campaigns.

During the next three days, the men of both ships, painted ship, and in the evenings the non-duty watches ashore in the fleet canteen did little to endear themselves, boasting with beer enhanced exaggeration of their ships successes in air, surface and underseas actions. Few ships of the fleet had seen recent action or had been in prolonged contact with the Japanese enemy, in fact several units had only recently returned from East African bases to Trincomalee as the Japanese threat to the Bay of Bengal and the Indian sub-continent had commenced to recede.

The officers of the two 'Ps' found that their new colleagues of the 11th Flotilla seemed disconcerted by the newcomers' record and tended to make in self defence, supercilious but good-humoured comments about the small and rather ugly 4 inch gun mountings. None could be perusaded to accept how fortunate the 'Ps' were to have such effective anti-aircraft guns as the main armament. Paradoxically the *Petard* was to find that because similar guns were only fitted and used in the ships of the fleet for AA defence, it was impossible to obtain semi-armour piercing (SAP) ammunition for use against surface ship targets from the Eastern fleet depot and ammunition supply ships; the ship was to be in trouble through this shortage before very long. *Petard* had not been able to replace the SAP ammunition expended in the Dodecanese before leaving Alexandria where stocks had run out.

On 5th February, Convoy KR 8 sailed from the East African port of Kilindini bringing some of the last naval and army support units back to the Ceylon and Indian bases as well as troop reinforcements for the army in Burma. *Petard* and *Paladin* were sailed from Trincomalee on the 6th to rendezvous with the convoy and escort it to Colombo. The 'Ps' emerged from the creek into the main anchorage, repainted and almost as if they had returned from banishment after they had learnt how to comport themselves in the company of their betters of the high seas fleet. They moved down the long lines of destroyers, cruisers, carriers and battleships somewhat chastened by the obvious inspection that they were undergoing. The two ex-Mediterranean fleets with ancient and ill regarded armament were being sent to carry out convoy escort duties, while the better armed destroyers of the 4th and 11th Flotillas remained behind to protect and exercise with the capital ships.

Passing out through the boom, then formed in line abeam the two ships turned south and a little west to follow the great curve of the island of Ceylon, turning south then east to make a departure from the southern tip of the island, Dondra Head, to steer south east for the remote coral island at the southern extremity of the Maldive islands, Addu Atoll. There was now little chance of air or surface attack, only the submarine menace on a reduced scale remained, requiring Brooky and his team to continue their vigil.

Petard making the second of many passages round the southern coast of Ceylon ran into a vast herd of whales who for an hour or more during the Dog watches alternatively fascinated and alarmed the crews of both destroyers. The sea out to visibility distance seemed populated by the huge creatures, water jets and vapour spray from blow holes appeared at all points of the compass, great tails thrashed the sea surrounding the ships. The sheer bulk of the 60 to 80 foot creatures surfacing close longside, alarmed the spectators, at times two or more rising from the depths each side of the ship as if the leviathans wished to sandwich it between their enormous bodies. The officer of the watch found the task of maintaining an anti-submarine zig zag course hazardous, because of the danger of collision with one of the apparently fearless marine mammals. To complete the awesome scene, the nine thousand foot Mount Pedrotallagallas summit inland from Dondra Head was lost in the dense mass of the Monsoon cloud which continued out over the sea to the south and discharged violent lightening flashes into the sea from an electrical storm that roared and crashed as the night closed in. With the darkness the sea became a brilliant area of phosphorescence resulting from the great convulsions caused by the whales until suddenly and dramatically they left the ships and the area.

For the next three days the destroyers steamed south east into an empty Indian ocean to thé Atoll almost on the equator, the great heat tempered somewhat by the NE monsoon wind, the ships rolling on a quartering sea.

Petard led the way in through the coral reef into the perfect circular lagoon of Addu Atoll and berthed on a fleet tanker stationed there to fuel escorts. *Paladin* secured on the opposite side of the tanker minutes later, by which time Simmons, wardroom chef and fisherman, had already caught his first tunny fish. Others were quick to follow the chef's example, the lagoon teemed with life and several tunny followed with many other fish, strange and some very beautiful lay on the hot iron deck gasping out their lives after being yanked inboard by the ship's piscators. The tropical atoll excited everyone's interest in both ships, it lived up to expectations and the imagination of all who had read of South Sea islands or who had seen location films. The deep entrance to the lagoon pierced the coral reef on the south, marred for the present by paraphernalia of war, the buoys and nets of the anti-submarine and torpedo nets of the boom defence. The east and west arms of the coral reef carried then little vegetation, the Indian ocean breakers crashed over into the calm of the lagoon in places, but most of the reef protected long strips of dazzling sand. The main portion of the island lay on the north of the lagoon, only a few hundred square yards of low lying land thickly covered by palms, hiding a small settlement from the ships at anchor. The palms grew out along the reefs, southwards for some distance getting fewer and smaller as the distance increased from the main part of the atoll. Only some outrigger canoes lying on the sand below the palm line indicated that Addu Atoll was populated.

Leave to land bathing parties given by Rupert to both ships quickly produced a rush from the non-duty watch to find places in the motor cutter and towed whaler.

Earlier on the same day that the crews of the two 'Ps' lazed, the anti-submarine escorts of Convoy KR 8 left the transports and returned to Kilindini; the first to leave at 0100 was the flower class corvette *Honesty*, later at 0620 the two ex-United States Cutters, *Lulworth* and *Sennen* departed leaving the five transports under the care of the old cruiser *Hawkins* until the arrival of *Petard* and *Paladin*.

At noon of the 10th the destroyers left Addu Atoll and sailed due west along the equator to rendezvous with KR 8, steaming at 20 knots through the afternoon and the night, making contact by an exchange of recognition signals at first light of the 12th with *Hawkins*. By 0800 *Petard* was in station 30 degrees on the starboard column leading ship three cables, with *Paladin* in similar station on the port column. For *Petard* to be again one of two destroyers sharing the escort duty of an ocean convoy with the cruiser, recalled the long seven week escort of Convoy WS 21 out of the Clyde to the Red Sea in 1942. Soon after joining, Rupert Egan adopted his predecessor's style by moving the destroyers out to a distance of four or five miles so that any submarine on the surface ahead and in the path of the convoy line of advance could be sighted before it had a chance of spotting its quarry.

Hawkins had escorted a series of convoys on long ocean passages without incident delivering her charges safely to destinations, the progress of KR 8 promised a similar successful conclusion, with nothing worse to combat than the blistering heat of the equatorial sun beating down on the ships in a flat windless ocean.

KR 8 consisted of five transports carrying mainly troop reinforcements for Burma. Four of the troopers* steamed in two columns 4 cables apart, and 3 cables between ships in column. Between the lead ship of the columns, ahead and 45 degrees on the bow, steamed the fifth and largest transport, the commodore's ship, the *Khedive Ismail*. The passengers in the commodore's ship consisted of a battalion of British officered African infantry, some artillery units and a number of miscellaneous groups of army and RAF personnel, naval support parties, WRNS and nurses. With the crew, the complement exceeded 2000 men and women.

On the morning of the 12th, the convoy was seven days out from Kilindini and as the day moved on under the relentless sun, the passengers in the crowded transports were listless, sought the shade where it could be found, and positions in the ships where the passage through the sea augmented the light surface wind. The sea continued flat and almost oily smooth, marked by an occasional ruffle where the variable gentle breeze played and touched the surface. In the cruiser and destroyers, warm sea water gushed continuously from the deck hydrants to reduce the heat of the iron decks which were otherwise impossible to walk on.

The noon position, 00 degrees 48 minutes north, 71 degrees 45 minutes east, course 075 degrees, speed 13 knots, placed the convoy just 48 miles north of the Equator, steering to pass through a gap in the long chain of the Maldive islands on direct route to Colombo. Afternoon watchmen had finished their midday meal and the forenoon watch looked forward to seeing their reliefs at 1200. The two destroyers maintaining a steady 15 knots, circled and zig zagged independently on station 4-6 miles out to port and

*SS *Ekma*, SS *Ellenga*, SS *City of Paris* and SS *Varsova*.

starboard ahead of the convoy's line of advance; ahead of *Khedive Ismail* the *Hawkins* moved in time with the convoy's zig zag pattern. At eight bells the watches changed, the forenoon watch came below to drink their tots, eat their lunch and with the remainder of the watch below, looked forward to a free afternoon; it was Sunday.

Petard's asdic watch in the stifling hot bridge control cabin settled down to the continuation of the endless underwater probing for submarines, the bridge lookouts scanned an empty and distant horizon without conviction of sighting anything, lulled into a relaxed calm after several weeks away from areas of high risk and the need of viligance against the immediate probability of enemy attack. Below in the boiler and engine rooms, the watch gasped out the afternoon in an inferno of heat and noise, standing whenever they could, under the forced down draught of warm air. Up in the blinding sunlight, 'B' gun crew, the oerlikon gunners, flag deck and depth charge team on the quarter deck, constantly shifted their positions as areas of shade changed in time with the frequent alteration of course made by the OOW to maintain position on the lookout patrol. Between and on deck, off watch groups sweated and dozed into the afternoon.

A wild cry from the port bridge lookout, '*Periscope bearing red 150, near*', exploded the senses and galvanised a startled ship's company into a scramble to action stations as simultaneously the whooping siren and the alarm rattlers warned the convoy and drove the watch below, clawing desperately up ladders and along decks now heeling over at an acute angle to starboard as *Petard* turned under full rudder with telegraphs clanging full ahead on both engines.

A great ball of black heavy smoke shot up into the still air from the funnel caused by the sudden emergency injection of furnace fuel into the boiler jets. Men fought their way along decks heeling thirty degrees and more with eyes searching with anxiety the sea and horizon for the cause of the alarm, ears and nerves braced for the expected crash from 'B' gun, the breech block had been heard to close and the shouts from the layer and trainer indicated that they were on target, the port oerlikon on the lower bridge wing started its staccato bark, shells foamed the sea and ricocheted where the periscope had been seen. The signalmen on the flag deck fought to hoist the submarine alarm flag signal to the upper yard.

While men still ran, fell and crawled over the heeling decks, the ship recoiled to a massive under water explosion, a huge sheet of orange flame and black smoke enveloped the after portion of the great bulk of the convoy commodore's ship, the *Khedive Ismail*, it was 1435. By 1438 the ship had gone, a salvo of torpedoes blew the bottom out of the ex-liner, and in one dreadful heave the great bow leapt out of the sea, exposing a third of the keel vertical to the surface, hung for a second then the entire mass vanished stern first below the smooth ocean. In *Petard* all now concentrated on the fact that the asdic team under Brooky's direction was in contact, and hardly noticed that *Hawkins* had ordered by siren and flag signal for the convoy to scatter. Searching from the plot position where the periscope had disappeared, the asdic team quickly established a firm echo indicating a large submarine moving from right to left towards where the transport had been sunk.

The ship now round and pointing to where the periscope had last been seen, reduced speed to 18 knots; Rupert Egan at his place standing by the polaris received firm ranges and bearings from Brooky and his asdic team, decided to attack. *Paladin* at the same time closed the spot where *Khedive Ismail* had vanished and was slowing to a stop with scrambling nets draped over her sides to pick up survivors who could be seen as concentrations of small blobs in a spreading expanse of oil and the debris of wreckage coming to the surface as it broke away from the submerged ship. With his ship now on a depth charge attack course, concentrating on the making of small adjustments to helm and engine revolutions, it did not require the near frantic calls from lookouts and gun crews that the depth charges would be close to the survivors, to realise that the Captain had allowed for this factor in his agonising decision to attack and prevent the submarine from taking refuge under the main concentration of swimmers struggling for their lives. The ship's company on the upper deck stood and crouched at their action stations with a sick numbness, carried by their ship remorselessly up to the depth charge release position, and listened in helpless despair to the buzzers on the quarterdeck ordering the crew to slip charges from the traps and fire·the throwers. The eight charge pattern seemed to erupt with greater than normal violence, and the pressure from the underwater detonations struck the hull with a shattering impact emphasising the effect it must be having on the pitiful numbers that had avoided going down with the torpedoed ship and still fought for their lives in the oil covered sea.

When Rupert turned his ship, with the asdic crew still with a firm grip on the target moving steadily on course, it was possible for a moment to take stock of what had happened to the convoy. The four remaining transports were steaming at full speed to four separate points of the compass, with the cruiser *Hawkins* legging it at top speed northwards to a preplanned rendezvous position laid down in the convoy orders. By the time *Petard* started to move in for the second depth charge attack all ships were hull down leaving the two destroyers alone in an empty ocean to avenge the dead and rescue the few living.

Paladin continued frantically to haul the living and dying out of the sea while Rupert directed his ship into two more deliberate attacks, transfixed with the horror and dilemma of his duty, his ship's company numbed by the sure knowledge that the attacks were destroying the lives of the few that escaped from the *Khedive Ismail*.

The depth charge throwers had been reloaded and other charges rolled aft into the stern traps while the asdic contact remained firm and true, ranges and bearings plotted the targets continuing movement to the fringe of the oil spreading out from the sunken transport. *Petard* ran in for the third attack steaming now through bodies, black and white, all young, men and girls, none alive to be rescued: the depth charges were launched to fall among the still forms floating in the midst of the debris of their ship. *Paladin* had completed the recovery of about 200 who had survived the sinking and the paralysing shock of the depth charge explosions, was under way manoeuvring to pick up asdic contact and join *Petard*'s assault on the submarine. The third pattern from Rupert's attack had twelve charges, the explosion of the massed depth charges threatened to tear off the ship's stern with the violence of the multiple detonations. The erupted sea still boiled, and wreckage thrown high into the air continued to fall back into the sea when a huge shape burst out from the depths in a welter of blown compressed air and spray, a black painted hull and grey casing exaggerated the menacing appearance of the U-boat, surfacing not to surrender but to fight.

The ocean submarine seemed as big as the hunting destroyers, on the casing it carried large chocks abaft the conning tower for a 2-3 man submersible, forward a large gun, probably 5 inch calibre, was already being manned and trained on *Paladin* by men falling out of conning tower openings. The submarine had begun to move ahead and quickly started to manoeuvre at speeds between 6-10 knots as the first 4 inch salvos from the destroyers fell round it. Hits immediately started to be scored on the casing, conning tower and the gun. The first gun's crew was eliminated before the weapon could be brought into action, but quickly others appeared from the tower structure and inside the submarine that now clearly was being conned to take avoiding action to upset the accuracy of the destroyer's 4 inch gunfire. Hits continued to be made at about 2500 yards, it soon became apparent that the submarine's gun had been damaged before the U-boat succeeded to getting it fully manned, the suicide attempts to reinforce the crew on the exposed casing stopped abruptly.

At this moment the *Paladin* started a chain of events that came within an ace of finishing in complete disaster for both destroyers. Checking fire to take stock of the situation and manoeuvring so as to not place his ship in a position vulnerable to a torpedo attack from the enemy, Rupert Egan took his eye off *Paladin*. His attention returned at the rush with Robert de Pass's shout, '*Paladin* is going in to ram, Sir', to see his consort crossing the stern, increasing speed with engines at full emergency ahead, and obviously on course to ram the submarine now 1000 yards on *Petard*'s starboard beam moving on the same approximate course at about 8 knots. Rupert instantly realised the danger, *Paladin* in the process of ramming through the pressure hull would with certainty damage itself grievously and even sink, putting at risk her ship's company and the survivors from the *Khedive Ismail*. In response to Rupert's urgent and repeated order to 'Stop her', emergency siren signals drew *Paladin*'s attention to Yeoman Bishop's rapid signal on the large bridge signal lamp 'Negative ram!' and the order repeated by a flag hoist.

Paladin responded at once, at 25 knots the destroyer heeled over under full port rudder putting the starboard iron and quarter deck lower guard rail below water as the ship forced itself round to avoid hitting the submarine. She almost made it, but the drift to starboard in the ramming course of the ship, drove the destroyer broadside on to the pressure hull of the Japanese, and before it could draw clear, the submarine's port forward hydroplane ripped into the belly of *Paladin*'s starboard side, aft of the engine room and tore out a straight 6 inch wide, 15 foot gash as effectively as a giant tin opener, through the length of the gearing room into two cabins in the wardroom flat and the intervening bulkheads before the ship tore itself free. Under forward momentum with engine and gearing room flooding up, *Paladin* came to a stop about 800 yards clear of the submarine that had been knocked off course by the collision and fortunately continued under way, away from the stopped and listing destroyer.

Paladin had a 10 degree list, the gash had been made when the ship heeled over at more than 20 degrees on the turn almost came clear of the calm still smooth sea now the ship was out of the turn but still listing to starboard. The luckless *Paladin* crowded with survivors making the task of the damage control party immensely difficult, moving portable pumps, shoring material and timber with the collision mat to stop the inrush of the sea through the long gash. The ship was also unstable, only the flat calm saved the destroyer from foundering. The greatest menace came from the huge submarine continuing underway and manoeuvring under the direction from someone who had at least a partial view of the sea and surroundings from inside the damaged conning tower; the periscopes had been shot away by the first 4 inch gun salvoes. The stopped and listing *Paladin* was desperately vulnerable to being rammed or torpedoed by the U-boat, once the commander had recovered from the temporary confusion caused by the collision with the destroyer; for the moment it seemed that he had not seen or interpreted *Paladin*'s predicament.

Rupert Egan saw the danger immediately, turned *Petard* to starboard at speed, passing under *Paladin*'s stern, placing his ship between the line of sight from the U-boat and the crippled ship as the submarine headed away still apparently unaware of what had happened to the destroyer. To prevent the submarine captain from recovering his orientation, the pom-pom and oerlikons drenched the conning tower with fire as *Petard* overhauled the Japanese, closing so fast that it was not possible to depress the forward 4 inch guns in time to open fire also; aft on the quarter deck Gunner (T) Mr Leuillete and his depth charge team raced to prepare a twelve charge pattern at shallow settings to be fired ahead of the submarine. The ship closed in on the port quarter then reducing to 18 knots passed less than 10 feet from the pressure hull, Rupert Egan taking a calculated risk that the submarine did not take a sudden violent turn to port or starboard and drive the forward or after port hydroplanes into *Petard*'s starboard side. It was a frightening eerie situation looking down at the pressure hull thrusting a way through the sea at 8 knots, nothing to be seen on the shell damaged casing and conning tower except for the remains of several members of the gun crew, but the certain knowledge of men enclosed in the steel cylindrical hull struggling to live long enough to destroy their hunters. As *Petard* drew clear ahead of the submarine, Rupert ordered the depth charges to be fired, the pattern from the traps and throwers fell into the sea in a great rectangle, into which the submarine moved as the shallow set charges exploded. The sea erupted into giant columns of solid water and spray blocking out the U-boat from sight until turbulence subsided back into the flat calm sea, to reveal the great black shape still apparently free from mortal damage, moving ahead. Twice more under the cloudless sky and tropical sun, *Petard* charged in to drop shallow set patterns in the path of the blundering half blinded giant until it was clear that the settings could not be adjusted shallow enough to destroy the enemy, but the attacks twice successfully turned and knocked the U-boat away when it seemed to have set course towards the helpless *Paladin*, or about to fire its torpedoes.

The contest had turned into a grotesque, bizarre and deadly cat and mouse situation, no one could guess the final outcome; one false move by *Petard* could result in the ship being crippled and put both destroyers at the mercy of the damaged partially blinded giant who would under no circumstances surrender. The First Lieutenant had earlier ordered the GI, Petty Officer Webb to prepare equipment for a boarding and demolition party, and was at this stage making up and arming hand grenades and sten guns, but no one had as yet solved the problem of boarding the enemy without hazarding the ship on the murderous hydroplanes; the motor cutter could not match the speed of the submarine. The Gunner had prepared a depth charge equipped with a timed fuse to act as a demolition charge but without a plan of how to get it onto the casing, earlier attempts to fire one out of the throwers to lodge a charge on the conning tower or casing had failed. The officers and men liable to form the boarding party knew that there was little chance of forcing an entry into the submarine and that the grim odds were that the Japanese hearing or sensing that their craft had been boarded would blow themselves and the invaders up.

While preparations continued to be made and methods considered how to board without putting the ship to unacceptable risk, *Petard* drew off to 3000 yards and reopened fire with the 4 inch. Hits were registered with almost every four gun salvo, flashes of the impact DA* shells appeared on the pressure hull, casing and conning tower, but making no vital impression or penetration of the immensely strong cigar shaped hull. Only semi-armour piercing

* Direct Action.

(SAP) could sink the submarine, but the magazines were empty of this vital ammunition. It was ironic that the guns and shells that would have sunk the U-boat with one salvo had disappeared from the scene with the *Hawkins*. At 1515, about the time that *Petard* had forced the Japanese to the surface, the cruiser was 12 miles away steering 073 degrees waiting for the four surviving transports to rejoin, her ship's company fallen out from action stations and reverted to 4th degree defence and cruising stations, with 7.5 inch guns, nearly twice the calibre of the destroyer's main armament, secured and unused.

The GCO and director's crew desperate with frustration, knew that without SAP ammunition there was little chance of sinking the submarine by gun fire, all that could happen would be a senseless expenditure of ammunition without reducing the threat of the submarine hitting one of the ships with a torpedo fired from either the fore or stern tubes. Checking fire, the GCO called down to the Captain suggesting that an attempt should be made with *Petard*'s torpedoes to sink the U-boat. Rupert agreed and his reaction was immediate, Robert de Pass received orders to train the two sets of quadrable tubes to starboard, and as torpedo control officer, to standby to fire from the bridge torpedo sights and control, the Captain started to turn the ship in a wide and complete circle to port, indicating to *Paladin* by a flag hoist of his intentions. The submarine at this point in time continued on a steady course at about 6 knots.

The standard drill for firing torpedoes, required them to be fired in salvoes of four or eight as the firing ship turned to port or starboard, the intervals for firing each torpedo in the salvo depended on the speed, course and range of the target, set against the speed and turning circle of the firing ship. The spread of the salvo would allow for any avoiding action taken by the target, one of the torpedoes should hit. The primary rule for a moving target was, a salvo of torpedoes, never single shots.

For some inexplicable reason, *Petard* failed to carry out the drill laid down by the torpedo school, HMS Vernon; perhaps it arose from the fact that Rupert Egan felt that because the enemy was less than 1000 yards distance, in conditions of flat calm, maximum visibility, he should not squander the MK IX** 40 knot torpedoes that cost so much, and over which his torpedo men lavished so much care with frequent tests and routines. Whatever the reason, Robert de Pass was given the task of firing a single torpedo with the ship steaming at slow speed on a course parallel to the Japanese submarine. At 1700, de Pass allowing a deflection of 6 knots, fired his first torpedo, No 1 from the forward set of tubes. The ships company held their collective breaths while the tin fish took three-quarters of a minute to cover the distance to the target. At two minutes it was clear that it had missed. The gun director range taker checked the range of the submarine against the gunnery radar set and called out a continuous series of ranges to Robert who checked the torpedo sight and control. Ten minutes after the first miss, the second torpedo was fired at the target still moving on a steady course, again the ship's company sweated and willed the long polished steel 21 inch diameter one ton torpedo running 6-8 feet below the surface to hit the black hull of the enemy. Again 2 minutes later, sick with apprehensive disappointment, the ship knew that the shot was a failure.

The Gunner (T) Mr Leuillete at his station as officer of the quarters at the torpedo tubes could not contain himself, rang the bridge to protest that firing torpedoes singly could only result in a total loss of the missiles without hitting the target. While he made his diffident objection, the third torpedo burst out of its tube into the sea and predictably missed, and ten minutes later so did the last and fourth out of the forward quadruple mounting. The tension on the bridge and the remainder of the ship reached an appalling pitch, everyone knew that if the remainder of the torpedoes missed, the ammunition available for the guns was incapable of sinking the submarine. There remained only two courses of action, a suicide attempt to board to blow the vessel up, or to ram.

By this time it seemed certain that the submarine had heard the torpedoes on the hydrophones, and now altered course and speed taking avoiding action. Mr Leuillete driven to a point where his outrage and concern that the principles and drills of his profession and specialist naval responsibility for the torpedo department, were being ignored, stood on the iron deck shouting up at the bridge asking for permission to take over the firing from the bridge to local control at the after torpedo mounting. It was a remarkable almost unprecedented incident for an experienced warrant officer to be driven to a point where he openly challenged his senior and commissioned officers, and the judgement of his commanding officer.

It is doubtful that the Captain heard the desperate appeal, he seemed caught in an inextricable dilemma and still shocked by the terrible decision forced upon him by his duty, to depth charge while survivors from the *Khedive Ismail* still remained in the sea. He could not bring himself to fire the remaining four torpedoes in a salvo, or to allow the Gunner to take over from the tubes; so the First Lieutenant desperate with anxiety, adjusted his bridge sight control, and forty minutes after firing the first torpedo, fired the fifth, followed by the sixth, both missing. The situation reached a terrifying point of no return as the seventh left the tubes into the oily calm sea, the morale of the ship was at a point of total collapse, when a huge column of water and flame blotted out the great semi-crippled submarine that had threatened the destroyers. When the water and spray subsided, the *I-27* had vanished for ever, destroyed by the seventh, one hour and ten minutes of agony after the torpedo attack had started; the time was 1755, three hours and ten minutes after the *Khedive Ismail* had been sunk, and two and a half hours after the submarine surfaced.

There were no cheers when the torpedo struck, men in both ships were physically sick from nervous reaction, while Rupert turned his ship and proceeded longside *Paladin*. During the long struggle played out by *Petard* and the submarine adversary, work had advanced to fit temporary seals along the gash in *Paladin*'s side. Hammocks had been jammed into the hole from inside the flooded spaces, rammed tight by planks and wedges backed by wooden damage control and repair stantions. The ship's pumps reduced the level of flooding, upperdeck weights and fuel had been transferred, reducing the list by about 5 degrees. On the fo'c'sle preparations for a tow were well advanced, while in the awful heat of the overcrowded and damaged ship, much had been done to help the 200 survivors. Oil fouled and most badly shocked, with several badly injured by their escape from the transport and later by the depth charge explosions.

Rupert with his men subdued and unhappy, closed *Paladin* to confer with Lieutenant E.A.S. Bailey DSC, quickly coming to a decision to transfer all the survivors and half *Paladin*'s crew into his ship to help improve the stability of the damaged ship and reduce the casualties if the ship sank under tow. The transfer caused little difficulty, the destroyers lay longside each other in the calm sea separated by several large fenders acquired by *Petard*'s Buffer on one of his foraging trips ashore at Brindisi. The long slow but slight ocean swell allowed the ships to lie easily together, *Paladin*'s list away from her consort assisted the evolution.

Before casting off, *Paladin*'s towing pennant had been passed across and secured to *Petard*'s towing slip, this helped the tow to get under way without difficulty, working up to ten knots, on course to Addu Atoll 100 miles distance.

In spite of the damaged ship's list to starboard the two ships arrived safely and passed through the boom, both anchoring by 1000/13th. On passage, working through the night into the next day, Doc Prendergast, his sickbay Tiffey and volunteers continued the task started in *Paladin*, cleaning off the oil fuel, giving first aid and medical assistance to the *Khedive Ismail* survivors. Only six girls had been rescued, WRNS and nurses, each owed their lives to men from *Paladin* who risked death from the paralysing crashes of the depth charges when they dived to the rescue into the oil fouled sea. The girls had been hauled half dead out of the oil fouled debris from the sunken ship, understandably could not be separated from their rescuers, like numbers of the survivors, were hostile and afraid while in the *Petard*, an attitude that added to the sense of failure and despair felt by the ship's company.

For Rupert, his ship crowded to suffocation, the situation and mental strain, when he considered the action in retrospect, must have been intolerable, now that his active role in events diminished, and he had to prepare situation signals and reports of proceedings.

The engine room staffs from both destroyers combined their resources to hasten first aid repairs and to prepare *Paladin* for the longest leg of the tow to the fleet base at Trincomalee.

In the meantime, two hours before the destroyers had anchored in the lagoon, at 0800/13th, *Hawkins* in position 02 degrees 41 minutes north, 74 degrees 49 minutes east had collected the convoy together and steamed at 16 knots, course 046 degrees. The cruiser continued with the reformed convoy until receiving a signal from the C-in-C to leave the transports and to proceed at best speed to Addu Atoll, render assistance to the *Paladin* and collect the survivors from *Petard*. At 1142, *Hawkins* turned and headed back the way she had come at 23 knots, course 210 degrees, arriving off the entrance to the atoll's lagoon at 0013/14th to anchor inside the boom half an hour later. *Petard* berthed on the cruiser by 0842 and commenced to transfer the survivors from the *Khedive Ismail* into the more spacious accommodation of the older and larger ship. By 1046 Rupert Egan had unberthed his ship from the cruiser, and commenced to assist *Paladin* to warp alongside the *Hawkins*. The damaged destroyer had steam on the capstan and in the calm conditions of the lagoon it turned out to be an easy evolution, completed by 1140. Once longside, the cruiser's pumps helped to clear the destroyer's flooded compartments, additional portable pumps as standby units were transferred from the cruiser, engineroom and shipwright artificers shifted welding equipment and plating to fit temporary patches to *Paladin*'s starboard side. The time available had to be short; many of the survivors were in poor shape for they had spent two days in very crowded conditions and in intense heat in the two destroyers, there were no facilities in the lonely atoll to help the injured and shocked, so at 1150/15th *Hawkins* weighed anchored, passed through the boom at 1200 and steamed at high speed for Colombo.

Petard remained at Addu Atoll with *Paladin* for a further four days, until a tug and corvette escort arrived on the 19th, then departed immediately at 28 knots, sailed direct to Trincomalee, arriving at the fleet anchorage in the dark of the early hours of the 21st. The ship fuelled and had secured head and stern to buoys in the destroyer trot before the fleet started the normal weekday harbour routine, escaping the curious and critical scrutiny by the ships who had heard of the long struggle to kill the submarine which had sunk the *Khedive Ismail*.

Following a five day break in harbour at Trincomalee, the ship sailed on the 26th, for Addu Atoll, this time one of three destroyers on passage to rendezvous with Convoy KR 9 on the 29th February. Captain D11 in *Rotherham* was in command of the escort, the third destroyer the Dutch ship *Tjerk Hiddes*. Apart for another encounter with a vast number of whales off Dondra Head, the operation passed off uneventfully. *Petard* arrived in Colombo on 6th March with *Tjerk Hiddes*, the cruiser *Frobisher* and the intact Convoy KR 9. *Rotherham* left the escort the day before arrival and returned direct to Trincomalee.

Petard and *Tjerk Hiddes* berthed together after refuelling during the forenoon, and shortly afterwards the two wardrooms received a joint RPC signal from the submarine depot ship, for drinks and one of the curry lunches for which the Netherlands ship's Javanese chefs were renowned. Doctor Prendergast led the rush of officers from the *Petard*, all welcoming a chance to break the gloom that had settled on the group since the sinking of the *Khedive Ismail*. About four hours later, in the heat of the mid afternoon, bloated with the splendid lunch, aglow and sweating with the drink generously plied by their hosts, the officers returned, clattered and slid noisily down the ladder into the wardroom flat to find the duty boy sitting on the club fender of the wardroom, chatting to a stranger, a Surgeon Lieutenant RNVR. The new man's name was R.N. Ticehurst, and Doc Prendergast's relief. Only the fact that they were awash with the Dutchman's drink enabled the doctor's messmates to weather the news, and to make boosy plans for a farewell party that evening ashore at the Galle Face hotel. But next day as the ship sailed leaving Doc ashore; the future seemed very bleak without the courageous, scruffy, anti-establishment but completely loyal and generous messmate. The watchkeepers coming off watch were going to miss the doctor and his endless store of outrageous and scandalous stories that accompanied his tireless capacity for liar dice and cammaroons. Doc deserved his release after two long and hard years; of those who joined the ship with him, only three remained out of the original complement of officers, Robert de Pass, Kenneth Brooksbank and the GCO feeling very lonely.

The ship made a run back to the fleet base, and almost immediately received orders to return with the *Penn*, who had very recently arrived from the Mediterranean, to escort a small aircraft carrier *Highway*, first to Colombo then on to Bombay. Off Colombo the group met *Paladin* leaving harbour partially repaired, bound for Durban and then home. For a short time, while waiting for the escort carrier to proceed ahead into harbour, three 'Ps' were in close visual signalling distance from each other, and for *Petard* and *Paladin* the last occasion together. The two ships steered to pass close, one bound home to the UK via South Africa for permanent repairs, the other still with an uncertain and indefinite 1st commission to run its course before a major refit had to be ordered. There were only a few shouts exchanged between the ships, all seemed preoccupied with the events that they had shared in the last year and a half, culminating in the long struggle to kill the Japanese submarine *I27*, west of Addu Atoll. Then a great shout roared over the space separating the passing destroyers, *Petard* spotted a familiar figure in crumpled tropical whites, the cap at an individual and undisciplined angle above a scruffy ginger beard, standing on the homeward bound destroyer's quarter deck. The coarse shouted messages of affectionate envy produced from the doctor a two fingered gesture in reply, not entirely as a ribald answer to the shouts, more as a benediction or blessing on his old ship and its company. Then the two ships drew rapidly apart, *Paladin* on course south west to Durban and *Petard* reluctantly into Colombo.

After only an overnight stay, the escort carrier sailed with *Keren*, *Penn* and *Petard* in attendance for Bombay, arriving on the 17th. *Penn* left almost at once with a return convoy to Colombo, BN 90A. *Petard* escaped the quick turn round and for the next nine days had a long break in harbour; the ship's company enjoying the new experience of being at the second city of India. The blackout ashore was on a reduced scale, not since Durban had it been possible to walk at night in a city with some street lighting, with shops and places of entertainment free from blackout enshroudments. The ship for the first time at night used reduced upperdeck lighting, and maindeck ports could remain open to improve ventilation, making living and sleeping conditions tolerable. Awnings were found and rigged over the fo'c'sle and quarterdeck.

Bombay lived up to the imagination and expectations of those who had not visited the east before, and had only dreamt of the promises the fabled far east held for the seafarer. It all came to an end on 26th March when *Petard* senior ship of the escort, lead two River class frigates, *Plym* and *Helford* also a Dutch ship *Derg* out to sea in charge of Convoy BA 66A, bound for Aden.

A six day uneventful passage across an empty Arabian sea, brought the convoy to Aden, arriving 1st April. There *Petard* found Captain D11 in *Rotherham* with another fleet the *Quadrant* waiting for her arrival. Refuelling during the overnight stop inside the arid surroundings of Aden, *Petard* was ready when *Rotherham* lead out through the boom and turned towards the Red Sea; the ships company puzzled and speculating on the purpose of their mission. Approaching Perim Island guarding the narrows separating the two continents Africa and Asia, the island and the entrance to the Red Sea was blotted out by a huge low black cloud of a desert storm that crouched over the land each side of the narrows and sea between. It sat like a great menacing barrier, the effect exaggerated by the clear weather above the cloud and in the area through which the ships steamed on course towards the violent but very localised storm; *Rotherham* ordered the ships to prepare to reverse courses, turning 180 degrees to starboard together, the flotilla leaders flag hoist 'Blue 18' at the dip on the starboard yardarm. In *Petard*, omitting the captain who was privy to the orders for the unit, some thought for a wild moment that the destroyers were about to run away from the storm ahead; at the instant that the signal went close up for execution of the turn, out of the murk into the sunshine appeared three new destroyers in extended arrow formation and astern of the centre leading ship came first a great trawler bow followed by a huge and spectacular hull, the French battleship *Richelieu* emerged suddenly out of the blackness before the startled destroyers from Trincomalee.

The great ship wore an enormous tricolour from the mainmast as a symbol of the French will to fight for freedom; to the men in *Petard* it was a strange almost unreal experience to be part of the escort under the command of a French flag officer in *Richelieu*; for almost two years they had associated France and her fleet with the sad emasculated ships of Admiral Godfroy's squadron that lay rotting in Alexandria harbour. The ship's part as one of the battleships escort lasted until that evening when *Richelieu* entered through Aden harbour boom to fuel, leaving next morning 4th April, with only three destroyers, *Rotherham, Racehorse* and *Quadrant*. Later that same day, in the blazing heat of the afternoon *Petard* with the two frigates, sailed for Cochin then on to Colombo where Robert de Pass was landed for hospital treatment. He had been unwell for sometime, not even the break from sea routine and the rest at Bombay had helped him to recover from an exhaustion state that continued to persist. Surgeon Lieutenant Ticehurst decided that hospital attention and a complete break from the ship was urgently required.

The GCO now found himself acting indefinitely as the First Lieutenant and second in command, Brooky moving up into the Second Lieutenant post but carrying on as navigator. The two lieutenants RNVR remained the only survivors out of the original nine who had commissioned the ship, and found themselves the senior members of the wardroom that with the exception of the Gunner (T) Mr Leuillete, was now entirely populated with temporary reserve officers.

The ship returned to Trincomalee on 11th April to find the land-locked harbour filled with great ships; the battleship *Richelieu* lay with the British capital ships, the American aircraft carrier *Saratoga* and a flotilla of United States destroyers had joined Admiral Sir James Somerville's Eastern Fleet, making the scene one of immense and crushing power. It seemed obvious to the thousands of men who manned the ships that the great fleet had assembled for a major operation; *Petard* found herself drawn into a day and night cycle of sallies from the anchorage to exercise with the battleships, cruisers and aircraft carriers operating in various squadrons and force groupings. Ships moved out and returned through the boom defences to and from fleet signalling and manoeuvring practice, gunnery and aircraft borne bomb assault situations with live ammunition used in great quantities.

While the fleet exercised, a conference held on the 12th at Trincomalee decided that an attack should be made on the Japanese air and fleet base at Sabang, Sumatra. The decision had been influenced by an urgent request made by the Chief of Naval Operations, Washington USA, for the British Eastern Fleet to cause a major attack diversion in Sumatra, Andamans and Nicobars on or soon after the 15th to reduce pressure on the American fleets operating further to the east.

1130/16th the entire Eastern Fleet, British and Allied ships sailed for Operation Cockpit. The fleet sailed in two units, Force 69 and Force 70, 8 miles apart, both on course due south east at 18 knots with squadrons of Liberator and Catalina aircraft flying out from Ceylon bases, keeping up a constant anti-submarine patrol round the two Forces until dusk of the 17th.

The fleet divided into two groups, one, Force 69 commanded by the Commander in Chief, Admiral Sir James Somerville, consisted of three battleships and four cruisers with a strong destroyer escort including *Petard*, and the second, Force 70 commanded by the fleets second in command, Vice-Admiral A.J. Power in the battlecruiser, had two aircraft carriers, one cruiser and a destroyer escort. The powerful fleet achieved a complete suprise, approaching Sabang without being detected, and on the 19th the seaborne aircraft attacked without opposition except from light anti-aircraft fire. One American plane was shot down ditching off shore within range of the Japanese shore batteries; the British submarine *Tactician* detailed for air-sea rescue, surfaced and under fire from the coastal guns, succeeded in recovering the aircrew uninjured.

The fleet returned unharmed and unmolested to Trincomalee during the afternoon and evening 22nd April.

The intelligence assessment of damage inflicted on the enemy by the mighty display of naval power was on a modest scale, but no doubt the show of allied sea strength had its effect on the Japanese General staff. The published results of the operation were distributed to the fleet:—

2   Merchant ships, 4000-5000 tons each, hit.
2   Destroyers strafed.

24 Aircraft destroyed on the ground.
 3 Aircraft shot down.
    Oil tanks set on fire.
    Bombs on the dockyard, power station and town causing fires.

Cockpit turned out to be the last fleet operation in which Rupert Egan, his men and ship *Petard* would play a part. They had finished with the breath-taking scenario of huge grey capital warships, battleships and aircraft carriers steaming in majestic ordered columns seeking battle with the King's enemies; the great ships supported by cruiser squadrons, and the whole formation encompassed by flotillas of sleek powerful fast fleet destroyers, moving with spray drenched precision to adjust to the main fleet manoeuvring in battle formation. The awesome heart stopping orange flashes, smoke eruptions and thunder crash of mighty 15", 16" and 18" gun broadsides, the prelude to the scream of huge shells passing over the screening destroyers; brilliant streamers of flag hoists originating in the Flag ships, squadron and flotilla leaders, to be repeated through the fleet by flag and light signals, directed and controlled the tactical movements of the entire fleet or lesser formations. *Petard* had taken her place for the last time in spectacular evolutions when destroyers in flotilla formation laid dense black smoke screens to hide the main fleet changing direction or battle formation, or to allow cruisers and destroyers to launch attack or counter attack through the smoke barrier with gun and torpedo. These fleet tactics were to disappear for ever as radar effectiveness and range improved, and sea borne air power replaced the battleship.

all 15"

Eastern Fleet operations continued from Trincomalee with battleship bombardments and carrier borne air attacks on targets in Sourabaya on 30th April and 17th May; on Fort Blair in the Anadaman islands 20th June, and again a further attack on Sabang 24th July.

The ship reverted to more mundane work of escort duties out of Trincomalee taking individual fleet units round the southern toe of Ceylon to Colombo and some beyond the Cochin and Bombay, returning with other units or fleet supply ships to the fleet base. 21st May *Petard* returned to Colombo after assisting with the escort of an escort carrier *Atheling* to Trincomalee.

By 1st July after escort duties to and from Bombay and to Addu

Atoll the ship arrived back at Colombo and gave leave to the watch that missed the first visit to Diyatalawa rest camp. While the watch was away Robert de Pass returned from his spell in hospital, looking and feeling better, and at the same time causing fresh speculation that the ship would soon return to the United Kingdom. It had been generally assumed that Robert would have returned direct home after discharge from hospital via the first available homeward bound ship, so his reappearance fuelled the imagination of the main buzz merchants, coupled to the fact that a number of the ship's company were overdue for discharge to UK depots for courses and promotion. The reliefs had in some cases joined the ship, but the men had not been landed for passage home.

The agony of suspense dragged on, the watch on leave returned from the hills near Kandy, and the ship sailed for escort duty, first to Cochin them on to Bombay with hopes high that it would be ordered to take a BA convoy to Aden, but again this did not happen; on the 11th Rupert turned his ship south for Colombo arriving there early on the morning of 13th. After lunch and refuelling completion *Petard* sailed again, this time with *Nizam* and a large transport, on course for Addu Atoll as a fuel stop for the two destroyers. *Petard* entered and left during the 17th, with no-one disappointed by the fact that the fast refuel prevented a visit to the reef or the beaches. The next five days at sea moving along and a little south of the Equator still kept the ship's company restless with uncertainty, not even Rupert seemed to know if he was taking his ship home to be paid off. Since the events of 12th February, the Captain had become very withdrawn, his exuberant energy and zest for life that had lifted and sustained his command during the Dodecanese operations had virtually disappeared; not even the publication that he had been awarded the DSO for his services in the Dodecanese and later, confirmation in the half yearly promotions signal, that his acting rank of commander had been made substantive, could lift the air of depression that had him in its grip. In the same issue of the *London Gazette* announcing Rupert's DSO, Ken Brooksbank's bar to his DSC was published. The award was for his brilliant and unflappable navigation inside the archipelago, night after night, under appalling and hazardous conditions; his DSC had been awarded when *Petard* scored her first success in October 1942, U-boat *U559*. 21st July the ship with *Nizam* arrived at the beautiful Seychelles and anchored off the island of Mahe still uncertain of what the future had in store.

Suddenly the news that all had hoped and waited so long came, Rupert ordered Robert de Pass to release the contents of a signal received from the Commodore Eastern Fleet Destroyers, *Petard* was to be sailed from Seychelles to Aden as part of the escort of US 24, then to be released for passage to Portsmouth, England. More than half of the original ship's company who had commissioned the ship on the Tyne remained in the ship, many of the reliefs who had joined since, had come from ships sunk or damaged in the Mediterranean station, there were very few who had been home inside of two years. The friendly Seychelle islanders and the men of *Nizam* were startled and overwhelmed by the eruption of wild spirits from the destroyer, from officers and men who until that moment had seemed collectively withdrawn and dispirited.

Nizam and *Petard* left the Seychelles on the 23rd, steering almost due north to cross the equator for the last time as far as the *Petard* was concerned; the group of ships arrived at Aden late on the 28th, with *Petard*'s men looking with their usual but this time rather thankful distaste on the tortured heat blasted landscape for a last refuel stop. Next morning, after first light, Rupert took his destroyer alone, with a feeling of liberation, out through the boom defences, turned west for Perim and the Red Sea, then at economical speed directed his course up the Sea to arrive at Port Suez on 1st August. The three day passage up the heat blasted sea allowed all to begin to speculate on the changes they would find in their war encompassed homeland and the possibility of an end to the interminable conflict. Scanty information had begun to come through to the Eastern fleet since the start of Operation Overlord and the success of the first assaults on D-Day, 6th June. It seemed that the German war machine was on its final retreat in north as well as the south of Europe.

At Port Said, on the 2nd August, after passing through a canal that clearly confirmed that the war had moved away from the Eastern Mediterranean, the great camps and dumps of war material were silent and many empty, even the Egyptian army who previously manned the canal banks in force had reduced its defences. A night in Port Said then west into a smooth tranquil azure Mediterranean sea that lulled the ship's company into a false dangerous feeling of security, a complacency that even the officers were at risk of adopting. The ship remained at relaxed cruising stations and only the asdic team continued their search for submarines which now seemed a remote risk in the enclosed

Mediterranean which was now, with the exception of parts of the Aegean, entirely in allied control.

The ship continued the lone passage west, at 22 knots carrying out a lazy zig zag, more as a habit than a serious tactic to confuse an underwater assailant, into the forenoon of the 5th a day of smooth sea and sunlit perfection, when the ship awoke to the cry of the starboard bridge lookout '*Object in sight green 50, far*'. It first looked like a submarine partially surfaced, and while the OOW turned the ship to point at the sighting, he pressed the alarm button. Every pair of binoculars trained on to the bearing trying to identify the suspect, and before the director's crew had fully closed up to bring the powerful gunnery optics into service, the bridge team identified the sighting as a ship's life-boat sitting motionless on the smooth unruffled sea.

Rupert brought the ship to a stop quickly and efficiently longside the craft and invited the large crew to use the scrambling net rigged from the starboard iron deck. Twenty-six men clambered up the netting, none had been hurt or appeared to have been in the sea, all carried a miscellaneous collection of hand luggage and personal possessions; there were six officers and twenty crewmen, all American.

The master was being conducted up to the bridge to meet the Captain when a new cry came from the port lookout that he had sighted the masts of a ship '*Bearing Red 80*', almost immediately from its higher position in the ship the director identified the mast, funnel and superstructure to belong to a Liberty ship. Rupert Egan moved away quickly from the abandoned life boat and steered towards the new sighting, at the same time listening to the American merchant seaman's account of what had happened to his ship. The Liberty ship, *Petard* was at that moment closing, was the *Samslarnia* that had been torpedoed during the middle watch of that day, the American master and his crew had abandoned ship soon after the attack because he expected either to be hit by more torpedoes or sunk by gunfire. They had got the boat away without difficulty or interference, suffered no casualties because the torpedo had struck aft near the rudder post, and had pulled away from the ship without seeing it sink or being intercepted by the U-boat. The *Samslarnia* lay at an even keel, down at the stern by about 5 degrees, and with the port anchor cable hanging out of the hawse pipe.

Rupert Egan signalled RA Malta, giving the damaged ships position 60 miles north of Benghazi, and asked for an armed tug with an escort. While waiting for the tug to arrive, *Petard* made an attempt to get the merchant ship under tow but the under water damage aft frustrated the destroyer's bid to earn salvage money. The Liberty ships forward hold contained a vast number of crates of silver bullion, loaded at Bombay and bound to the United Kingdom. The brief moment of excited calculations of salvage money shares ended with the arrival of the tug and escort. The American master and his crew were soon transferred to the new arrivals and *Petard* left the scene.

A brief stop at Malta to land despatches, embark mail for the UK, fuel and top up with victualling stores, there was no time to visit familiar and favoured bars or to swim at St Paul's Bay. The ship sailed two hours after arrival, with no one regretting the short pause; all were still fearful of a recall until safely past Gibraltar.

Again alone, *Petard*'s long slim hull cut a path through the incredible blue of the Mediterranean sea leaving a creamy wake soon to vanish with no sign or mark of the ships passing. In board, the BBC overseas forces programme was again heard, and had brought back Vera Lynn's nostalgic voice and songs of home and family that matched the still half fearful elation and emotion of the homeward bound sailors. Only a fuel stop at Gibraltar and miraculously the ship received onward routing orders, still alone for Plymouth then Portsmouth, ETA 1400/15th August.

Out into the Atlantic, steering north 50 miles out from the mainland of Portugal, even the hardcore pessimists could not hold out against what now seemed inevitable, the return to the United Kingdom to pay off and leave. One or two made a half hearted rally with an attempt to start a buzz that the ship would be diverted to one of the Overlord Normandy beaches, but this effort foundered when the coxswain's schedules appeared in alll the messes requiring the entry of names and addresses, with details of the nearest railway station so that leave passes and railway warrants could be prepared by the time the ship arrived at Portsmouth. Volunteers were also called for, to remain in the ship after paying off to assist the Gunner, Buffer and Chief Stoker to supervise the destoring of the ship and prepare for the refit. Chief Petty Officer Haustead, a local man from Copner, Portsmouth, knew that by sticking by the ship for the long refit it would reduce the risk of an early draft back to sea, it was also a job that suited this splendid practical seaman, better than a routine barracks duty, and he would virtually be his own master.

The middle watchmen during the second part of their watch sighted Eddystone light transmitting on reduced power, guiding supply convoy trains in and out of Plymouth Sound to and from Normandy beaches and Mulberry Harbour. Rupert Egan below the bridge in his sea cabin was roused for the last by the officer of the watch voice in the pipe close to his ear, this time a hushed voice full of suppressed emotion and excitement reported the sighting of the English mainland as a dark loom in his binoculars. The OOW knew also that he was keeping his last middle watch after more than two years of watchkeeping and seatime, his next watch seemed a long way off, following foreign service leave and perhaps a course or two. With a following southwesterly wind force 5, Rame Head was abeam by 0530, and nearly the entire ship's company on the upperdeck in the thin drizzle looking at Cornwall, the coastal battery and ancient chapel high on the spine of the headland that protected the approaches to Plymouth sound. Low cloud touched the high places of the ridge, but visibility was clear enough for the exiles to feast their eyes on the greens and browns of the Cornish coast line close on the port hand, then the twin villages of Kingsand and Cawsand nestling inside Penlee point and at the head of Cawsand Bay.

Past the boom entrance between the west Breakwater light and Fort Picklecombe, *Petard* threaded a way through a mass of anchored shipping in the sound, part of the supply and reinforcement armada for Overlord, the operation that had emptied Devon and Cornwall of the American invasion army since D-day on 6th June. *Petard* was just another destroyer in the busy movement of shipping within the base, and if she had been noticed it was because of her Eastern fleet ship side and superstructure colours that contrasted with the home fleet dark grey. The ship's company fell in for stations to enter harbour wearing and itching in blue serge No 3 uniform and blue caps, unfamiliar dress for men long accustomed to white tropical rig. The ship turned to port passing Drake's Island into the tide rip in the narrows off Devil's Point, saluting with piping party on the bridge wing, and ships company in ranks and at attention on the upperdeck, the C-in-C's flag on Mt Wise lawn before Admiralty House, to finally berth in the dockyard near Flag Staff steps. The large piles of mail bags that had crowded between deck spaces, collected from every port since departure from Seychelles, disappeared into the waiting mail transport on the quay. Non-duty watches were ashore by noon for all night leave and into the pubs of Devonport, Stonehouse and Plymouth's Union Street which had escaped destruction by the Luftwaffe.

Taste buds and gullets responded to the almost forgotten flavour of English beer, even the war diluted west country variety seemed to be a nector infinitely better than the pale imitations found the length of the Mediterranean and Eastern Fleet stations, including the best known brand of onion beer served in the Fleet Club, Alexandria, 'Stella'. The first afternoon and night ashore in the UK was a confused rush of contacting surprised family and friends, by telephone and telegram to inform them of the returning destroyerman, and attempts to sample all the frugal and rationed pleasures that remained in Plymouth after five years of war and the departure of the invasion army and supporting armada. Only the GCO had someone to see, the girl he met during a week of live gun firings at nearby Wembury point, part of the GCO gunnery course more than $2\frac{1}{2}$ years before.

Leave expired at 0600/15th, it was Sunday, a wet west country August morning, no one was adrift when the ship unberthed and headed down the Hamoaze for the last leg of the long voyage to pay off. At 0700 the rain washed Hoe was empty except for one small figure, the lovely girl who remembered and waited for the fo'c'sle and gunnery control officer of the destroyer slipping out to sea through the misty rain, below the Belvedere where she stood. Outside the breakwater, Brooky's asdic team lowered the dome for the last and final round of asdic watchkeeping in the run up channel. The watch below were in a frenzy of activity, packing 'rabbits' and presents, sorting out kit and equipment that would go with kitbags and hammocks into store at the RNB; it still seemed improbable that by the Dog watches, three quarters of the ship's officers and men will have departed for leave never to return to *Petard*, and that very few who had shared messes and action stations for so long would meet again.

The 140 mile passage to Portsmouth via the coastal searched channel slipped by in a little over six hours, the grey day doing nothing to depress a morning of barely suppressed excitement flavoured with the final of often repeated extravagant declarations how the now imminent leave would be spent and what the priorities, mainly physical, should be. The Sunday morning routine of a ship at sea on active service proceeded through habit and discipline, the midday meal in each mess was prepared by the messcooks as usual and put up to the galley, but the 'straight rushes' of meat and potatoes, were no doubt straighter and more rushed than usual and few were garnished with the essential onion and Bisto, messdecks and flats got scrubbed and cleaned, 'up Spirits' piped and grog issued to the messes. At noon, the afternoon watch closed up to relieve the forenoon cruising station watchmen, as the Isle of Wight appeared out of the light mist on the port bow.

1300 hours, special sea dutymen closed up and the cruising watch secured the 'B' gun mounting and unarmed the depth charges, then fell out and stood by for 'stations for entering harbour'. The ship's company responded to the last call on the pipe of the commission to man the upper deck, with extra speed and animation as the Nab Tower appeared abeam, *Petard* had arrived for the first time at her manning port and depot. A similar scene to the one at Plymouth appeared to the returning ship, a great mass of supply and reinforcement shipping for the armies in France, moved in and out of the Cowes roads, Southampton and Portsmouth, all occupied with the reality of supporting the immense Overlord operation. Very few noticed the light coloured destroyer slipping quickly through towards the narrow entrance to Portsmouth and Salley Port, perhaps one or two as piping courtesies between junior and senior ships were exchanged, commented on the vivid rust stains marking the light sea stained paintwork and flowed from many of the 49 assorted patches that pocked the destroyer's hull, superstructure and funnel.

The asdic dome raised and housed, the headphones hung up in the cabin until the new asdic team of the recommissioned ship remanned the bridge hut; someone from the final watch ringed three dates painted on the forward bulkhead, dates that would only survive until the new crew repainted the asdic hut, 30th October 1942, 15th December 1942, 12th February 1944 when *Petard* and her crew destroyed three submarines.

1500 hours, *Petard* berthed on the North wall, Tidal basin, Royal Dockyard, Portsmouth, minutes later Rupert Egan called down the voice pipe to the coxswain in the wheel house 'Finished with main engines Coxswain' and the ship was at rest. In another half hour with dockyard electrical and steam supply connected to maintain domestic services, the boiler and engine room commenced to shut down. At 1600 about 150 of the ship's company filed onto the jetty to place kitbags and hammocks into the transport parked clear of the railway lines, the men dressed in No 1 uniform, gas masks carriers slung on canvas slings across their chests, oilskins folded over right arms, carrying small brown cases in their left hands, many with parcels lashed to the cases, fell in three ranks facing the ship waiting for coxswain to check off names and read out instructions for reporting back to depot and training establishments after leave. A brief nod from Robert de Pass, the coxswain ordered the senior Petty Officer in the party, to take charge and march the libertymen away to the harbour station. With hardly a backward glance they were gone, a few shouts from the Buffer's party of volunteers and the handful of specialist senior ratings remaining behind until the refit started. On the upper deck, the Captain, 1st Lieutenant and Engineer officer were already greeting the Foreman of the yard and his associates who had arrived to take charge of the ship.

An end of a commission, commonplace and unemotional, unmarked by ceremony, repeated many times in Royal and civilian dockyards the length of the Kingdom, *Petard* was just another ship requiring a major refit and brought in by a weary crew desperate for leave and reunion with family and land based relaxations, free from the threat of the enemy and the elements.

Rupert Egan returned once to the ship during the early part of the refit, to congratulate the Buffer, Chief Petty Officer Alfred Haustead on the award of his DSM, published in the *London Gazette* after the ship had paid off. The graceful tripod foremast had gone, and the ugly lattice work replacement that would carry improved radar was in course of construction, the decks and between spaces were carpeted with air and power leads, the ship rang with riveting hammers where new ship side plating had replaced the older splinter damaged plates. The ship lay in dry dock gutted and stripped of boats, with a nucleus of the new ship's company standing by to supervise *Petard*'s return to the operational fleet. Not long afterwards the Buffer handed over to his replacement and reported to the Royal Naval Barracks to await training duties and redraft.

Petard recommissioned in mid 1945 and returned to the far east in time for the last few weeks of the conflict with Japan, remaining out on the station until 1946. In 1950 the ship was converted to an anti-submarine frigate and remained in this new role until 1963 when the ship was sold and broken up, twenty two years after the launching on the Tyne.

SOURCES

BOOKS

A Sailors Odyssey	Viscount Cunningham of Hyndhope.
HMS Coventry	A narrative by George Simms
Sicily, whose victory?	Martin Blumenson
Eisenhower	Martin Blumenson
Salerno, foothold in Europe.	David Mason
War in the Aegean.	Peter C. Smith. Edwin Walker
The Second World War.	W.S. Churchill

Cryptologia Oct 1987 Vol XI Number 4

DOCUMENTS, PAMPHLETS, DIARIES and LETTERS.

PUBLIC RECORDS OFFICE.

ADM1/14255   Sinking of Italian U-boat by HMS PETARD and HHMS QUEEN OLGA.

ADM53/115353   HMS ARETHUSA log 16-20 November 1942.

ADM53/116041/116042/116043.   1942 HMS HAWKINS Log July, August and September.

ADM53/119538   HMS HAWKINS Log February 1944.

ADM119/258.   1943-4. Naval operations in Mediterranean.

ADM119/639/640/641/642/643.   Mediterranean and Eastern Fleet War Diaries.

ADM119/940.   Naval operations in the Mediterranean. 1941-43 reports.

ADM119/943.   Husky.

ADM119/975.   19423 Mediterranean convoy reports.

ADM119/976.   1943-4 Mediterranean convoy reports.

ADM119/1040.   1943-1945 HM and Greek ships, East Mediterranean reports of proceedings.

ADM119/1044.   1943. Naval operations in Aegean. Reports and remarks.

ADM119/1138/1139/1140.   W S convoy reports.
ADM119/1388.   1944. Eastern Fleet war diaries.
ADM119/1428.   1944. Levant and Eastern Fleet war diaries.
ADM119/14402.   Two enemy destroyers sunk by PAKENHAM and PALADIN.

MINISTRY OF DEFENCE. NAVAL HISTORICAL SECTION.

Operation reports, Husky and Avalanche.
Admiralty war diaries.

CENTRAL CHANCERY OF ORDERS AND KNIGHTHOOD.

Checking awards and citations.

IMPERIAL WAR MUSEUM.

Articles of war 1943.
510.4. Control of the Sicilian straits. A.B. Cunningham.
Invasion of Sicily. Supplement to the London Gazette, 38895   2077.
Janes Fighting Ships, 1952.
King's Rules and Admiralty Instructions, 1942.
Operation Retribution. Supplement to the London Gazette, 38423   5322/5373.
Navy Lists, 1942-1944.

LETTERS AND DIARIES.

Letter from HMS Vernon dated 12th June 1975, Captain G.D. Trist.
Letters from HMS Excellent dated 15th May 1975, Captain R.S. Falconer, dated 4th July 1975, Captain M.C.M. Mansergh.
Personal Diary, R. Chapman.
Description of 14th/15th September 1943, written by J.H. Hall.
Other letters written by J.H. Hall.
Extracts from 1942/43 diary kept by C.A. Sewell.
Recollections written by A.E. Haustead.
Letter from Neil Allen.

Index